Praise for *The AI and Data l*

'We are all becoming awar[illegible]ys in driving the digital economy and powering AI. Yet too few of us can articulate what "good data" is and how it should be managed. This book shines a light on the issues that matter and offers an excellent introduction to the topics that will help you understand how to deliver greater value from AI and data-driven decision making.
Alan Brown, Professor in Digital Economy, University of Exeter

'De Saulles offers an eloquent and clear entry point for understanding the commercial and regulatory dynamics at play when organisations encounter AI-related innovations. Combining history and timely case studies, he shines much needed light on the opportunity niches afforded by these encounters and their implications for how we live and work with information. Whether subject matter expert or novice, there is much in these pages to contemplate.'
Daniel J. Paré, Director (Arts), Tri-Faculty Digital Transformation and Innovation Program, University of Ottawa, Canada

The AI and Data Revolution

The AI and Data Revolution

Understanding the New Data Landscape

Martin De Saulles

facet publishing

Published by Facet Publishing
c/o British Library, 96 Euston Road, London NW1 2DB
www.facetpublishing.co.uk

Facet Publishing is wholly owned by CILIP:
the Library and Information Association.

British Library Cataloguing in Publication Data
A catalogue record for this book is available from the British Library.

ISBN 978-1-78330-708-1 (paperback)
ISBN 978-1-78330-709-8 (hardback)
ISBN 978-1-78330-710-4 (PDF)
ISBN 978-1-78330-711-1 (EPUB)

First published 2025

FSC
www.fsc.org
MIX
Paper | Supporting responsible forestry
FSC® C013604

The manufacturer's authorised representative in the EU for product safety is Logos Europe, 9 rue Nicolas Poussin, 17000 La Rochelle, France (contact@logoseurope.eu, www.logoseurope.eu).

Typeset from author's files in 10/13 Palatino and OpenSans by Flagholme Publishing Services.
Printed and made in Great Britain by CPI Group (UK) Ltd, Croydon, CR0 4YY.

For Denys and Kate

Contents

Figures and Case Studies **xi**

About the Author **xiii**

Introduction **xv**

1 How Did We Get Here? **1**
A brief history of the information industry 1
The role of technology 3
Data-driven innovation 5
A brief history of AI 9

2 The Current AI and Data Landscape **15**
How much data is there? 15
Sources of data 16
How data is used 24
Changing business models 30
The AI landscape 49

3 The Emerging Data-Driven AI Revolution **55**
AI opportunities 56
AI challenges 69
Prompt engineers: the new librarians? 72

4 Ethical, Policy and Legal Issues of Data-Driven AI **77**
Ethical concerns 77
AI and data policies 80
AI and data legislation 93

5 Looking Ahead **107**
Predicting the future 108
Social and economic implications of the AI and data revolution 109
Data and AI technologies to 2030 117
AI in the real world to 2030 129
The regulatory and commercial environment to 2030 132

6 Pulling the Threads Together **135**

References **137**

Index **163**

Figures and Case Studies

Figures

1.1	Branches of AI	11
2.1	Sources of data	17
2.2	Information intensity matrix	25
2.3	ICE automotive value chain	26
2.4	EV ecosystem data flows	29
2.5	Business Model Canvas	31
2.6	Porter's Five Forces model	34
2.7	Google data flows	38
2.8	Apple revenue breakdown	39
2.9	Apple data ecosystem	40
2.10	Mobile data flows	43
2.11	Data exchanges and marketplaces	48
2.12	Large language model (LLM) variables	51
2.13	Large language model (LLM) bottlenecks	52
3.1	Retrieval-augmented generation (RAG)	59
3.2	AI healthcare and medical research applications	64
3.3	Translating ethics into legislation	78

Case Studies

2.1	The London Datastore	20
2.2	Strava	44
2.3	Harbr	49
3.1	SinglePoint	59
3.2	WPP Open	61
3.3	The NHS AI Lab	64
3.4	A&O Shearman	67

About the Author

Dr Martin De Saulles is a technology analyst and writer who focuses on the impacts of digital innovations on organisations and the broader economy. He has worked in several management consulting firms, where he led research on the telecommunications and internet sectors. Until 2024, he was a Principal Lecturer at the University of Brighton, where he taught modules on innovation and marketing to computer science and media students. He is the author of several books on the data and information industries as well as academic journal and conference papers. Further details can be found at https://martindesaulles.com.

Introduction

We are entering a new phase in the information revolution driven by the introduction of new artificial intelligence (AI) technologies and how they are being used to transform the data amassed within organisations over the previous 30 or so years. This revolution started hundreds of years ago when moveable type was used to print books at a scale and speed not previously possible. The rise of mass media and then mass communications in the form of telecommunication networks, coupled with the data processing capabilities of computers, powered the next phases. Thirty years ago, the expansion of the internet and the widespread adoption of the World Wide Web (WWW) as a means to publish and share information brought the digital revolution into our homes and businesses. Mobile computing has put powerful, always connected computers in the pockets of most people in the industrialised world and social networks have provided platforms for individuals to reach billions of others with their thoughts and ideas.

A result of these innovations and the ways they have been used is a world awash with information, most of which sits unused, unstructured and hidden away in archives and data silos within the organisations, public and private, that created it (Lange, 2023). Despite significant advances in information management techniques and technologies, only a fraction of the value of this data is being realised. However, we are now at an inflection point where much of the infrastructure is in place to begin the process of changing that. AI and associated technologies will play a key role in this new phase of innovation through their ability to extract meaning and value from the information assets accumulated over the previous decades.

Objectivity, as far as this is possible, is important when ascribing transformative attributes to new technologies. How technologies are adopted, and the uses to which they are eventually put, may not always tally with the predictions made by commentators at their inception. In the 1940s, IBM's president, Thomas J Watson claimed there was only a world market for about five computers, a prediction he abandoned a few years later, much to IBM's benefit, when mainframes became popular with businesses (Carr, 2008). In 2007, the then CEO of Microsoft dismissed the newly launched iPhone for not having a keyboard and being 'a not very good email machine' (Reisinger, 2017). Microsoft abandoned its efforts in making smartphones with keyboards several years later. Conversely, there are many examples of commentators being overly enthusiastic about the potential of new technologies. This was particularly true in the early days of the internet and social media. Their potential to encourage social reforms through the free exchange of ideas from and between those not normally given a voice was seen by many as heralding a new age of democracy. The reality has been rather different, with social platforms often amplifying authoritarian views as well as becoming shopfronts for retailers and marketers (Srnicek, 2016).

The core thesis of this book is that the current wave of AI-driven innovations represents a step-change in how organisations can extract value from data and that this will have significant implications for business innovation and how companies compete. The current commercial and regulatory environments around the world will shape how these changes evolve and will, in turn, be impacted as companies find ways to monetise their AI investments. These are all topics that will be discussed in the following chapters.

While there are many potential social implications of these changes, particularly if large-scale unemployment is a result of AI taking over human jobs, these are not the primary focus here. A short discussion on AI and employment is presented in Chapter 5 but only to illustrate some of the difficulties in linking new technologies to job losses. This book also stays away from anticipating what might happen if artificial general intelligence (AGI) were to become a reality as it leads down philosophical and technical paths that others are far more qualified to take. The potential dangers of uncontrolled AI and how it might be deployed are real, however, and do need addressing. When the so-called 'godfather of AI' quits Google because he is concerned about the risks AI poses to society (Waters and Murgia, 2023), we need to take note. The core aim of this book is to provide students of business and technology as well as practitioners with a better understanding of what AI and the data behind it means for organisations in the public and private sectors.

Chapter 1 sets the scene with a short history of the information industry and the role of technology in making data a core asset for organisations to compete with in the 21st century. It also discusses the key milestones in the history of AI that have led to the current wave of innovation. It should be noted that the terms 'data' and 'information' are used relatively interchangeably throughout the book. This is deliberate and should not be taken as a refutation by the author that there are no differences between them. The short section on knowledge management in Chapter 3 acknowledges the value of the conceptual framework of the data, information and knowledge pyramid. However, the semantics of whether something should be classified as data or information would add an unhelpful layer of complexity to the discussions presented here. For example, where the training inputs for large language models (LLMs) have come from scraping websites containing vastly different types of content, definitions start to blur. An academic paper hoovered up by one of these models might be seen as information, or even knowledge, in that it has meaning and context, while a table of numbers with no contextual explanation of what it means could be better described as data.

In Chapter 2, an overview of the AI and data landscape is presented with explanations of the key sources of data that organisations as well as AI developers rely on. Several frameworks are presented to illustrate how data is used within businesses and how it drives innovation and competitive activities. There is a particular focus on the rise of platform-based businesses that have harnessed network effects to attract users and, as a result, capture valuable data for commercial use. A discussion of generative AI (GenAI) and its core components follows to provide readers with an understanding of how these services work. Of course, AI encompasses a wide range of technologies and activities but the prime focus of Chapter 2 is LLMs and GenAI and the machine learning (ML) and deep learning (DL) technologies that power these models. The current wave of GenAI innovations offers organisations potentially transformative ways to manage and extract value from their data as well as presenting challenges to publishers, regulators and some of the technology giants that profited from the first wave of internet innovations.

These opportunities and challenges are the focus of Chapters 3 and 4 where the capabilities of GenAI and natural language processing (NLP) are explored in the context of different applications from medical research to publishing. Policies and legislation from Europe and the US are considered in terms of what they seek to achieve as well as their potential impacts on developers and users of these technologies.

In Chapter 5, scenarios for where the AI and data revolution may be heading up to 2030 are discussed as well as what the potential bottlenecks are that might hinder these developments.

Chapter 6 pulls together the core threads from earlier chapters and presents readers with some thoughts and questions to keep in mind as AI starts to permeate our professional and personal lives.

Underpinning this book are tried and tested theories and frameworks as well as evidence from the real world of how data and AI is being used across a range of settings. This, combined with a historical perspective, form an important part of the book and underpin the discussions on how AI and the data revolution are impacting organisations and society today. They also inform the discussions presented towards the end of this book about where this current wave of innovation may be heading and the questions and issues we need to think about. Some of the products and companies mentioned in this book will no doubt have disappeared within a few years of publication and others will be very different to their current form. New services and companies will have emerged to replace those that have left the stage, but the aim is to help the reader have a broad understanding of the forces currently driving the AI and data sectors and where it all might lead.

Om Malik, a long-time and wise observer of the digital revolution going back to the early days of the internet, expresses well the sentiment of this book when he talks about the current wave of GenAI innovations: 'How we interact with information and data is set to transform, just as it did with the web and smartphones' (Malik, 2023).

The tools are being developed and deployed to radically alter how we create and use information and, for better or worse, we need to understand the forces driving these changes and what they mean for how we work. This book aims to be a useful starting point.

CHAPTER 1

How Did We Get Here?

A brief history of the information industry

Before considering the business and social impacts of the current data-driven AI revolution, it is worth considering how our use of information has evolved over the last 5,000 or so years. In many ways, the forces that led to the rise of information being transcribed for the first time are not too dissimilar to those driving change today. Commerce and the desire to maintain power over disparate groups of citizens have always required the creation, storage and distribution of information in multiple forms and across a variety of media.

One of the earliest forms of transcription was discovered in 1929 by Julius Jordan, a German archaeologist who excavated a collection of clay tablets over 5,000 years old in what is now Iraq. It took almost 50 years for researchers to decipher the markings on the tablets, which turned out to be records of the sale of commodities such as sheep, grain and honey. What many archaeologists had thought were early forms of poetry or personal correspondence were, in fact, much more mundane, but vital to the orderly flow of goods across the region (Harford, 2017). Further study of the tablets revealed an unexpected sophistication in the way information was transcribed in the clay. As higher quantities of goods needed to be recorded, new ways of representing larger numbers were needed. For example, the sale of three sheep involved the sheep being pressed into the clay three times, but when quantities grew above ten, other symbols were required. These symbols allowed records of ever-larger exchanges to take place. Harford (2017) recounts that one tablet recording a war reparation demand amounted to 4.5 trillion litres of barley, approximately 600 times the current annual US production of the crop.

Increasingly sophisticated record keeping developed over the next thousand or so years with the so-called Code of Hammurabi being widely used in Babylon by 1800 BCE. This represented the first known use of formalised rules around the granting of credit. Under this code, the maximum rate of interest that could be charged on, for example, loans on grain was set at 33.3% per year, with 20% for silver. Such loans were only legally valid if witnessed by a public official and recorded formally as a contract (Desjardins, 2017). Commerce in ancient Rome relied extensively on credit notes, with the poet and philosopher, Cicero, noting in 50 BCE that his neighbour had recently purchased 625 acres of land for 11.5 million sesterces. As Desjardins (2017) observes, that many sesterces would have weighed more than 11 tonnes, an unmanageably large amount of coins to transport across Rome. In such instances, credit notes facilitated the orderly transaction of business in a way recognisable in today's financial markets.

Although the medium on which commercial transactions was recorded has changed in the last 5,000 years, the reasons for collecting and storing this information has not. The key difference is scale, with the expansion of global trade from the 16th century necessitating internationally recognised financial agreements. Since the 19th century, the rise of more affluent middle classes in industrialised economies extended financial services to individuals, forcing ever-more elaborate forms of record keeping.

As well as scale, the speed with which data is collected and shared has also been a defining feature of the evolving information sector, particularly in financial services. Timely access to sets of data can be a defining competitive advantage for financial services firms. This is well illustrated by the company Spread Networks, which, in 2010, completed a US$300 million project to drill through several mountains and lay an 827 miles long fibre optic cable between Chicago and New York. The sole purpose of this undertaking was to shave four-thousandths of a second off the time it takes for financial data to be transmitted between the Chicago Mercantile Exchange and New York's Nasdaq Stock Exchange. The exchange of data between these institutions had been taking place for decades prior to Spread Network's project but the cables used had not followed an exact straight line, diverting in sections to avoid mountains and other obstacles. The new cable went through these obstacles, albeit at great expense. However, the time saving of 0.004 seconds was sufficiently attractive for banks to willingly spend tens of millions of dollars to access the data (Lewis, 2015, 22).

The following section will explore how innovations such as the printing press, telecommunication networks and computing technologies have been drivers of innovation in the creation, distribution and storage of information, but have also been shaped by these processes.

The role of technology

A defining feature of how new technologies have transformed the information landscape is their ability to both speed up the process of creating information records whilst also lowering the costs of storing and distributing these outputs. For several thousand years, clay and then papyrus, vellum and paper were used for codifying and transcribing information. A common feature of these media is the time-consuming nature of their production. Each must be written by hand, forcing a restriction on how quickly they can be created and how they can then be used and accessed. In the first millennia, this began to change. Printing presses were developed in China, radically transforming the speed with which information could be created and shared. However, this process required the creation of wooden printing blocks that took time to carve.

It was the invention of the moveable type printing press in China at the end of the first millennia, where individual carved letters could be set and re-used, that allowed a much faster and more flexible form of printing (He, 1994, 158). In the 15th century in Germany, this was improved by Johannes Gutenberg when he replaced wooden letters with metal ones. This allowed a more robust printing process with books and pamphlets being reproduced at a faster rate. A side-effect of the less expensive books produced by these more efficient printing presses meant ideas could be spread more quickly, leading to political and religious beliefs taking hold among the more educated sections of society. In 1501, Pope Alexander VI decreed that anyone printing texts without the church's approval would be excommunicated. As it turned out, this was an ineffective order, with printed texts by Martin Luther and John Calvin splitting the Catholic church a few years later (Rayward, 2014).

The 16th and 17th centuries saw the rise of the Age of Enlightenment across much of Europe, where the mass printing of scientific and philosophical texts allowed scholars to share information in a way not previously possible. According to Rayward (2014):

> Of central importance in understanding the emergence of the Gutenberg-based information and communications infrastructures and what these infrastructures supported was the fact that they were an integral part of the general secularisation, modernisation, and industrialisation of Western capitalist economies.
>
> (Rayward, 2014, 682–3)

As scientific methods evolved and people had a better understanding of the natural world and the forces of physics that defined our place in it, the industrial revolution was kickstarted, first in England and then across the US and much of Europe. The resulting rise in economic activity required ever-more accurate and detailed record keeping as trade increased and workers moved from rural to urban settings.

A positive feedback loop also emerged with new scientific knowledge and industrial practices being applied to the printing industry itself. Steam-powered machines and rotary presses were developed that could print millions of pages a day. Such scale enabled the printing of mass-distribution newspapers that could be transported across the country overnight. Books became a relatively cheap commodity, allowing the masses to access literature that had previously been the preserve of the rich. New genres of literature emerged to cater for broader tastes, encouraging new publishing companies to be created that specialised in increasingly niche areas.

In financial markets, information became an increasingly sought after commodity as banks and other institutions looked for new sources of competitive advantage. In 2016, the global expenditure on financial, credit and compliance data was estimated to be $168 billion (Watson Healy, 2017, 8). Adjusting for inflation, this figure would be $223 billion in 2024. The origins of this market can be traced back to 16th-century Amsterdam when networks of traders and financiers emerged to share proprietary information on prices and financial deals among themselves for mutual benefit. Similar networks arose in other cities around the world, with the London Stock Exchange emerging from an information sharing club of 150 men in 1761 and a similar arrangement in New York in 1792 (Donnan, 2011, 8).

As the global trade in physical goods grew through shipping routes, the international exchange of information was limited by the speed with which a human could travel either by boat over the sea or horse over land. These limitations were challenged in the mid-19th century when the German Paul Julius Reuter used carrier pigeons to fly stock prices between markets in Aachen and Brussels. In 1851, he opened an office in London to transmit data between London and Paris over the newly laid Dover–Calais telegraph cable (Reuters, 2008). The Spread Networks cable linking Chicago and New York (discussed above) is a natural progression of this trend to speed the flow of information for commercial purposes.

Information for entertainment purposes has also been transformed by new technologies, particularly through the rise of mass media. It has already been noted that the building of railway networks in Europe and the US in the 19th century allowed the distribution of national daily newspapers printed on steam and then electric-powered printing presses. The business models of news publishers changed as they realised that revenues could also be generated from carrying advertising. In New York in 1833, print shop owner, Benjamin Day, looked for ways to make newspapers affordable to the masses.

At the time, newspapers in the city were selling for around six cents a copy, putting them out of reach of many potential readers. Day planned to sell his newspaper for one cent and make up the shortfall in production costs by carrying advertising. On 3 September 1833 he launched *The New York Sun* and within months it was selling thousands of copies a day. The advertising revenue it generated more than offset the losses from its low cover price (Wu, 2016, 12). The rise of advertising-driven mass media had begun.

Advertising also drove the rise of mass radio audiences in early 20th-century America and television audiences in the second half of the century. By 1930, radio advertising in the US was generating US$60 million. By 1940, it had risen to US$600 million (the equivalent of US$28 billion in 2024) (Wu, 2016, 96).

At the heart of the rise of mass media is the data used to justify the advertising costs to marketing agencies and the brands they represent. The methods and technologies used to measure audiences have often been crude and not always accurate. A newspaper publisher knows how many copies they have sold in print but does not know who bought them (unless the sale is via a subscription) or what parts of the newspaper the purchaser read. Similarly, the nature of terrestrially broadcast radio and television means that a broadcaster does not know how many households have tuned in to their programmes or who is watching. Surveys and sample households with set-top boxes have been used to try and measure audiences but the rise of digital media and the back-channel enabled by internet connectivity has transformed this (as we shall see in the following section).

Data-driven innovation

An oft-quoted phrase is that 'data is the new oil', alluding to the fact that oil has powered economic growth across developed economies for much of the 20th century while data will do the same in the 21st. Countries with oil reserves reaped massive dividends and continue to do so. If we acknowledge that data is the new driver of growth then organisations with access to data will be the winners. As *The Economist* put it:

> This abundance of data changes the nature of competition . . . . By collecting more data, a firm has more scope to improve its products, which attracts more users, generating even more data, and so on. The more data Tesla gathers from its self-driving cars, the better it can make them at driving themselves – part of the reason the firm, which sold only 25,000 cars in the first quarter, is now worth more than GM, which sold 2.3m. Vast pools of data can thus act as protective moats.
>
> (*The Economist*, 6 May 2017)

Is that comparison still valid today? On 11 July 2024, Tesla was worth 13 times as much as GM, as measured by the companies' market capitalisations, while selling less than a third of the number of vehicles (GM, 2024; Kolodny, 2024). How far this massive difference is due to Tesla's access to 'vast pools of data' is not obvious, but it does indicate that not all businesses within the same industry are considered equal. In Chapter 2 we will look in more detail at the ways data can confer a competitive advantage and how business models are built around it. However, it is worth considering in this section the ways data has helped drive innovation over the last 150 years.

We saw in the previous section that the exchange of data for financial and commercial purposes has resulted in new industries, from stock price compilers to mass media. Technology facilitated these innovations as telegram, telephone and broadcast systems allowing the distribution of information at speed and scale. The first telegraph systems were deployed in the mid-19th century and allowed, for the first time, the transmission of messages over long distances faster than a horse and rider. In many ways, this was more radical a transformation than the arrival of the internet 140 years later. As *The Wall Street Journal* proudly announced in 1889:

> Today it takes less than 30 seconds for the price of the latest trade to travel the 216 miles between the Boston Stock Exchange and the NYSE. From almost anywhere in the US with telegraph service, an order can be sent to New York and confirmation of the executed trade received back in less than 90 seconds. Trades cross the Atlantic in under five minutes.
>
> (Zweig, 2014)

Just as commerce soon moved onto the internet when it was made accessible to consumers in the early 1990s, so the telegraph networks were quickly flooded with businesses and individuals looking to make a profit. Early telegraph fraud centred on the transmission of horse racing results to towns many miles from the racetrack allowing punters to place bets on winners before local bookmakers had access to the same information. Similar scams involved the exchange of stock market data between London and Edinburgh by stockbrokers looking to exploit information asymmetries around share prices (Standage, 1999, 102–3).

Later in the 19th century, telephone networks were built out across developed economies and, for the first hundred years, were used primarily for voice communications. In the second half of the 20th century, dedicated data networks were installed by telecommunication operators and private businesses. These deployed new data exchange protocols, such as packet switching, to route data more efficiently across dispersed systems. The invention of the World Wide Web (WWW) by Sir Tim Berners-Lee in 1989 and the opening of the internet in the US to commercial operators allowed the digital revolution to establish itself among consumers rather than being the preserve of corporations.

A key feature of the internet that has driven much of the innovation we take for granted today has been its data backchannel. Combined with the opening of telecommunication networks to third parties, this has transformed the communications sector beyond recognition since the late 1990s. We have moved from a broadcast model of information exchange to a distributed and more democratic one. Until the 1990s, most countries had a single, often government controlled, telecommunications provider that had a monopoly on providing telephone services to individuals and businesses. The US had a less concentrated market but the public was mostly confined to one or two telecommunication providers in their locality. Deregulation across Europe and other countries from the late 1990s, coupled with the growth of internet services, provided a platform for companies to build businesses on top of this new landscape. These ranged from the deployment of entire new telecommunication networks, fibre optic and wireless, to service providers offering internet access and startups building businesses to provide digital services.

The backchannel feature of the internet facilitated the rise of many of today's most valuable companies. Notable among these companies are Alphabet (Google), Amazon, Meta (Facebook, Instagram) and Apple. The first three of these were only created because of the interactive nature of the internet, while Apple resurged from near bankruptcy to become, on and off, the world's most valuable company.

Alphabet, the parent company of Google, is the world's largest advertising platform. By developing a superior web search algorithm in 1998 it offered users a better way to find the information they needed in a rapidly growing WWW. Their PageRank algorithm looked beyond just the content of websites when compiling the Google index and included a measure of quality as expressed by the number and reputable external links going to individual web pages. This thinned out much of the spam content that had sprung up as content creators tried to trick their way into search results pages.

The data that Google collected from its users helped refine the quality of search results while also providing a highly targeted platform for advertisers. Rather than advertising to consumers across the broadcast systems of a traditional media owner, brands could reach potential customers based on the words they were typing into the Google search box. The brands and their agencies could then measure how often their ads were clicked on and whether that led to sales on their websites. None of this was possible under the broadcast model where targeting was less precise and knowing what a consumer did after seeing a print or television advertisement was impossible. From Google's perspective, it had created an almost perfect advertising platform. While mass media enterprises had to create expensive content to attract audiences, Google only had to crawl and index third-party websites and then sell advertising on top of that. This has been highly profitable for the company, with its annual global advertising revenue reaching US$238 billion in 2023 (Alphabet, 2024, 35).

While Amazon is a very different business to Alphabet, it too has relied on the interactive nature of the internet to make it a global leader in ecommerce. Not only does the data backchannel allow consumers to order goods from the company or its marketplace vendors, but the company also benefits from the information it collects about users' behaviour on the website and the products they order. On top of this, the company has information about users' home addresses and payment details. Amazon has built even closer ties with its users through the Prime subscription service and hardware products such as the Kindle e-reader, Alexa home devices, Ring video-doorbells and Fire tablets. All these products and services 'lock' customers into the Amazon ecosystem and provide an ever-richer source of data for the company. Less obviously, Amazon has also built a large and highly profitable advertising business that sits on top of its ecommerce business. Many third-party sellers on the Amazon Marketplace now pay the company to have their items listed at the top of product listings. In 2022, this generated US$37 billion for the company, making Amazon's advertising business larger than the entire global newspaper industry's advertising revenues (Evans, 2023). By 2023, this figure had grown to US$47 billion (Amazon, 2024, 3). Like Alphabet, it is Amazon's ability to offer data-driven, highly targeted advertising and its dominant ecommerce platform that puts it in such a strong position.

Meta, owner of Facebook and Instagram, has also built a highly profitable advertising business on top of the social media services it offers to consumers. It harvests data from the internet backchannel through the social graphs built out by its social media users. Like Alphabet, the company does not need to create expensive media assets to attract its users but relies on user-generated content to bring consumers onto the platform. Building an understanding of psychological triggers into the user experience (UX) design of its social networks, including an endless scroll of content, makes Facebook and Instagram highly addictive for many users. ByteDance's TikTok social app has followed this pattern with, arguably, even more addictive results. Collecting data on who users are connected to, the types of content they like and what they share across the network with others makes for a rich environment for advertisers. Campaigns can be targeted at very niche groups of users via the digital tools provided to advertisers from Meta and ByteDance.

Apple offers a good example of a technology company that was created long before the internet revolution, but that has reinvented itself by building physical products that harness the opportunities offered by the data backchannel. Created in 1976 to build and sell personal computers, the company was innovative and successful in bringing user-friendly devices to end-users. However, by the 1990s, the company was in financial difficulty as the PC revolution had been won by computers running Microsoft's Windows operating system and Intel's microprocessors. As a result, Apple saw an 80% drop in their share price between 1992 and 1997 (Martins, 2023). The return of Apple co-founder, Steve Jobs, in 1997 began the rebirth of the company as it expanded into new product categories that made use of the rapidly growing internet. The launch of the iPod in 2001, the iPhone in 2007 and the iPad in 2010 transformed mobile entertainment and communications through a combination of superior UX and the harnessing of third-party content from music and video to easily installable apps adding functionality to the hardware. While Apple still generates most of its revenue from hardware sales, particularly the iPhone, it is the data that flows across these devices that keeps users within the Apple ecosystem. This extends to app stores, Apple Watches, home devices such as Apple TV and the HomePod, AirPods and AirTags. As we will see in Chapter 2, data-driven platforms have the power to lock out competitors and accelerate profits through the harnessing of network effects.

The next wave of data-driven innovation is being led by the development and deployment of AI technologies. The next section considers how AI has evolved over the last 70 years to get us to this stage.

A brief history of AI

The notion that a computing device might attain intelligence comparable to a human's goes back to the earliest days of the modern computing era. In 1943, McCulloch and Pitts (1943) outlined a simple model that made use of Boolean logic to mimic the processing that takes place in the brain by neurons. The idea of a computer operating in a similar way to brain neurons took hold and, in 1958, Rosenblatt (1958) described a more intricate system he called the 'perceptron'. This extended the processing functionality to include inputs beyond the simple Boolean operators of AND, OR, NOT.

As researchers further developed systems designed to imitate the human brain, a debate emerged around how the 'intelligence' of systems might be measured. Computing pioneer Alan Turing sought to provide an answer and his 1950 paper, Computing Machinery and Intelligence (Turing, 1950), considered the question, 'Can machines think?'. While Turing considers in depth the theological and philosophical questions about what a machine might be capable of and what we mean by 'think', he posits a simple test to measure if a machine can think. In simplified terms, the test involves a human judge communicating in writing via teleprinter with another human and machine. If, from the answers the human and the computer give to questions posed, the judge cannot tell which is which then the machine might be deemed to be intelligent. While the Turing test is no longer considered by many researchers to be the authoritative measure of whether a computer has achieved 'intelligence', it has provided a useful framework for later research, both technical and theoretical.

Perhaps the defining moment in the history of AI came in 1956 at the Dartmouth workshop in the US. This was a summer workshop organised at Dartmouth College by some of the key figures in the field of computing and communications research, Marvin Minsky, John McCarthy, Claude Shannon and Nathaniel Rochester. The objective was to gather key thinkers and researchers together for eight weeks to explore practical and theoretical ideas around the concept of 'thinking machines'. The phrase 'artificial intelligence' emerged from the workshop as a term to describe this emerging discipline (Solomonoff, 2023). Charting the history of AI in his 2021 book *Genius Makers: The Mavericks who Brought AI to Google, Facebook, and the World,* Cade Metz argued that the 1956 workshop 'set the goals for this field. The way we think about technology is because of the way it was framed at that conference.' (Friel, 2023).

A number of the Dartmouth workshop organisers and attendees went on to become leading lights in the AI field and refine what intelligence really looks like in the context of computing devices. Marvin Minsky defined AI as 'the science of making machines do things that would require intelligence if done by men', while John McCarthy described it as 'the science and engineering of making intelligent machines' (Toosi et al., 2021, 3). The main impact of the conference was that it made AI a more defined and concrete field of study for future research. Over the coming years, advances were made in designing and building AI systems that could simulate aspects of human reasoning, but overly ambitious expectations and hype often led to disappointment and claims that AI was always going to be a shimmering mirage on the horizon. These so-called 'AI winters' diverted attention and funding to other areas of computer science. However, several universities, including the Massachusetts Institute of Technology (MIT) and Stanford in the US and Edinburgh and Cambridge in the UK as well as defence-related projects, continued to explore the potential of reasoning machines.

Following Joseph Wizenbaum's demonstration at MIT in 1966 of Eliza, a chatbot that could mimic a psychotherapist engaging with a patient, excitement grew about how near computing systems were to passing the Turing test and achieving intelligence. However, advances were much slower than expected and the first AI winter took hold in the early 1970s as hardware limitations and poorly performing models forced researchers to realise that little progress had been made since the 1960s (New Scientist, 2022, 21). A scaling back of ambition from trying to create systems that thought in human ways to more focused efforts around areas such as speech recognition and computer vision delivered better results. In 1997, a landmark demonstration by IBM reignited excitement in this area when its Deep Blue system beat world chess champion Garry Kasparov. However, it was increases in computer processing power and new approaches to helping machines make inferences, coupled with the rise of internet-generated data, that has driven the more recent advances in AI.

To understand what AI means in 2025 it is important to define some key terms and show how different areas of research relate to each other. Figure 1.1 provides a high-level illustration of the key branches of AI research and how they relate to each other.

AI can be thought of as the overarching term to describe efforts to create machines that can think like humans. There are numerous practical and philosophical debates as to what that really means and whether a machine

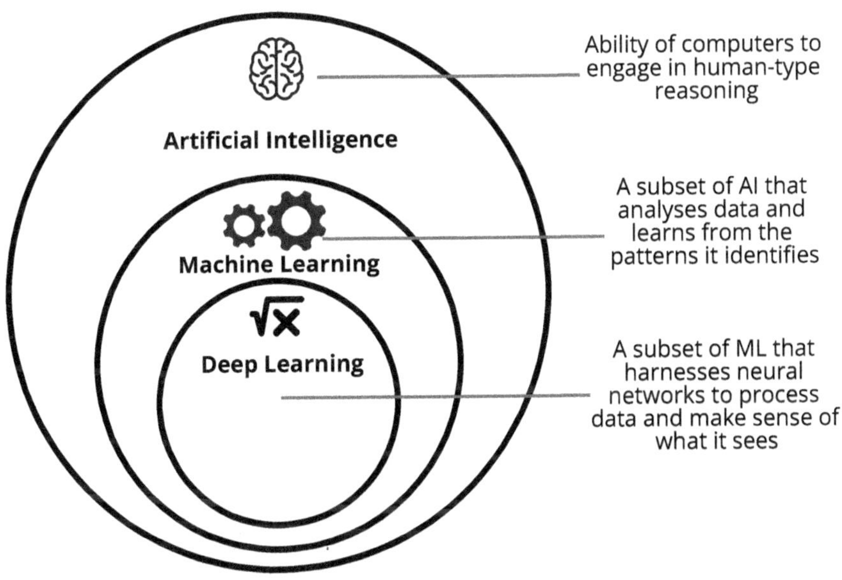

Figure 1.1 *Branches of AI*

would ever be able to think and reason in the same way as humans. Artificial General Intelligence (AGI) is a phrase used to describe this state, but it is unclear if or when we might see such systems in action. However, machine learning (ML) is a reality in that the application of ML techniques has enabled computers to make sense of large data sets and learn from what it observes. Recommendation engines deployed by firms like Amazon, Netflix and Spotify use ML algorithms to spot patterns in the types of products we buy, films we watch and music we listen to and then suggest similar items we might be interested in. Spam filtering in e-mail systems and fraud detection within financial services operate in a similar way. Deep learning (DL) is a subset of ML and utilises neural networks to go deeper into pattern recognition and understanding than more basic ML approaches. The number and depth of node layers within a neural network separates a single neural network from a DL algorithm and there must be more than three (IBM, 2024a).

The current revolution in AI has been driven by the rise of generative AI (GenAI), which can be seen as a subset of DL. Whereas ML and DL systems are able to analyse and make sense of massive sets of data, GenAI systems are able to go a stage further and generate new content based on the patterns it has observed from the data it was trained on and the prompts entered by users. Key to this massive change was the development of a tool known as a 'transformer' that accelerated the ability of computers to understand language. Being able to make sense of large groups of text and not just individual words or phrases allowed context and meaning to be interpreted by machines for the first time (FT, 2023). The research into transformers was led by researchers within Google and published in 2017, leading to the rise of GenAI services from companies such as OpenAI, Anthropic and Mistral (Uszkoreit, 2017).

Launched in November 2022 by OpenAI, ChatGPT immediately caught the public's and journalists' attention by its ability to create paragraphs of text from simple prompts typed into the chatbot. While Google had, for over 20 years, been efficient at translating search terms into links to relevant web pages, ChatGPT appeared to bypass the need for users to click through links to find the information they needed and provide relatively detailed answers itself. OpenAI's Dall-E appeared to be even more magical as it could generate original images from text prompts in just a few seconds. Almost immediately, concerns were raised about what this might mean for artists and content creators and their livelihoods. Schools and universities expressed worries about the potential for such tools to encourage academic misconduct among students. These and other issues surrounding the adoption of AI systems by organisations and individuals will be explored in more detail in Chapters 3 and 4 but it is worth considering here the role of data and the internet in the development of GenAI technologies.

We've already seen that the development of the transformers within Google was a pivotal advance in AI research that enabled larger bodies of data, particularly text, to be understood by machines and then that understanding used to create original outputs. This approach has also been applied to images through vision transformers that break images down into smaller segments for analysis and processing (Houlsby and Weissenborn, 2020). The key to training these models is feeding them enough appropriate data, whether text, numerical or images. According to Hughes (2023), OpenAI's GPT-3.5 was trained on 570Gb of data obtained from web articles, books, Wikipedia and other public sources, amounting to over 300 billion words. GPT-4 processed trillions of words during its training phase and, reportedly, cost over US$100 million (Knight, 2023).

Content owners have become concerned that their data is being unfairly and, in some cases, illegally scraped by OpenAI and other GenAI companies with no financial compensation. Although Google has been criticised by some news providers for the content the search engine has indexed, Google does at least provide links to the original sources in the search results. For many website operators, these leads provide a key source of income. If a GenAI chatbot is providing answers to users' prompts without driving traffic to the original content it was trained on then there is a real risk of disintermediation. Content creators could be bypassed in this new information value chain. As a result, several larger news providers and popular websites, such as Reddit, are striking deals with OpenAI and its competitors to ensure some financial compensation. We will examine how business models and value chains may change in this emerging landscape in Chapters 2 and 3.

CHAPTER 2
The Current AI and Data Landscape

The data landscape has changed almost beyond recognition over the last 30 years. Established methods of collecting, compiling and publishing information have either been made redundant or radically transformed. We have looked at the drivers of these changes in the previous chapter, with the internet and, more recently, AI reconfiguring data value chains and business models in the process. This chapter explores the current state of the information landscape and considers how much data is being created in the mid-2020s, where it is coming from and how it is being used.

How much data is there?

Precisely mapping and measuring the global information economy is impossible as countries measure things differently and many of the inputs and outputs are hidden behind firewalls and corporate networks. However, approximations can be made based on publicly reported data, government statistics and technology sales. Broadly, we can attempt to measure the monetary value of data and information products produced each year as well as the quantity of data produced, distributed and stored. For the purposes of this book, the utility of considering such figures is to help us better understand broader trends in the production, distribution and use of data and what this might mean for the future of information professionals from a range of disciplines. Understanding the shifting sands of our data-driven environment can help us make better decisions about where to invest our time and resources going forward.

One of the first comprehensive and rigorous attempts to measure the volume of information being generated each year was carried out by economists Peter Lyman and Hal Varian at Berkeley University in 2000 (Lyman and Varian, 2000). They calculated that in 1999 the world produced between 2 and 3 exabytes of unique information. This figure was arrived at by estimating the digital equivalent of analogue outputs, such as paper and film, and adding that to natively digital media, such as magnetic and optical drives. A follow-up study in 2003 resulted in a total figure of up to 5 exabytes (Lyman and Varian, 2003). It is important to remember that these figures refer to the amount of unique information created each year and not the volume of data that was transmitted across networks such as television, radio and the internet. In 2002, they calculated this was almost 18 exabytes.

So how big is an exabyte? In technical terms, an exabyte is equivalent to 1,000 petabytes or a billion gigabytes. But these are abstract measures for the human brain to comprehend. It may help to know that if 5 exabytes were burned onto DVDs, the stack would reach to the moon and back and then halfway back again (Davis, 2024).

However, the digital world has changed considerably since 2002, with technology consulting firm, IDC, claiming that by 2026 221,000 exabytes will be created globally (Burgener and Rydning, 2022, 3). The DVD metaphor starts to unravel at this scale, but the key message is that data volumes have increased exponentially over the last 20 years. Interesting questions emerge from this: why has it increased so much, where has all this new data come from, what formats is it being stored and transmitted in and how is it being used?

Sources of data

Before looking in detail at where all these exabytes of data are coming from, it is worth noting that there are two broad types of data that make up what IDC calls the 'global datasphere': structured and unstructured data. According to IDC, unstructured data makes up more than 90% of the data being created each year (Burgener and Rydning, 2022, 3).

Structured data fits easily into tabular format and includes types such as numbers, dates and short text descriptors. Unstructured data cannot be slotted neatly into tables and comprises formats such as audio and video files and large quantities of text. The processing of structured data is straightforward using tools such as standard query language (SQL) databases. Making sense of unstructured data requires more elaborate approaches, including data visualisation, programmatic manipulation and machine learning (ML) (AWS, 2024). Figure 2.1 opposite presents examples of structured and unstructured data from both the public and private sectors.

From a user perspective, structured data allows organisations to build workflows more easily around their information, but the predefined structure constricts users to a more limited range of functionality. Unstructured data is more complex to manage and extract value from but, once harnessed, can be put to a wider range of purposes (IBM, 2021). Much of data gathering and

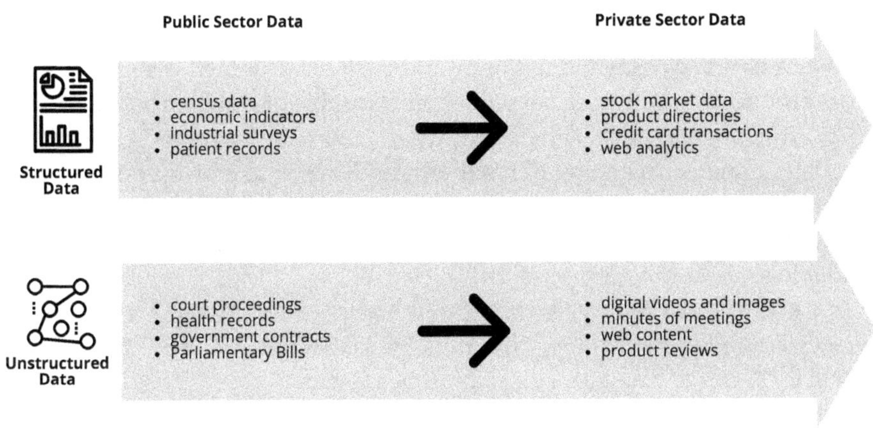

Figure 2.1 *Sources of data*

processing carried out by AI firms such as Anthropic and OpenAI has involved collecting disparate sets of unstructured data from websites and feeding it into their large language models (LLMs).

While differentiating between structured and unstructured data is a useful way of thinking about data at a meta level, it does not help explain where the data came from and why it was collected. The following sections explore the key originators of data and how it is used by others to create information products that organisations can incorporate into their workflows.

Public sector data

Government and public bodies are the largest collectors of data in many developed economies. Such data includes information on employment, tax collection, social demographics, economic indicators and health records. In a 2021 written submission to a UK government consultation, open data advocates, the ODI, concluded that there were over 100 different public bodies with significant responsibility for data. These included more than 65 national departments, 12 cross-government bodies and over 30 advisory boards (Freeguard, 2021, 6). Providing greater access to this data is essential, the ODI argues, for both social and economic reasons. The EU has implemented a number of initiatives since the early 2000s to unlock the value of public sector information (PSI), including the Gaia-X project, which aims to help business, science and political bodies work more closely to build 'an open, transparent digital ecosystem, where data and services can be made available, collated and shared in an environment of trust' (Gaia-X, 2024).

The US has a longer history of opening PSI to citizens and third parties. The 1966 Freedom of Information Act allowed any citizen to request records held by executive agencies. This has established the principle that PSI can be seen as a national asset and a vibrant industry has emerged over the last 50 years around the commercial exploitation of public information assets. Third-party innovators have created value-added information services by combining and repackaging PSI and selling them on to end-users. The most recent US legislation on PSI reuse was the 2017 OPEN Government Data Act, which requires open government data assets to be published in machine-readable formats (US Congress, 2017).

In the UK, until relatively recently, there has been more of a culture of secrecy among public bodies, with the Official Secrets Act of 1911 making it illegal for civil servants to share any public information about the operations of state even down to the colour of the carpets in a minister's office. This was only repealed in 1989. However, since then there has been at least an acknowledgement by those in power that the benefits of sharing non-sensitive data more broadly can have a range of social and economic benefits. In 2020, the UK government launched its National Data Strategy with Mission 1 aiming to 'unlock the value of data across the economy' (techUK, 2021). Central to this objective was to: encourage public bodies to store data in accessible and reusable formats; store data on resilient infrastructure that third parties can access; encourage best practice among public bodies regarding data access; and co-operate internationally to encourage data sharing more broadly.

Not all types of PSI are considered equal when it comes to the value it presents to third parties aiming to build commercial information services. Over the last decade, data collected by mapping agencies, statistical offices, meteorological services, company registers, legal bodies and transport agencies have offered the most commercial potential. Products built on these types of data are often of value to businesses for logistics, compliance and credit checking purposes. The value to national economies of such PSI can be enormous, with estimates for the value of open public data as a percentage of GDP ranging from 0.1% to 7.19% (Bennett Institute for Public Policy, 2020, 10).

The single most valuable source of public data is mapping agencies whose geospatial data is a key resource for organisations, public and private, in planning and operations. An early pan-European study on the value of PSI found that geospatial data was worth €36 billion in 2000 (€66 billion in 2024), more than half of the total European PSI value of €68 billion. Since 2000, the collection and use of such data has grown rapidly with a number of private companies, such as mobile operators and software companies including Alphabet and Apple, now rivalling public organisations in the volumes and granularity of mapping data collected. In the Netherlands, the national statistical body uses private vessel-tracking data as a measure of economic activity. In the UK, the public agency overseeing 4,300 miles of road, Highways England, has partnered with a mobile operator to share phone usage data to improve road and transport infrastructure planning (OECD, 2022).

While there is little debate as to the value of PSI to the broader economy, questions are raised about whether it is appropriate for private companies to generate profits from the resale of data that was collected at public expense. If public data has value, so the argument goes, then it should not be given away for others to profit from. Companies should be charged for using PSI or government bodies themselves should be the ones to commercialise these assets. In the UK, different approaches have been tried with some public bodies operating as quasi-commercial entities and tasked with generating income from their data assets. The Land Registry and Ordnance Survey fell under this category and operated as so-called 'Trading Funds'. However, government policy has changed in recent years with semi-commercial Trading Funds being replaced by more open regimes but still imposing conditions on how their licenced data may be used by third parties.

Perhaps a reflection of this more open approach was the creation in 2010 of the data.gov.uk portal that offers access to more than 80,000 public data sets. These can be downloaded in a variety of common formats (such as CSV and PDF) and republished within the conditions of the Open Government Licence. With the primary exception of personal data, users are granted a 'worldwide, royalty-free, perpetual, non-exclusive licence to use the information . . . (providing you) acknowledge the source of the information.' (National Archives, 2024). There are few restrictions on what can be done with the data with third parties free to "copy, publish, distribute and transmit the information; adapt the information; exploit the information commercially and non-commercially for example, by combining it with other information, or by including it in your own product or application." (National Archives, 2024).

The data.gov.uk portal has been acknowledged as a major step forward in opening up public data assets but there are still criticisms that licencing costs and usage restrictions from bodies including the Ordnance Survey and Hydrographic Office are holding back progress. The EU's Open Data Maturity index measures the progress member states have made in releasing their PSI. The last index to include the UK (Brexit has removed the UK from the index) showed it had fallen behind most other European countries with a score of 62% against 95% for Spain, 98% for France and 89% for Germany (EU, 2021). The EU index considers national data policies, open data impact, the quality of public data portals and data quality when comparing countries. A concern with the UK's PSI was the quality of the public data being made available, particularly the currency and completeness of the data.

Case study 2.1 – The London Datastore

PSI is collected by regional bodies and authorities and used to help policy making and encourage businesses and citizens to engage more closely with their local environment. London has been a leader in making the data it collects available for social and commercial uses, with the London Datastore (LDS) being set up by the Greater London Authority (GLA) in 2010. By 2024, the LDS hosted over 2,000 data sets with more than a million downloads of data and two million page views in January 2023 alone (Chief Digital Officer for London, 2023).

The data sets cover a wide variety of activities related to the governance and operations of a city of nine million people. These range from monthly aggregated statistics on vehicles entering London's Congestion Charge zone available in CSV and XLS formats to structured data on London's Wellbeing and Sustainability index. From a logistical perspective, the benefits of providing detailed data on London's infrastructure through data sets such as the National Underground Asset Register (NUAR) and the Infrastructure Mapping Application (IMA) have been quantified by the GLA. The NUAR allows over 26 public authorities and utilities to share data on street works such as laying and repairing water and gas pipes and, it is estimated, has saved 426 days of disruption on the road network and added wider benefits to the London economy of £4.1 million (Chief Digital Officer for London, 2023). Complementing the LDS is the open data made available by Transport for London (TfL), including details of timetables for buses and underground trains, service status data and planned engineering works. These are offered via APIs for developers to feed into real-time applications and are part of digital offerings from Google, Apple and Citymapper. Research by Deloitte estimated that making this open and freely available for reuse has added up to £130 million a year to the city's economy (Deloitte, 2017, 5).

Later in this chapter, we consider in more detail how PSI is used, particularly by third parties that repackage and combine public data sources to create commercial data products.

Private sector data

Broadly, there are two types of data created by private organisations: data created for the sole purpose of selling on to third parties and data created as a by-product of an organisation's core activities. Since commerce began more than 5,000 years ago, information has been generated to track sales made and credit given. More recently, as we have seen, businesses such as newspapers and entertainment providers have made the creation and distribution of information their core offering.

Consulting firm, Outsell Inc., has calculated that in 2022 the global value of both these types of information and the services surrounding them amounted to US$2.2 trillion (Phillips, 2023, 160). Breaking out each type of data created within the private sector is difficult as there is a degree of duplication from companies collecting data from various sources and repurposing and reselling it to interested parties.

A company's internal records of business meetings, product sales, staffing and recruitment, financial accounts and marketing activities generates huge quantities of data. Depending on the sector involved, there may be a legal requirement to hold certain types of information in specific formats and for predefined periods of time.

While much of this data may seem mundane and of little value beyond the purpose for which it was originally created, internal information assets are increasingly seen as a valuable commodity that can be exploited for competitive advantage. The rise of knowledge management (KM) in the 1990s as a set of tools, techniques and frameworks for creating value from these assets can be seen as the beginning of this trend. KM sought to create systems within organisations that could capture the collective knowledge of employees and codify it into actionable and shareable information resources. Davenport and Prusak (1998) were proponents of this approach and sought to explain the differences between data, information and knowledge. They argued that data formed the building blocks of an organisation's knowledge system and could be seen as discrete and objective facts about events, such as structured records of transactions or employees' personal details. Data becomes information when it has meaning attached and becomes valuable in some form to the organisation. This might include adding contextualisation such as why it was gathered, why it is relevant or who, within the organisation, might find it useful and for what purpose. Things become a little fuzzier when we talk about the next stage, turning information into knowledge. The authors provide the following definition:

> Knowledge is a fluid mix of framed experience, values, contextual information, and expert insight that provides a framework for evaluating and incorporating new experiences and information. It originates and is applied in the minds of knowers. In organisations, it often becomes embedded not only in documents or repositories but also in organisational routines, processes, practices, and norms.
>
> (Davenport and Prusak, 1998, 20)

The idea that knowledge management systems could combine the information held in company files with the accumulated experience of employees to create a unique and valuable resource for an organisation was a powerful one. Technology vendors and consultants were quick to offer solutions and systems, but the promise of KM never really materialised. In his critical look at some of these promises and the reality of what was actually on offer, Wilson (2002) pointed out inconsistencies with this 'nonsense' as he saw it. At the heart of Wilson's critique was his argument that, by definition, knowledge could not be managed as it was unique to the individuals from where it originated.

Knowledge management fell out of fashion throughout the 2000s and 2010s as new technologies caught the imagination of technology vendors and users, including smartphones and mobile apps, social media platforms and Web 2.0. However, as we will see in Chapter 3, the new generation of AI technologies and services has the potential to help businesses get closer to a number of the promises of KM. Putting philosophical questions about the nature of knowledge to one side, AI may be able to extract more value and meaning from internal data assets than more traditional information systems have been able to.

Synthetic data

The rise of GenAI over the last few years and the development of the large language models (LLMs) powering this step change in content creation has seen a new type of data appear. Emerging in the early 1990s to help with privacy concerns over the collection of census data, computer-generated synthetic data has become an important component in the training of LLMs (Rubin, 1993). According to Jordon et al. (2022):

> Synthetic data is data that has been generated using a purpose-built mathematical model or algorithm, with the aim of solving a (set of) data science task(s).
>
> (Jordon et al., 2022, 5)

Whereas real data is generated by events in the real world (for example, e-mails, web pages, financial transactions and medical tests), synthetic data, as we use the term in an AI context, is created by computers and aims to help solve the following issues:

- Privacy – training AI models on real data that includes personal information such as names, addresses and health records raises obvious privacy concerns. Synthetic data can be designed to mitigate this but, as we shall see, is not perfect.
- Data scarcity – LLMs such as OpenAI's ChatGPT and Anthropic's Claude have been trained on massive data sets, much of it scraped from

the open web. As content owners start to lock down their content from being freely absorbed into these models, training data is becoming scarcer. Being able to quickly generate synthetic data has obvious advantages.

- Costs – finding, absorbing and processing real-world data can be expensive and time-consuming. Much of the data is unstructured and may require expensive inputs from data scientists and computing infrastructure to get it into a usable format that the training models can understand. Designing synthetic data that can be fed straight into these models saves time and money.

In 2022, technology consulting firm Gartner forecast that by 2024, 60% of the data used in training AI models would be synthetic and that by 2030, synthetic data will completely overshadow real-world data for AI developers (Gartner, 2022). Synthetic data can be generated on demand through services such as MOSTLY AI's Synthetic Data Platform, which, in their words, 'generates data that is highly representative, highly realistic, and considered "as good as real"' (MOSTLY AI, 2024). Alternatively, developers can buy off-the-shelf synthetic data from marketplaces such as Datarade, where users can buy, for example, one million synthetic credit card statements, 200,000 images of damaged cars or AI voice data in multiple languages for training customer service bots (Datarade, 2024).

Although synthetic data may seem to provide solutions to many of the concerns surrounding AI LLMs and the inputs used to train them, there are issues which need to be considered:

- Privacy cannot be taken as a given. Synthetic data may disclose confidential information if it was derived from inputs containing private data. A research report from the Alan Turing Institute and The Royal Society concluded that synthetic data should be used as a tool to accelerate LLM development but any AI products that will be used in the real world need to be carefully checked and, if required, should be fine-tuned on real data (Jordon et al., 2022).
- The real world is messy and unpredictable and LLMs designed to help make decisions within organisations need to be trained on data that takes this uncertainty into account. Replicating these outliers in synthetic data is difficult as, by their very nature, they are hard to predict.
- Data inbreeding and model collapse. Just as diversity is important in making animal populations sustainable, so there is a danger of synthetic data derived from other synthetic data risks becoming too far divorced from reality. Inbreeding within groups of animals may result in

deformities that become worse with each generation. Similarly, defects in synthetic data sets may become amplified if fed into subsequent models. This may happen directly through synthetic data being fed straight into training models or indirectly where GenAI-created content is published on the web and then scraped by developers for training purposes. Researchers writing in Nature believe this can lead to model collapse:

> We discover that indiscriminately learning from data produced by other models causes 'model collapse' – a degenerative process whereby, over time, models forget the true underlying data distribution, even in the absence of a shift in the distribution over time.
>
> (Shumailov et al., 2024, 755)

How data is used

In his seminal paper of 1937, Ronald Coase sought to explain why businesses are formed when it could be possible for the functions of a firm to be carried out by independent individuals (Coase, 1937). At the core of his explanation was the issue of transaction costs incurred in creating products and services and then launching them into the market. By performing these functions within a single legal entity, these costs could be reduced due to the bargaining power of a corporation and the ability to use in-house experts to carry out specialist tasks. Two of the key factors where a company has an advantage over an individual are search and information costs. These include costs incurred finding information about competitors and their products, identifying potential firms to partner with, understanding pricing levels in the marketplace and forecasting where consumer demand might be going.

The 20th century has seen information become a key asset for organisations as technologies have emerged, such as computers and telecommunication networks, to speed up its creation, processing and distribution. The rise of the post-industrial or information society has been long discussed (Machlup, 1962; Toffler, 1970, Bell, 1976; Porat, 1977; Stonier, 1983; Miles, 1993), with the rise of computing technologies forming a central role in this transformation. Much of this literature focuses on the social impacts of digital technologies as well as attempts to quantify the size of the 'information economy'. In the context of commerce, Peter Drucker saw the implications of these changes for companies and how the shift from manual to knowledge work would change the dynamics of business (Drucker, 1969). At the heart of his argument was the prediction that the critical resource for competitive success would shift from capital and land to knowledge. He saw knowledge as information that was put to productive use in helping with more effective corporate planning, decision-making and innovation.

Porter and Millar (1985) also argued that information was a key resource for organisations to outcompete their rivals and mapped how different industries and product categories used and embodied information in different ways. Their information intensity matrix (Figure 2.2) is a useful tool for thinking about the importance of information to different types of business.

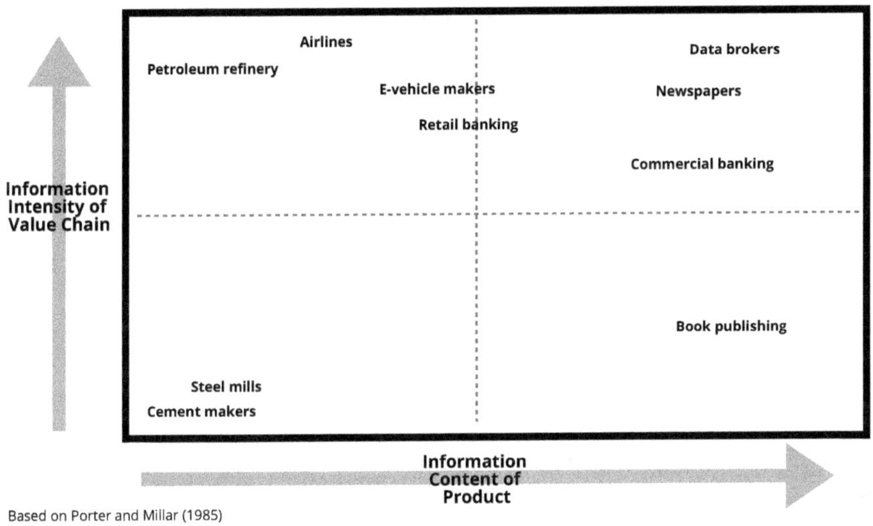

Figure 2.2 *Information intensity matrix*

The matrix maps the extent to which information plays a role in the overall value chain within which the business operates as well as the importance of information to the product or service being produced. Oil refining, for example, creates a product that contains no information itself but requires large amounts of information in its production, from exploration to drilling to transportation and finally to refining. Similarly, the creation of newspapers, physical or digital, requires a complex value chain of gathering multiple types of information from diverse sources, processed by journalists and editors. However, the end product differs in that it embodies this processed information for readers to consume. Interestingly, a number of physical products that traditionally contained little or no information in their final form are increasingly vessels of as well as producers of data. Automobiles, while complex to produce and being part of information-intensive value chains, have generally made little use of information in their operation. Speedometers, rev counters and fuel gauges were the more information-intensive elements of a car. However, the embedding of computer chips and sensors for gathering a multitude of data sources as well as the wireless transmission of this data, particularly in e-vehicles, have changed this. These connected cars, forecast to make up 95% of all vehicles on the road by 2030, are generating an estimated 25Gb per hour (Afshar, 2024).

Data value chains

Following on from Porter and Millar's demonstration of the role of information in industry value chains, this section considers in more detail the increasing importance of data in the ways services and products are created and industries structure themselves. Staying with the automobile industry, we will look at how information is used and shared by the different stakeholders to better understand how value creation and capture is changing in a traditional sector.

Figure 2.3 shows a simplified version of the key stages and activities traditionally involved in the production of internal combustion engine (ICE) vehicles. Since the early 20th century, the ICE with a gearbox/transmission system driving four wheels has been the dominant design for automobiles. It was not always clear that this would be the configuration that would prove most popular, with electric and steam-powered cars enjoying equal sales at the turn of the century. Ultimately, the ICE proved the winner due to its longer range and the greater power-to-weight ratio offered by petroleum. Once these core design elements had proven a winning combination among consumers, the focus in the auto industry shifted to making cars more cheaply and quickly. Henry Ford of the Ford Motor Company and Alfred P. Sloan at General Motors devised and refined the system of mass production. Rather than a group of workers putting together a vehicle in a single space, Ford and Sloan discovered that creating an assembly line along which the car in its various stages passed and was worked on by assemblers who focused on a

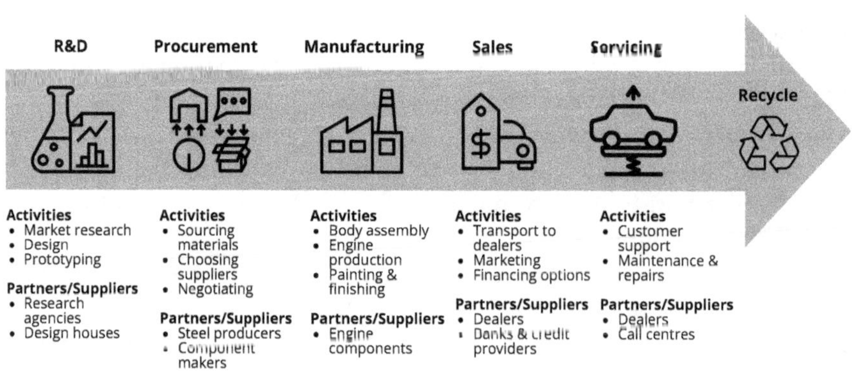

Figure 2.3 *ICE automotive value chain*

specific task was much more efficient. The first Ford Model T was sold in 1906 for US$850 and by 1914 the company was producing 265,000 cars a year. During this eight year period, the price dropped to US$490 and then to US$260, with Ford taking 55% of the US automobile market (Hargadon, 2014, 169). The only way for manufacturers to survive in this market was to use economies of scale and mass production techniques to beat competitors on price. The collapse of smaller manufacturers illustrates this: the number of active manufacturers in the US fell from 253 in 1908 to 44 in 1929, with three companies accounting for almost 80% of the total market (Abernathy, 1978, 89). Over the course of the 20th century this was the model for car makers around the world, with the exception of niche and premium brands such as Rolls Royce and Ferrari.

Over the last 20 years, the role of data in the operating and maintenance of automobiles has become more prominent. Sensors installed around the car to monitor engine performance and component wear and tear have become common. However, the rise of electric vehicles (EVs) and autonomous vehicles (AVs) is seeing data become a key factor in competitiveness for manufacturers and a value-added service for drivers. This is impacting elements of the value chain and challenging established, legacy auto makers as they compete with new entrants such as Tesla and Rivian in the US and BYD and SAIC in China. Sourcing sufficient batteries and developing reliable software are now hurdles that manufacturers need to overcome alongside capturing and using data to create competitive advantage.

The key changes to the vehicle production value chain brought about by the rise of EVs are:

1. Research and Development
   - Development of advanced driver assistance (ADAS) systems and software
   - Incorporating battery technologies and associated energy management systems
   - Integrating AI and ML capabilities
   - Linking with connectivity modules and wireless updating capabilities.
2. Procurement
   - Securing reliable supplies of sensors, semiconductors and wireless chips
   - Sourcing increasingly scarce materials for batteries including nickel, cobalt and lithium
   - Finding experienced software developers.
3. Manufacturing
   - Integrating sensors, microprocessors, software and advanced electronics into the vehicles

- Replacing ICEs with battery packs and electric powertrains
- Integrating new safety procedures associated with handling high voltage components
- Activating software elements and integrating with computing hardware components.

4 Sales
- Offering value-added software/data services to purchasers
- Integrating subscription services and payments.

5 Servicing
- Collecting and storing vehicle data
- Ensuring reliable over-the-air software updates
- Maintaining cybersecurity systems to protect vehicles from hacking
- Integrating with smart grid and home charging systems
- Maintaining applications for users' smartphones.

Manufacturing scale is still important for EV makers as this drives prices, a key factor in purchasing decisions. While individual vehicle ownership is the dominant model for personal transportation in most economies, the rise of autonomous vehicles (AVs) and sustainable vehicle sharing schemes (VSS) threatens to change this. Data and who controls it will become a key input as well as output of AVs and VSS and this will lead to new value chains, with the dynamics of competition changing. Figure 2.4 opposite shows the key data flows required to maintain the infrastructure to charge EVs. The efficient exchange of this data is essential for electricity generators and grid operators to deliver the energy where it is needed and forecast demand. EV drivers need to be connected to pay for electricity used, while charging station operators act as intermediaries between drivers and those managing generation and the backbone grid.

The addition of efficient, electric motors coupled with energy-dense lithium-ion batteries and wireless connectivity has also led to a massive growth in urban areas of pay-as-you-go electric bikes and scooters. In the US in 2018, 60% of all trips were between zero and five miles, a distance well suited to such journeys (Binder, 2018, 9). Micromobility operator, Lime, is one of the largest service providers globally and operates 200,000 e-bikes and e-scooters in over 30 countries and 230 cities. The company claims its subscribers have taken more than 394 million rides and, in New York City alone, covered more than 2.4 million miles (Lime Micromobility, 2024). This and other similar systems only work because each bike and scooter are constantly being tracked via GPS and sharing data over cellular networks about location and range left in the battery. Users can then access this data via an app on their phones and discover whether a suitable vehicle is nearby.

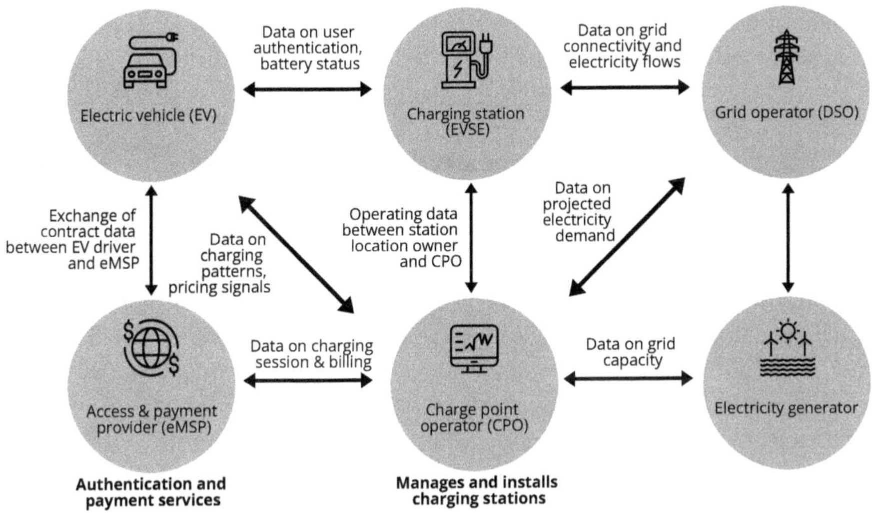

Figure 2.4 *EV ecosystem data flows*

The feedback provided to operators on the location of bikes and scooters and patterns of usage allows them to refine their operations with respect to ordering new items, repairs and recharging.

The increasing flows of data generated by electric vehicles of all types exposes an interesting tension among:

- the companies building the vehicles
- the people driving/riding them
- the businesses acting as intermediaries and offering services such as ride hailing, car sharing and e-bike/scooter on-demand subscriptions
- policy makers and politicians tasked with improving transportation systems, powering pollution and lowering carbon emissions
- electricity generators and grid operators.

A challenge for all stakeholders in this system is the extent to which data can be shared across multiple systems and operators. The use of different and often incompatible data formats and standards can make this impossible where commercial stakeholders are unwilling to share data for commercial reasons. A recent report from consultants, EY, made the case that great data interoperability would increase the speed of the take-up of EVs across Europe:

> eMobility is about more than just the technological switch away from combustion engines. It's about connecting the worlds of transport, energy and the built environment. This, however, depends on data interoperability and

> information sharing and getting there is a challenge. Overcoming this will help improve the overall EV experience and unlock value for ecosystem players.
>
> (EY, 2024, 8)

The benefits of common data standards and protocols have been demonstrated across a number of technologies and services. While proprietary formats may confer benefits to commercial entities in the short term, they may benefit more in the longer term by adopting a common standard. This is certainly usually true for the end-users of those services. E-mail is a good example where the common use of non-proprietary and free-to-use protocols such as POP3, SMTP and IMAP opened electronic communications to the masses in the 1990s. An earlier generation of e-mail services, such as those provided by AOL, CompuServe and Prodigy, used proprietary and closed systems that restricted electronic messaging only to users on the same network. The commercial incentive for this was to grow their subscriber bases and, depending on the critical mass they achieved, to become the de facto provider of electronic entertainment and communication services. However, the open standards underpinning the internet, where no single entity controlled access or the services it could offer, undermined the closed models of AOL and its competitors. Eventually forced to open their networks to the internet, their walled garden approach to the services they provided users became unsustainable. The power of network effects, whereby a communications platform becomes exponentially more valuable to users as connections grow, was better suited to an open architecture than a closed one. In the case of the web, a virtuous circle emerged as new services were built on top of open protocols, including e-mail and the World Wide Web (WWW), and then applications such as Amazon, Gmail and Facebook on top of those layers. We will explore the dynamics of network effects and their impact on data-driven business models in the next section.

Changing business models

While the fundamentals of how businesses operate have changed little over the last century, being able to succinctly define the core activities and processes within an accessible framework is relatively new. Breaking down these elements into what is often referred to as a 'business model' makes it easier to understand why some businesses succeed while others, in the same sector, fail. A business model describes what a business does, how it does this and how revenues and, hopefully, profits are generated. Teece (2010) provides a clear and broadly accepted definition of the term:

> The essence of a business model is in defining the manner by which the enterprise delivers value to customers, entices customers to pay for value, and converts those payments to profit. It thus reflects management's hypothesis about what customers want, how they want it, and how the enterprise can organise to best meet those needs, get paid for doing so, and make a profit.
>
> (Teece, 2010, 172)

In practice, the business model concept helps leaders and strategists dissect a firm's activities and, if required, reorder them to cope with changing markets, technologies and economic environments. Osterwalder and Pigneur (2010) took this module approach and created a conceptual framework they called the 'Business Model Canvas'. This can be used to analyse, describe and define business models in a practical way that is accessible to managers. Their framework expands on Teece's definition of a business model and breaks the activities of a firm into nine core elements, from defining customer needs, explaining the firm's value proposition in response to those needs, where revenue will come from and what costs will be incurred. Figure 2.5 lays out these nine components and how they relate to each other.

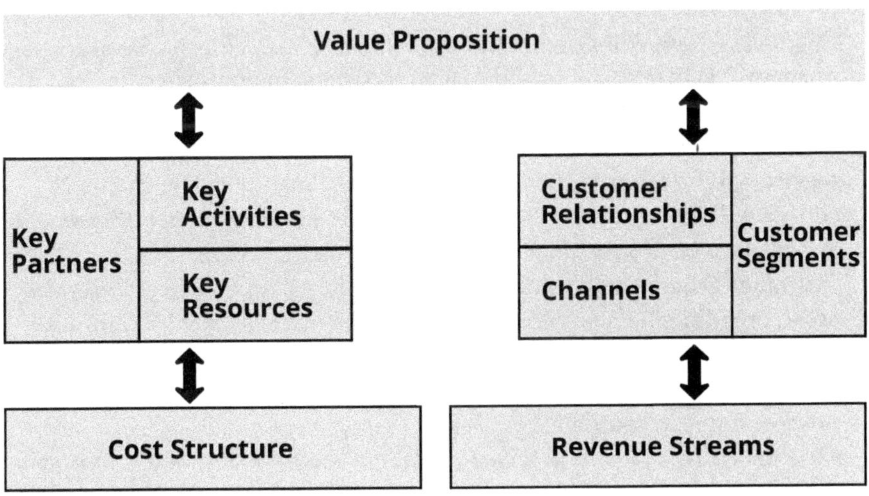

Adapted from Osterwalder and Pigneur (2010)

Figure 2.5 *Business Model Canvas*

Following is a brief explanation of what each of the nine elements of the Business Model Canvas describe and how they relate to each other:

1 Value proposition – this is at the core of the model and defines how the company's product or service differs from its competitors and why

customers might want to buy it. Most companies will have multiple customer offerings so each division or product team may have their own framework. The value proposition may be a unique set of features, a certain pricing point that appeals to a specific customer segment or a level of quality that others cannot match.

2 Key activities – what will this company or product team need to do to deliver on their value proposition?
3 Key resources – what staff, equipment or investment might be needed to produce the product or service? This may be sourcing premium materials or employing sufficient staff to offer a superior customer experience, depending how the value proposition has been defined.
4 Key partners – what help might be needed from outside the organisation? This might involve contracting legal help, consultants or technical expertise.
5 Customer relationships – what type of relationship will the company have with their customers? It might be indirect if they are selling through third-party retailers or direct if selling via their own website. Companies engaged in selling to other businesses may employ agents on a commission basis.
6 Channels – how will potential customers be reached for marketing purposes? Will it be via traditional advertising channels such as mainstream media or via more direct means such as digital and e-mail marketing? Channels also encompasses the ways that the product or service will be put into the hands of the end consumer. The channels chosen will influence the type of customer relationships that then emerge and need to be appropriate to the market being targeted.
7 Customer segments – customers are ultimately people, even if the sales are to other businesses. People are complex and have many needs and wishes. Segmenting your target market(s) and devising sales and marketing approaches appropriate to each is important if the value proposition is to resonate.
8 Cost structure – what will it cost for all the above and does the company have the necessary resources?
9 Revenue streams – how will the products or services generate income for the company? Will it be one-off sales of products where marketing efforts are directed at creating repeat sales? Or will there be a recurring nature to the revenues, such as subscriptions?

The concept of a business model serves as a vital tool for entrepreneurs and executives in crafting and managing thriving enterprises. It offers a conceptual framework for strategising various aspects of operations. By employing this tool, leaders are compelled to consider all the necessary processes their organisation must engage in to attract clientele and deliver market-demanded goods or services. Successful business models invariably revolve around a core principle: articulating how value will be generated and conveyed to customers while ensuring profitability for the company.

As consumer preferences evolve and become more refined, coupled with the emergence of novel distribution channels like ecommerce, the significance of innovative business model design intensifies for firms seeking to distinguish themselves from rivals. Organisations that fail to adapt to these shifts risk falling behind and, as evidenced across various industries, may ultimately face failure.

Teece (2010) highlights several historical instances where industries underwent transformation due to the introduction and implementation of innovative business models by forward-thinking companies. One such example dates to 19th-century America, involving Swift and Company's reimagining of meat transportation from Midwestern cities to burgeoning East Coast markets. Traditionally, livestock was transported live and processed locally upon arrival. Swift Company, capitalising on advancements in refrigeration technology for railcars and warehouses, revolutionised the industry by processing the meat before transport, achieving significant economies of scale and offering more affordable products to consumers. While this innovation proved highly profitable for Swift Company, it severely impacted local butchers and slaughterhouses reliant on the conventional system.

Business model innovation has repeatedly reshaped industries throughout history. Two notable examples include the advent of container shipping in the mid-20th century and the emergence of low-cost airlines in the late 20th century. The introduction of standardised metal containers revolutionised maritime transport, significantly reducing labour costs associated with cargo handling and enhancing port efficiency and delivery speed. Similarly, the aviation industry was transformed by low-cost carriers offering no-frills, point-to-point flights, challenging the traditional hub-and-spoke model employed by major airlines.

A frequently cited example of business model innovation is the razor-and-blade strategy, often attributed to the Gillette Company. This approach, adopted across various industries over the past century, involves offering a low-cost or subsidised primary product that requires consumers to purchase more expensive complementary items. In the razor industry, this manifests as inexpensive razors paired with costlier replacement blades, with proprietary fitting systems and intellectual property protections ensuring customer loyalty. While this model has proven successful for companies like Gillette and Wilkinson, new variations are emerging. One such innovation is the subscription-based model, where replacement blades are regularly delivered to consumers. This shift fundamentally alters the manufacturer-consumer relationship, creating closer ties and opening avenues for marketing additional products and services.

While a business model explains what a company does to build products and services and attract customers, it does not help us understand what is going on outside the organisation and how external forces might impact on internal decisions and strategies. Michael Porter's Five Forces model (Figure 2.6) is widely used by businesses to make sense of external challenges and help managers adapt their strategies accordingly (Porter, 1979). Designing a business model in the abstract without considering how competitive forces in the real world may impact it is like trying to climb a mountain without any training or equipment, you will likely fail. Although Porter's model has faced criticism for being rather static and lacking in sufficient granularity for use by practitioners, it offers a valuable, high-level framework for thinking about competitive challenges (Grundy, 2006). This will be useful later in this section when we look at data-driven business models and why some have found spectacular success while others have stagnated or disappeared. Other widely used frameworks such as PEST (Political, Economic, Social, Technological)

Adapted from Porter (1979)

Figure 2.6 *Porter's Five Forces model*

and SWOT (Strengths, Weaknesses, Opportunities, Threats) can help organisations understand their place in a market but Porter's model is more focused on the dynamics that drive business success.

1 Rivalry among existing competitors – some markets are more competitive than others. For example, the markets for low-cost smartphones or cars are highly competitive, with manufacturers operating on very low profit margins selling products that are broadly similar. Conversely, the market for internet search services, being dominated by Google for the moment at least, is less competitive as network effects and a superior algorithm locked out other search engines.
2 Threat of new entrants – some industries are very difficult for new entrants to make inroads. The pharmaceutical sector, for example, is dominated by a relatively small number of competitors as the costs of research and development (R&D), marketing and regulatory compliance is beyond many startups. The banking and financial sectors are also difficult for new entrants to gain traction in due to the high capital requirements and regulatory pressures. At a local level, retailers and catering establishments are always threatened by new entrants, where opening a new store or coffee shop is relatively inexpensive.
3 Bargaining power of buyers – unless you are a large manufacturing enterprise with loyal customers, selling your products into large retail chains such as Walmart or Tesco can be extremely difficult. The power balance between an artisan cheese producer and a company with hundreds of stores and millions of customers obviously does not favour the cheesemaker. Similarly, a company buying laptops for thousands of employees can strike a much better deal on price than a lone individual buying directly from the manufacturer, however good the product is.
4 Bargaining power of suppliers – all products are made within a broader industry supply chain and where bottlenecks exist in those chains, suppliers can exert an upward pressure on prices. Where demand outstrips supply or where a supplier offers a unique product, this can have a negative effect on profit margins further down the chain. Nvidia's dominance in the graphic processor unit (GPU) market has seen its sales and profits surge, first from the cryptocurrency boom around in the early 2020s and more spectacularly from the AI boom post-2022.
5 Threat of substitute products or services – some markets are more vulnerable to product or service substitution than others. The costs for a large enterprise to switch over the software it uses for key business functions may be too expensive to be justified and so it will stick with an

existing supplier even though its software may be inferior. Apple has adopted a strategy of creating an ecosystem of products and services that work well together, making users reluctant to use other devices. Where products are more commoditised and easily substitutable then competition may be much fiercer. Office supplies such as paper, desks and drinks machines are seldom unique and relatively easy to source, so price rather than features often drives customer choices.

Data-driven business models

While the core principles of what makes a successful business model have changed little over the last century, one of the inputs driving success has changed. The shift from raw materials and/or labour as key resources feeding into what a business does to data as a driver of differentiation and profitability has been exemplified over the last 20 years with the rise of companies like Alphabet (formerly Google), Meta (formerly Facebook), Amazon, Uber and Spotify. While they may not all be selling information directly to their customers, their use of data has made them the most successful companies in their sectors. Below these companies are ecosystems of smaller, data-driven businesses that provide supporting services across sectors such as marketing, banking and finance, retail and hospitality. Even product-focused companies such as Apple are increasingly using data to offer differentiated services and lock out potential competitors. To explore how data has been used to create some of the most valuable companies in the world today, we will look at two of the largest – Alphabet and Apple – and consider how they have exploited network effects and the benefits of operating platforms. We will also consider some of the smaller companies that have built successful business models within the ecosystems of these giants.

Alphabet

Formed in 1998 by two Stanford PhD students, Larry Page and Sergey Brin, Google quickly established itself as a superior search engine compared to rivals such as AltaVista, Lycos and Excite. This was largely due to its PageRank algorithm, which was able to present more relevant results to users than its competitors. Traditionally, search engines have used the information their web crawlers found on websites when they scoured the web. This would include any text or metadata, such as page titles and keywords. When the WWW was relatively small such results would often suffice, but as it grew from 130 websites in 1993 to more than 100,000 at the beginning of 1996 (Science and Media Museum, 2024). Website owners with commercial incentives to increase visitor numbers quickly discovered that tricking search engines into ranking their sites higher than competitors for certain keyword searches was relatively easy. Packing web pages with these keywords in the main body text as well as within the metadata pushed them higher in search engine results pages (SERPs), good for the website operator but not for the searcher who was increasingly presented with irrelevant results. Google added another key variable into their PageRank algorithm that helped weed out low-quality, spammy results from their SERPs and did a far better job of presenting users with the information they wanted. This extra ingredient that favoured quality over quantity was measuring the number and quality of links from other websites that went into the one being indexed. Like citation analysis of academic research papers, the rationale was that if other sites thought it worth linking to a page on another website, then that must be an indicator of quality. Additionally, links from sites that themselves were widely linked to were considered more important than those with less inbound links.

Very quickly, this approach made Google the most popular search engine, with its competitors quickly disappearing. By the early 2000s, Google's global market share of search engine traffic was more than 80%, with a share of more than 90% in 2024 (Statcounter, 2024b). During its first years of operation, Google had no way of monetising its users as its search page was kept free of advertisements to provide a cleaner user experience than the ad-filled pages of its competitors. However, in 2000, the company launched its AdWords (now Google Ads) product where marketers could bid online for their advertisements to show when certain keywords were typed into the search box. In an important move away from more traditional forms of banner and display advertising on websites, marketers only paid Google when someone clicked on their advertisement. By making it a self-service product that marketers engaged with and paid for via the web, setting their own spending limits and bids for certain keywords, the barriers to usage were very low. Coupled with only charging when ads were clicked on and providing analytics data to the advertisers and the fact that searchers were only shown ads relevant to what they were looking for, Google AdWords became an instant success. Data was at the core of the product: the search terms being typed into the Google search box, the budgets and bids set by the advertisers, and the analytics on how many times an ad appeared and was clicked on. Figure 2.7 on the next page illustrates the core flows of data that are generated by users' search inputs and how these are then monetised by Google.

This provided a virtuous circle for advertisers as they refined their approaches and the design of their ads and a virtuous circle for Google as they cemented their place as the internet's most effective advertising platform. Revenues rose from almost zero in 2000 to US$440 million in 2002 and US$258

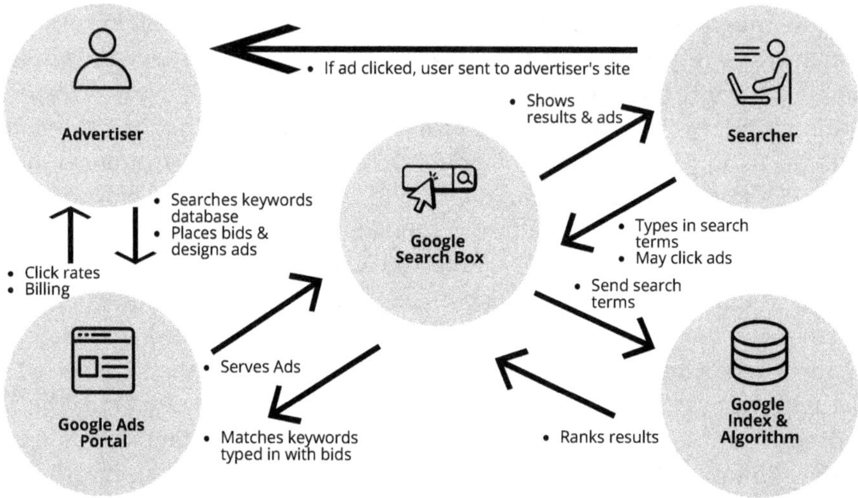

Figure 2.7 *Google data flows*

billion in 2021, with the company's value (measured by its market capitalisation) increasing to more than US$2 trillion by mid-2024 (GlobalData, 2024; Google Finance, 2024a). Although Alphabet is engaged in other commercial activities, from mobile phones to cloud computing and driverless cars, its advertising business is by far the most important and accounted for almost 80% of the company's total revenues in 2023 (Alphabet, 2024).

Protecting its dominant position in search and the associated revenues has been key to Alphabet's business strategy over the last 20 years. The company's move into smartphones with the acquisition of Android in 2005 was a belief that mobile computing could become another source of search traffic for Google. This has proven to be a smart strategic move with searches from mobile devices overtaking desktop traffic in 2009 (Gibbs, 2016) and Android's share of global smartphone operating systems rising to over 70% in 2024 (Statcounter, 2024a). Owning the Android platform allows Alphabet to make Google the default search engine on all compliant devices while it pays Apple more than US$20 billion a year for the same privilege on all iPhones (Nylen, 2024).

Apple

While Apple is another global technology giant like Alphabet, the way it uses data to drive its business model is very different. We have seen that Alphabet's main income is derived from its advertising platform that monetises search results and its core strategy is to maintain that revenue stream through ensuring Google remains the most popular search engine whatever device people are using. Apple's main revenues come from the sale of physical devices, primarily the iPhone. Its business model is focused on finding new buyers for its products and persuading existing customers to upgrade their devices as frequently as possible. On the back of this, the company sells a range of supporting software and data services to users, creating a platform that has the effect of 'locking' customers into the Apple ecosystem. In 2023, 78% of Apple's total revenues came from sales of physical products such as the iPhone, iPad and iMac while the rest was from services such as App Store commissions and iCloud subscriptions (Apple, 2024; Conte, 2024).

Figure 2.8 shows the steady growth of revenue from services as the company uses the data generated from device usage to create a richer user experience. Whereas Alphabet harnesses user data to sell advertising services to third parties, Apple tends to keep user data within its ecosystem. Maintaining a loyal and stable customer base is a core strategy for most companies. Customer acquisition costs (CACs) can be significant depending on the markets, products and customers being targeted. The longer a company can keep its customers before they go to a competitor or substitute the product for something else, the higher the profits that can be generated. Ultimately, the lifetime value (LTV – the total amount of revenue generated while the person is a customer) of a customer needs to exceed the CAC.

There are no shortages of similar products to iPhones, iPads, Apple Watches and iMacs that Apple's customers can switch to should they wish. So, how has the company managed to create one of the world's most valuable and

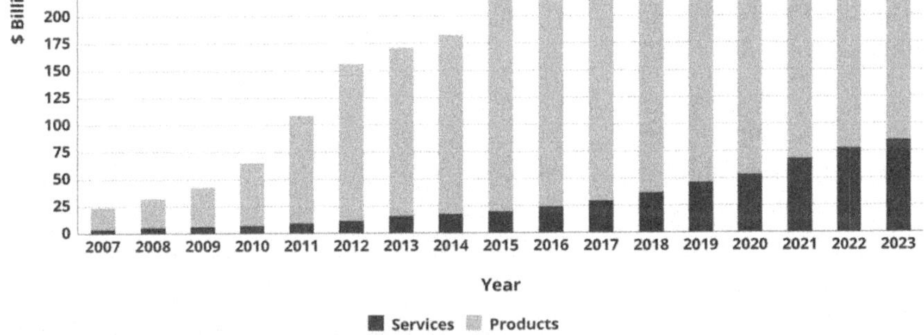

Figure 2.8 *Apple revenue breakdown*

profitable companies selling products in a highly competitive market? Innovation in terms of building software interfaces that people like to use and offering products built to high standards is certainly part of the answer. But the key factor in its success is how Apple uses the data that flows across its devices and that is generated by their use. This, coupled with network effects, creates a hardware and software environment that aims to satisfy users' information and communication needs. Figure 2.9 illustrates how the physical products made by Apple, and the way they interconnect and share data, make it increasingly difficult for customers to move to competitors' offerings.

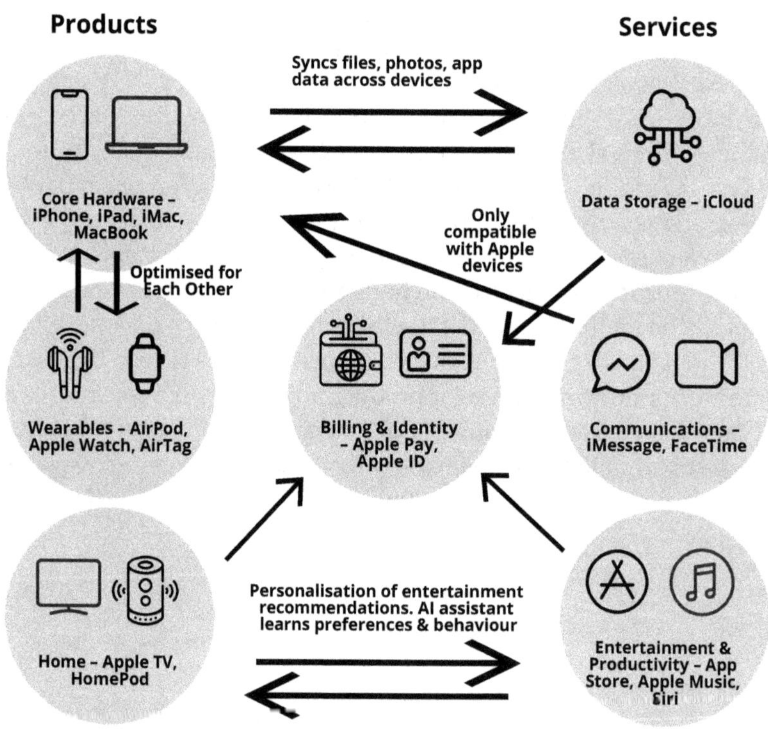

Figure 2.9 *Apple data ecosystem*

In terms of functionality, nothing in Figure 2.9 is unique to Apple products. Alphabet offers its own cloud data storage solution for mobile users; WhatsApp, Facebook Messenger and texting are like iMessage and Facetime; and Android has an app store and billing solutions for its devices. The difference is that some of the apps and peripherals in Figure 2.9 will either only work on iOS devices or are integrated in a way that makes them operate more effectively. An Apple Watch will not pair with an Android phone, making it far less useful to non-iOS users, while iMessage and FaceTime only run natively on iOS. Once a user becomes used to communicating with family and friends via those apps, there is little incentive for them to switch to a non-compatible platform or system such as WhatsApp and persuade others to do the same.

While Apple and Alphabet maintain control over the shape and evolution of their mobile operating systems, there is a key part of their ecosystems, apart from the wireless networks, that has accounted for the rapid adoption of smartphones since 2007. These are the app stores hosting almost two million downloadable applications on iOS and over two million on Android. Like the rise of personal computers (PCs) in the 1980s and 90s, third-party applications have substantially increased the functionality and value of these devices in a way that would not have been possible by the operating system owners themselves. The so-called 'killer app' that made the PC indispensable to businesses was the spreadsheet, created in 1979 by Harvard Business School student, Dan Bricklin, after he thought there must be a better way to record numerical data than in rows and columns on paper. His VisiCalc software, written for the Apple II computer, became an instant success and spawned even more successful imitators such as Lotus 1-2-3 and then the final winner, Excel (Harford, 2019). It is useful to think of PCs and smartphones as platforms for innovation where, if the platform owners manage them in a certain way, massive profits can be made.

Platforms

Today's most successful technology companies owe much of their success to their ability to create and run hardware and software platforms that offer utility value to users and incentives for other companies to develop applications and products that increase that value. Through their extensive research on platforms, Gawer and Cusumano (2002, 2008, 2014) have identified two main types: (1) internal platforms where a company organises a set of assets into a common structure from which the organisation can develop and produce derivative products; and (2) external platforms that allow outside firms to build complementary products and services (Gawer and Cusumano, 2014, 418). Internal examples include Volkswagen's MQB platform, comprising of a shared modular design that has been used across a range of vehicles such as the Audi A3, SEAT Leon, Skoda Superb and VW Golf. This has helped the company cut development and design costs by sharing common architecture. Boeing did something similar with its Dreamliner platform, which was used across variants of its 787 series of aircraft (SP Airbuz, 2018). While internal platforms have become vital elements to business success for many companies, we are more interested in external platforms and the ways they manage data to add value to product and service offerings.

There are several key characteristics that can be found across most external platforms:

- Modular design – a modular structure makes it easier to integrate complementary products and services developed by third parties
- Open architecture – elements of the platform are open to third parties through sharing information about the technical architecture and ways to interconnect and/or by providing mechanisms such as app stores for external developers to offer services to platform users
- Network effects – many platforms benefit from network effects whereby its value increases as more users join and more developers build complementary assets
- Governance structure – rules are established and enforced about what can be done on the platform and how the platform owner interacts with external developers
- Core and peripheral structure – there is usually a central and stable core maintained by the platform owner (for example, iOS, Android, Windows) and a constellation of peripheral innovations built and maintained by outside developers.

A key challenge for platform owners such as Apple, Alphabet and Microsoft is to be open enough so there is an incentive for external developers to invest time and resources in building applications while maintaining sufficient control to prevent any external firms taking over the platform. IBM faced this challenge in the 1980s with the PC. Although behind the launch of the most successful personal computing platform in 1981, the company lost control of the PC's evolution and the bulk of the profits it generated over the subsequent decades to Microsoft (that built the operating system) and Intel (that made most of the microprocessors powering the devices). IBM let Microsoft maintain ownership of the operating system, DOS, as its primary aim was to make profits from selling the PCs themselves, a strategy that had made it the world's largest computer maker from the 1950s to the 1980s. Similarly, Intel controlled the design, manufacture and intellectual property behind the 8086 chips at the heart of the machine. This created an incentive for Microsoft and Intel to encourage other companies to build PCs around this architecture, which IBM had left open enough for clones to enter the market.

Despite attempts by IBM to prevent competitors such as Compaq and HP from using elements of the original PC design architecture, the battle was lost by the late 1980s. Under the so-called 'Wintel' partnership, Microsoft and Intel steered the PC revolution by sharing technical data with other software and hardware developers about the x86 chip instruction set architecture (ISA) and other elements of the device to encourage third parties to build applications and peripherals that would enhance the utility of the PC (Yoffie and Cusumano, 2015, 93–8). This created a virtuous circle of innovation and profits as purchasers were attracted by the range of software available for PCs and developers were encouraged to build more applications by the growing base of users. By the late 1980s, Wintel PCs dominated the market for personal computers. They have maintained that position, with 72% global market share in 2024. However, the personal computing market branched off from the PC after 2010 with the rise of mobile computing, namely smartphones. As we have seen, Apple and Alphabet have gone on to dominate that category by adopting similar strategies. By 2024, just over 4.7 billion smartphones were in use globally, compared to 1.5 billion PCs (Canalys, 2024; GSMA, 2024).

Once the mobile computing market became concentrated around two platforms, the data generated by usage of iOS and Android phones helped cement their dominance by creating a vibrant and highly profitable ecosystem for the platform owners, app developers and advertisers. Figure 2.10 illustrates some of the key data flows within these ecosystems that sustain the platforms' business models.

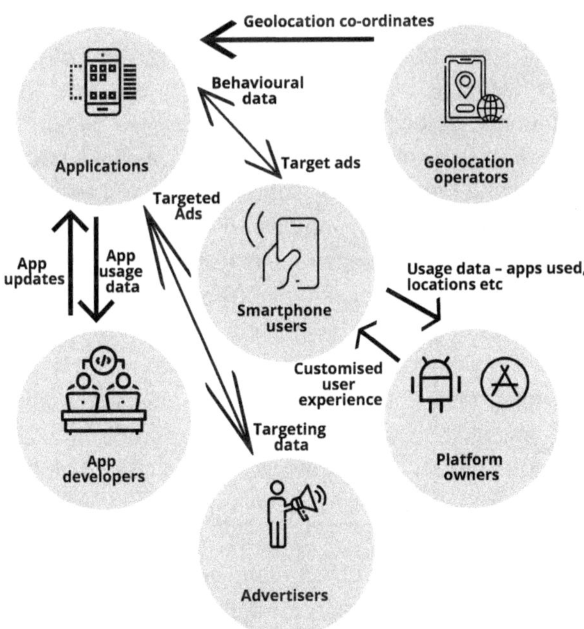

Figure 2.10 *Mobile data flows*

Each phone user is unique and uses their devices in different ways and for different purposes. Based on the apps downloaded and how they are used, the platform owners seek to customise the app store user experience to highlight apps that may be most relevant. This helps increase usage and makes it more likely that further apps will be downloaded and used. For Alphabet and Apple, this is important as the more their phones are used, the more likely it is that customers will stay on their platforms. There is also a direct financial incentive as paid-for apps, or those which generate revenue through in-app purchases, must pay a commission to the platform owners. This has been the subject of much complaining and litigation on the part of app developers as well as legislators. Traditionally, the commission rates have been set at 30% but recent moves by Apple and Alphabet have reduced this for some apps to 15%, with sliding scales for different types of purchases and based on developer revenues. However, as the two companies generate an estimated US$200 billion annually from their app stores with third-party developers doing most of the work, it remains a highly profitable part of their businesses.

Case study 2.2 – Strava

Fitness app Strava was formed in 2009 and by mid-2024 had more than 100 million users and had tracked over 8 billion activities (Strava, 2024). The Strava app, available on iOS and Android, utilises the geolocation capabilities of phones to track and map user activities and also integrates with other tracking devices to measure variables such as heart and recovery rates. These metrics are useful for athletes wanting to track their progress but it is the aggregated data that adds another layer of value for users. Strava allows users to share data with others to create a social element to the app and also creates segment challenges where specific walking, running and cycling routes are tracked for fastest times. This is a popular competitive feature of the app and elevates it beyond being just a solitary user experience. There is also a discovery element to Strava that produces heatmaps showing popular activity routes, helping users find new places to exercise. All these data streams add to the network effects, which discourages users from switching to alternative apps as well as acting as a strong incentive to upgrade to a paid subscription to unlock some features. It is reported that in 2023 Strava generated US$275 million in revenue, with the company being valued at US$1.5 billion in 2020 (Curry, 2024).

The combination of network effects and applications optimised to keep users scrolling and sharing has created some of the most popular and profitable technology platforms during the first 20 years of this century. Data from UK media regulator, Ofcom, shows that, in 2024, adults over the age of 18 in the UK spent an average of 167 minutes per day using their phones, with this figure rising to 231 minutes for the 18 to 24 age group (Ofcom, 2024b). The most popular apps were Instagram, Facebook, TikTok and YouTube. TikTok users over 18 spent an average of 1,011 minutes (almost 17 hours) on the app during March 2024 (Ofcom, 2024c). The application of behavioural science to the design of these apps, combined with the social dimensions of the user experience, explains their popularity and profitability. Instagram generated an estimated US$71 billion in advertising revenue in 2024 (WARC, 2024). All these factors make it incredibly difficult for new entrants to compete in this market where the platform owners have deep pockets to defend their positions and network effects help lock users into the most popular apps. However, new competition is emerging from applications utilising more open technology architectures and which, for the most part, are not driven by commercial motives.

The fediverse

The network that is the internet is founded on protocols and standards that are open and free to use, with no commercial entity exercising overall control of how the network evolves and adapts to changing conditions. A number of quasi-public and voluntary organisations made up of experts from industry, academia and government have set and maintained standards as the internet has grown and been used for purposes not originally anticipated. This flexible and open structure has been a key driver of innovation as individuals and companies are free to build services and applications at various levels of the technology stack. Zittrain describes the internet as being 'generative', whereby specialists and enthusiasts can build products and applications to run on the internet without needing permission from any central authorities (Zittrain, 2008, 67–73).

When Tim Berners-Lee invented the World Wide Web (WWW) in 1989, he chose the internet as the platform on which it could be used because the network was already in operation, could scale globally if the WWW became popular, offered flexibility for implementing the new protocols that the web would require and was decentralised, which fitted with Berners-Lee's vision of an open-decentralised system that anyone could contribute to. He saw the WWW as a collaborative environment for sharing information and his original design allowed web users to edit the web pages they were looking at (Berners-Lee and Fischetti, 1999, 41–2).

While the internet has remained an open platform for innovators and users, the reality of how most people use it has not matched Berners-Lee's vision of a read-write web but instead has become more of a platform for entertainment and information consumption. Alongside that, a small number of application providers have gone on to dominate where most people spend their time online and, as we have seen, have very successfully monetised that. In the UK in 2023, UK adults spent an average of 3 hours and 41 minutes online each day, with 2 hours and 14 minutes of the total being spread across apps and sites of just 12 companies and 1 hour and 20 minutes being spent on properties owned by Meta and Alphabet (Ofcom, 2023). The picture is similar in much of the rest of the world, albeit with different mixes of companies. It seems that the internet has been colonised by a handful of technology giants that have a vested interest in maintaining their control and finding ways to keep users on their platforms for as long as possible. Bearing in mind the often trivial and increasingly misleading nature of much of the content being consumed across these platforms, a number of commentators, policy makers and developers have become concerned that society is not well served by this development:

> Ultimately, it is not our nation or culture but the very nature of our lives that is at stake. For how we spend the brutally limited resource of our attention will determine those lives to a degree most of use prefer not to think about. As William James observed, we must reflect that, when we reach the end of our days, our life experience will equal what we have paid attention to, whether by choice or default.
>
> (Wu, 2016, 7)

One response to these concerns has been the rise of more open and decentralised applications that run over the internet, a constellation of new ways to communicate and share information often referred to as the 'fediverse', a combination of federation and universe. In many ways, these applications share the ideals of many early internet and web developers such as Berners-Lee who saw the interactive and open nature of the developing network as a way for individuals to gain agency in a world dominated by the commercial concerns of big business.

In simple terms, the fediverse is a set of interconnected social platforms that can communicate with each other primarily using the ActivityPub protocol for publishing and sharing information. Unlike Facebook, Instagram or X (formerly Twitter) there are no central organisations that control fediverse platforms such as Mastodon, Diaspora or PixelFed. Instead, each platform consists of many independent servers known as 'instances'. New users of any of these services must choose an instance from which they can post and share content. Different instances may have specific rules and guidelines about the types of content they allow based on the preferences of whoever set the instance up. This decentralised structure creates some key differences from centralised platforms such as Facebook, including greater privacy and personal data control, less vulnerable to large-scale hacking attempts, no centralised content policies and a sense that one's data is not being used for commercial gain.

However, the relative complexity in accessing and using a fediverse platform for most non-technical users has seen slow growth in user numbers. By August 2024, there were approximately one million active users of the different services running across just over 20,000 servers around the world (Fediverse Observer, 2024). The network effects and user lock-in that benefits established, large-scale networks, such as Instagram, makes it difficult for new entrants operating in the fediverse, such as Mastodon, to make significant inroads. This may change as older, established platforms from outside the fediverse start to connect their networks and users. The world's most popular website development and blogging platform, WordPress, now offers a plugin for site owners to connect their properties to the fediverse. Content sharing platform Flipboard has begun to do something similar with segments of its portfolio, while Threads, the social networking site owned by Meta, has been actively testing federation via the ActivityPub protocol.

Whether the fediverse gains enough traction to start benefiting from network effects itself remains to be seen but the engagement of already successful platforms such as WordPress and Flipboard could provide the trigger to growth that is needed. Innovation and the development of new services and applications built on top of the internet has slowed since the early 2000s as large corporations have dominated what individuals do online. Their platforms have become isolated, often barren, islands of content which, although popular with many users, do not allow others to innovate on. In many ways, it is like 1993, when most people's online experience was confined to the walled gardens of CompuServe, AOL and Prodigy. However, in that year, Mosaic, the first widely available web browser was launched and those closed platforms quickly disappeared. Perhaps the fediverse and the innovation that is occurring around and within it will have the same impact.

Data exchanges

Just as stock exchanges and other trading marketplaces provide liquidity for the financial services sector by facilitating the trading of assets such as company shares, commodities and government bonds, so data exchanges have arisen to do the same for the digital economy. If data is the new oil, it needs to flow from where it is produced, be refined and then put in the hands of those that need it. Exchanges and marketplaces play a key role in this process as they offer centralised hubs for data transfers to take place between producers and users.

Figure 2.11 summarises the key data exchange archetypes, how they are used and some of the organisations that provide them. Public data exchanges are open platforms that anyone can access and are typically provided by government and public bodies. We looked at the types of data they provide earlier in this chapter. Private exchanges are closed with access only to specific members or organisations; they may also be used internally within larger organisations that manage proprietary data sets used for functions including product development and marketing. Real-time data exchanges are particularly prevalent in the financial and marketing sectors. Banks and financial services firms subscribe to such services from companies like Bloomberg, S&P Global and Reuters for the real-time data on stock prices, share indices and news. Real-time or programmatic advertising is founded on the trading of personal browsing and searching data in the few

Type	Uses	Examples
Public Data Exchanges	• Public policy making • Academic / scientific research • Journalistic research	• Data.gov • Eurostat • NASA Earth Data • Google Public Data Explorer • OpenStreetMap
Private Data Exchanges	• Healthcare providers • Supply chain management • Automotive industry	• Snowflake Data Marketplace • AWS Data Exchange • Dawex Data Exchange Platform • Harbr
Real-time Data Exchanges	• Financial markets • Marketing sector • Weather forecasting • Airline industry	• Nasdaq Last Sale • Google Ad Exchange • FlightAware Global Aviation Data Services
Personal Data Exchanges	• Individual consumers • Data broking • Social media marketing	• Caden • Solid (Social Linked Data) • CitizenMe

Figure 2.11 *Data exchanges and marketplaces*

milliseconds it takes for a web page to load and uses third-party or cross-site tracking cookies to achieve this. Personal data exchanges are less common but offer ways for individuals to sell their personal data to market research and advertising targeting firms. While platforms like Facebook and TikTok generate significant revenues from the aggregate sale of user data to marketers, it is more difficult for individuals to do the same as, on its own, it is worth very little. Personal data exchanges are an attempt to rectify this but have not managed to attract significant numbers of individual users. However, increasing concerns about online privacy may encourage more people to use services such as Solid that offer greater personal control over online data.

Case study 2.3 – Harbr

London-based Harbr was founded in 2017 and describes itself as a data commerce platform company that helps organisations share, collaborate on and distribute data. Rather than running a data marketplace itself, the company provides a platform for other enterprises to create their own exchanges and marketplaces. Their secure platform and supporting tools allow companies to brand, customise and monetise their data assets both for internal and external purposes. Financial data provider, Moody's, has used the Harbr platform to integrate a number of their data assets and offer their customers a more unified portal for accessing Moody's data products. Harbr describes its platform as solving the 'last mile' problem for data by offering a solution that closes the gap between data producers and consumers. This is an important function as data has no value if it is not in the hands of those that need it or can extract value from it. Such marketplaces and exchanges will become increasingly important as data assets become a competitive differentiator for many companies wanting to integrate AI into their product and service offerings.

The AI landscape

In Chapter 1, we looked at the evolution of AI from its conceptual underpinnings in the 1940s, to the rise of different branches of AI research, including ML and deep learning (DL), and up to 2022 with the launch of OpenAI's generative product, ChatGPT. This is a rapidly changing and dynamic sector that will have evolved considerably from the time this book is being written to when it is published. However, there are some clear trends emerging as well as several interesting questions regarding the potential impact of AI over the next five to ten years that we will consider here.

In the immediate excitement of the potential of GenAI, a number of analysts and consultants attempted to predict the impact it would have on organisations and economies. Consultants McKinsey estimated in 2023 that GenAI could add the equivalent of US$2.6 trillion to US$4.4 trillion annually to the global economy (Chui et al., 2023). McKinsey argued that 75% of this value would come from four key areas within businesses: customer operations; marketing and sales; software engineering; and R&D.

Since then, there has been a little cooling of some of the more extravagant predictions on the impact of AI as the initial hype settles and the hard work of building products and services that harness the potential of AI begins. The focus of this book is on the changing data landscape and AI is playing a significant role in this. While ML and other approaches to integrating AI into solving routine issues, such as pattern recognition and interactive chatbots, have been in use for a number of years, the current wave of LLMs and their ability to produce text, image and video-based content have resulted in a step change in the potential of AI to transform business processes. This transformation will take place over the next five to ten years as models improve and organisations learn from experimentation and implementation how to optimise their deployment. Replacing tried and tested business processes with more automated systems powered by AI is not something organisations will undertake without extensive testing, particularly in heavily regulated sectors such as healthcare and finance.

Understanding at a high level how GenAI products like ChatGPT and Claude work helps us understand what some of the limitations and bottlenecks are and how this might evolve over the medium term. Figure 2.12 opposite illustrates this by showing some of the key parameters that define the effectiveness of LLMs, while Figure 2.13 highlights the main key factors constraining model improvements.

Broadly, there are three categories of variables that determine the effectiveness of a LLM: (1) volume and breadth of training data; (2) parameters making up the processing of the training data within the LLM; and (3) context window limiting the prompts and inputs making up queries of the LLM.

Training data

Early versions of LLMs were trained on scraped content from websites, including Wikipedia and news sites, digital books, social media content, computer code repositories such as GitHub, public data sets, transcripts of videos and podcasts and academic papers. Concerns over copyright and privacy have seen a number of websites and other sources of training data imposing restrictions on how their content can be used by LLM developers. It is likely that accessing training data will become an increasing problem for developers as content owners seek to either block access or begin charging for their intellectual property to be used. Financial deals have already been announced by content creators, including the Financial Times, Reddit and NewsCorp (Tong et al., 2024). New data marketplaces, such as Dappier and Corpus, also started to appear in 2024 providing platforms for content owners to licence their assets to LLM builders (Barker, 2024). For general-use LLMs, the greater the volume and breadth of data used in training the more likely it is to produce useful answers, providing the parameters defining how that data is processed are sufficiently defined.

Parameters

Parameters is a fairly broad term and refers to the numerical values that define an LLM's learned knowledge and capabilities. They include the adjustable weights and biases set within the neural network that comprises the AI model. When the model is being trained, these parameters can be varied to identify patterns and relevant information from the training data. As the model is being tested, these parameters will be fine-tuned by setting specific tasks and training on specific data sets. As Figure 2.12 shows, the number of parameters within a given model may run into the billions, with an estimated 500 billion

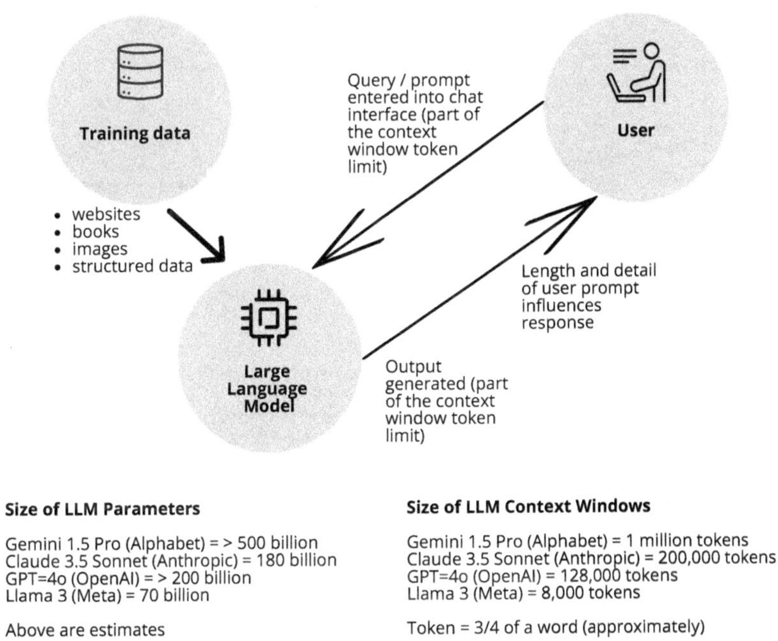

Figure 2.12 *Large language model (LLM) variables*

or more parameters in Alphabet's Gemini 1.5 Pro LLM. In general, the more parameters put into a model, the greater its ability to capture more complex patterns and useful information from the training data. However, this comes at the expense of requiring more computing power, which can become very expensive. Alphabet's Gemini Ultra model, which predates Gemini 1.5 Pro, cost an estimated US$191 million in compute power to train, while its original 2017 Transformer model had cost a much more modest US$900 (Lazzaro, 2024).

Context windows

The 'context window' is the amount of text an LLM can consider in a single operation when generating or processing language. This limit is measured in tokens, which are typically three to four characters in English or about three-quarters of a word. The context window comprises both the length of the prompt or question a user types into the model and the length of the response it then provides. Like parameters, these limits have increased with each new generation of LLMs, with Gemini 1.5 Pro being able to handle 1 million tokens. It is important to note that any documents or files that a user uploads to an LLM as part of their query also count towards the context window limit.

Figure 2.13 highlights how the variables described above present challenges, both technical and financial, that LLM developers are dealing with as they seek to improve their models.

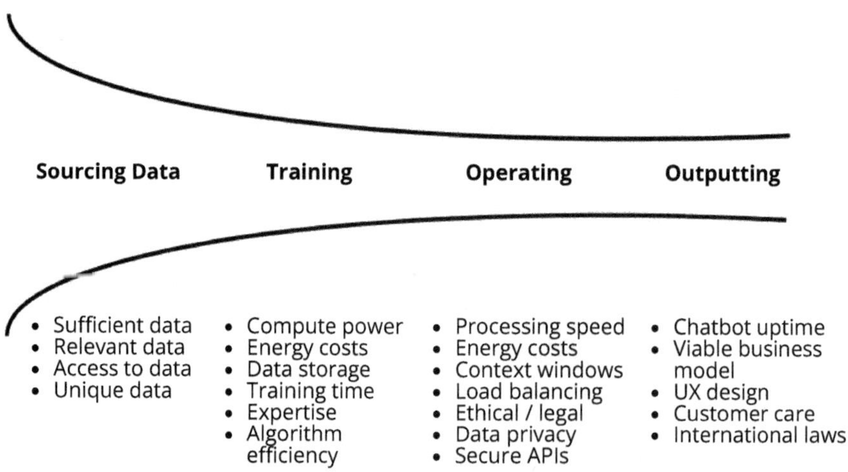

Figure 2.13 *Large language model (LLM) bottlenecks*

From a technical perspective, there is intense competition among LLM vendors to launch ever-more powerful models that can outperform competitors. Four key resourcing constraints limiting this are access to data, staffing, finance and energy.

An LLM is only as good as the data it was trained on. As the old saying in the computer industry goes: garbage in, garbage out. We've already seen that securing access to the necessary quantities of suitable data is becoming more difficult as some important content owners restrict access and/or have started to do financial deals with LLM developers. An issue with widely used LLMs, such as ChatGPT and Claude, is the recency of the data on which they were trained. This may not be an issue for evergreen reference topics, such as historical or scientific facts, but where currency of data, such as news or financial information, is involved this can be a problem. For example, the GPT-4o product released in May 2024 was trained on data up to October 2023 (Kerner, 2024). There are techniques and approaches that go some way to mitigate this problem such as fine-tuning, external plugins and continuous pre-training but these add to the complexity and costs of maintaining models.

Finding suitably qualified AI experts is difficult and demand is forecast to outstrip supply for the foreseeable future. A 2022 survey by Deloitte estimated there were 22,000 AI specialists worldwide, with demand for these experts coming from businesses looking to deploy AI internally as well as the LLM companies themselves (Deloitte, 2022). This shortage is inevitably pushing up the salaries AI specialists can command. Another growing expense is the compute power required to train and run these models. It has been estimated that graphic processing unit (GPU) maker, Nvidia, controls between 70% and 95% of the market for AI chips (Leswing, 2024). Other chip manufacturers, including Intel and AMD, are developing their own offerings, but Nvidia's position is likely to remain dominant for a number of years due to its supporting ecosystem of software and developer tools. Being in such a strong position alongside unprecedented demand for AI chips allows Nvidia to maintain high prices for its products and is reflected in its share price, which rose almost ten-fold in the 18 months between January 2023 and June 2024 (Google Finance, 2024b).

There is a growing concern about the amount of energy required to train and operate LLMs as the GPUs and other supporting computing hardware can be power hungry. Training GPT-3 consumed an estimated 1,287 MWh (megawatt hours) of electricity, equivalent to the energy consumed by a typical US household over 120 years (Mehta, 2024). Deploying and running these models consumes even more energy, with a single LLM interaction consuming the same power as an LED lightbulb (Wells, 2023). When this is scaled up to the millions of users interacting with LLMs daily, the total power requirements are substantial. It has been calculated that if Google incorporated AI inference into all its web searches it would cost Alphabet

US$100 billion in server costs alone, with ChatGPT requiring 15 times more energy than a traditional web search (Hetzner, 2024). How sustainable this all becomes if LLMs are deployed more widely across businesses and society has started to raise alarm in terms of its impact on climate change. As we've seen over the last 20 years with the building of large-scale data centres in colder parts of the planet to benefit from natural cooling, it is possible that some countries and regions will become hubs for AI infrastructure. Iceland, in particular, with its cold climate and abundance of clean, geothermally-generated electricity is becoming a focus for new data centre installations. It has been estimated that running a data centre in Iceland can save 84% in costs, with an accompanying 92% carbon reduction and 32% energy saving (Moss, 2024). We will investigate these broader investment and policy issues in more detail in Chapter 4.

Hallucinations

So far, we've looked at some of the issues involved in developing and running an LLM but an important factor limiting their adoption, particularly within organisations, is the problem of hallucinations. LLMs produce outputs and answers based on patterns they have observed in the training data and generate responses that 'look' accurate. With AI-generated images and videos, it may be easier for humans to spot where something has gone wrong. Dogs with five legs or cars with no doors are examples of hallucinations where the generated artefact looks broadly correct but has telltale errors. Spotting this in text-based responses can be far more difficult as we do not have the visual cues. In an academic context, hallucinations may extend to the creation of fake citations. A study looking at this problem in research proposals generated by ChatGPT discovered that of the 178 sources cited, 69 had no digital object identifier (DOI) and 28 were completely made up (Emsley, 2023, 1). Another study found that of the 115 references generated by ChatGPT for a medical article, 46% were genuine but inaccurate, 7% were authentic and accurate while 47% were completely fabricated (Bhattacharyya et al., 2023, 4). Clearly, the consequences of such errors could be catastrophic if decisions about medical procedures or aircraft design choices are made on the basis of hallucinated AI outputs. We will consider some possible solutions to mitigate these problems in Chapter 3 when we consider the challenges facing organisations that are incorporating AI into their workflows.

Now that we have a picture of some of the key parameters of the current data and AI landscape, it is time to consider how organisations are incorporating these innovations and opportunities into their operations as well as examine the challenges this throws up.

CHAPTER 3

The Emerging Data-Driven AI Revolution

The title of this chapter may be provocative to some as it suggests radical change driven by data and AI are leading a revolution in how organisations will operate in the near future. Caution over analysts and pundits calling technological advances 'revolutions' is wise (as we shall see in Chapter 5) and there is no shortage of examples where irrational exuberance has got the better of writers and forecasters. As the management guru, Peter Drucker, is quoted as saying, 'Trying to predict the future is like trying to drive down a country road at night with no lights while looking out the back window' (Guber, 2014). This is particularly true with trying to forecast how new technologies will evolve and whether they will succeed in the marketplace. Established technology vendors may have a vested interest in playing down the significance of a new innovation developed outside their own company, while businesses launching new products may go in the opposite direction.

Over-confidence in the existing order was demonstrated in 1876 when the president of the telegraph giant, Western Union, was offered the patent on the telephone for US$100,000 and stated, 'This "telephone" has too many shortcomings to be seriously considered as a means of communication' (Yeuh, 2019). Less than 30 years later, his company was bought by telephony 'upstart' AT&T. On the other side, we have WeWork, once valued at US$65 billion by Goldman Sachs for its innovative use of technology to revolutionise office-letting but sold for approximately one hundredth of that figure a few years later (Neate, 2019; Sherman, 2024). Hubris and a confused business model were to blame there.

While acknowledging the difficulties of predicting technology adoption curves, the contention of this book is that we are at the start of a revolution in business practices driven by data and AI. Chapter 5 will explore how this may take shape over the coming five to ten years. This chapter examines a number of current developments and how organisations are already experimenting with and deploying data-driven AI services.

AI opportunities

The WeWork debacle mentioned above shows how the laws of physics limit the extent to which digital technologies can impact the physical world. Office buildings are still buildings no matter how clever the apps are for workers to book desk space in them. Data can be used in clever ways to track and predict demand for office space across various locations and at different times of the year but the core business of companies like WeWork is to provide clean and comfortable spaces in convenient locations for people to sit at desks and do their work. As with the internet revolution of 20 years ago, the greatest and most immediate impact of the current AI revolution is to be found in businesses and workflows which are focused on the processing of information. The digitisation of data coupled with the distribution capabilities of the internet have already transformed how we consume news and find information. When information was primarily in analogue formats, such as books, newspapers and magazines, the physical world dictated the speed and ease of access of such resources. We might say this was an age of information scarcity where finding the information required for research projects often required visiting multiple libraries and combing through catalogues and shelves of books and journals. With the rise of the internet as a network for distributing digital data and the WWW as a protocol for publishing it, we have entered an age of information abundance. Finding the information we need is often just a couple of clicks and taps on a keyboard. In this environment, Google and a few other access providers have dominated with their abilities to index vast quantities of data and provide easy-to-use search interfaces.

AI in the form of LLMs and chatbot interfaces has the potential to take information management to the next level. Whereas Google and other traditional search engines provide links to web pages where they believe the answers you seek can be found, AI solutions are starting to offer users answers without making them click through links. Google's Knowledge Graph database, launched in 2012, could be seen as a stepping stone to this as, for certain straightforward queries, it provided snippets of web pages in its search engine results pages (SERPs), saving users from having to click on any of the results. This worked well for queries such as the population of a country or weather forecasts.

Answer engines or search engines?

Established search engines such as Google and Bing as well as new entrants like Perplexity are where many people will have their first experience of receiving AI-generated answers. Google, for example, started showing 'AI

Overview' answers on SERPs to some queries in 2024. These make use of Google's Gemini AI model as well as aspects of its existing Knowledge Graph database to provide answers above the list of traditional search results (Rogers, 2024). AI Overview results are more commonly shown when interrogative words such as 'why', 'what', 'when' and 'who' are part of a search query. Microsoft has done something similar with its Bing search engine by adding its Copilot AI chatbot as a feature. How these AI technologies are integrated into search results will likely change over the coming years as they struggle with balancing a value-added user experience with advertising-driven business models. This is particularly true for Alphabet that relies on the cash-generating Google search engine for the bulk of its revenues. If users can find the answers they need without having to click on paid-for advertisements placed above and beside search results then the company may have serious problems. This would also spill over into the website operators that rely on traffic from Google and Bing to fuel their advertising-driven sites.

As well as the incumbents in the search engine space, there are new entrants offering AI-powered answer services. Perplexity, launched in 2022, is more akin to products such as ChatGPT and Claude as it offers more of a conversational experience for information seekers than traditional search engines. The company describes its mission as:

> There has been a paradigm shift in how information can be organised, consumed, and created. The way that everything works can be reevaluated by going back to first principles: everyone in the world should have the information they need, as fast as possible. At Perplexity we are leading this change by building great software, in-house AI, and powerful infrastructure.
>
> (Perplexity, 2024)

Using its own LLM as well as others, including GPT and Claude, the service generates answers from sources it has indexed on the web using natural language predictive text. While this is similar to the AI search capabilities offered by Google and Bing, the company's business model differs slightly. It operates a freemium model where non-paying users only have access to its proprietary LLM while subscribers to Perplexity Pro can utilise models from OpenAI, Anthropic, Mistral and Meta. The company is also introducing advertising to some answers but the number of users required to attract advertisers means it will struggle to compete with Google, as Bing has found to its cost. Whether Perplexity manages to survive the highly competitive search engine sector remains to be seen but its experimentation with a subscription-based revenue model may herald a shift away from the advertising-driven models of the last 20 years. ChatGPT and Anthropic offer similar freemium models but have not marketed themselves as such direct competitors to Google in the same way as Perplexity.

A new age of knowledge management?

Knowledge management is one of the more obvious areas for AI to have an application. Over the last 30 years, many approaches and technologies have been adopted by organisations wanting to better manage and extract value from their information resources as well as the collective wisdom of employees. However, the early promises of vendors and consultants that systems could be developed to do this have not been effectively realised. Organisations preside over ever-larger silos of data, but real knowledge still resides within the humans doing the work. Chapter 2 touched on this disillusionment with knowledge management as a goal that could be achieved with better database-driven systems for organising information (Wilson, 2002). However, some of the technologies emerging from the current wave of AI-driven innovation may bring organisations closer to extracting more value from their information assets. We will avoid the semantic debates about what we mean by knowledge in the context of the Data-Information-Knowledge pyramid and instead focus on how information can be put to work more effectively through the application of AI technologies. These changes should be viewed as an evolution in the practice of knowledge management rather than a revolution as many of the information management techniques and technologies developed and adopted over the previous 20 years are complemented by AI rather than replaced by it.

An early business application of AI has been the use of LLMs and chat interfaces to help employees find the information they need from internal documentation. Rather than using the search function of a company intranet to identify relevant documents, a chat interface similar to ChatGPT offers a more user-friendly method. However, simply using an existing LLM such as GPT-4 to perform this task is not appropriate. These models are trained on public data and are prone to hallucinate where answers that look correct are given but have been made up by the model based on patterns it has observed in the training data. Internal knowledge systems need to output accurate as well as relevant answers, particularly where critical decisions may be made based on those answers. This is particularly true in a medical context or highly regulated industries such as finance. A promising approach to solving this problem is retrieval-augmented generation (RAG), which is an AI framework that combines more traditional information retrieval systems such as databases with the power of LLMs. Figure 3.1 illustrates the key processes at work in a RAG system where a user question is fed first into an organisation's knowledge base comprising cleaned and vetted data. Traditional search processes are applied to locate relevant information from the knowledge base, which is then fed into the pre-trained LLM as a full prompt. Because the LLM has been trained to understand the context of the organisation's work and the types of data it holds, it is able to produce more accurate and informative responses. The output of this is then presented to the user via the interface in which the original query was entered.

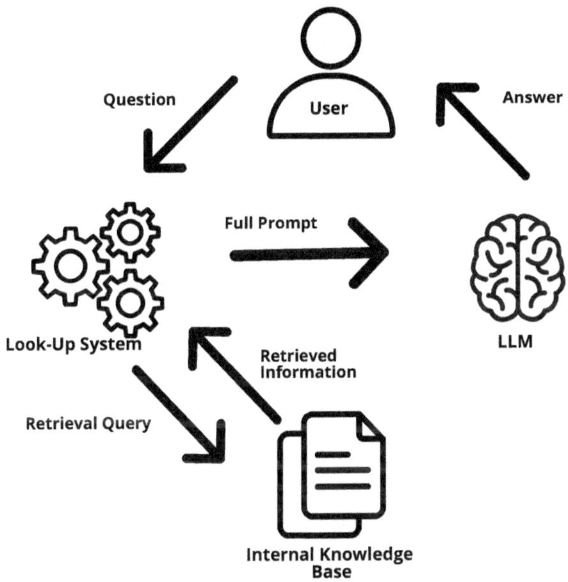

Figure 3.1 *Retrieval-augmented generation (RAG)*

Case study 3.1 – SinglePoint

Since 1996, Northern Light has offered knowledge management platforms for organisations based on enterprise search technologies. Its SinglePoint research product offers customers a centralised portal for searching across multiple internal and external data sources. Typical uses include tracking competitors, analysing markets and helping with new product development. In 2023, the company announced SinglePoint would incorporate a GenAI answering capability built on top of OpenAI's GPT-3.5 Turbo LLM. Adopting a RAG approach, SinglePoint only provides answers based on approved sources, with explicit instructions programmed in not to rely on the training data that the model was originally trained on. In this way, it is expected that hallucinations can be minimised or even avoided altogether. The company claims its AI Insights feature within SinglePoint can reduce the time taken to produce competitive intelligence insights from two hours to 20 seconds (Northern Light, 2024).

These knowledge management techniques can also be applied in an externally facing capacity to help an organisation's current or prospective customers. Running call centres to deal with customer enquiries is expensive and not having enough trained staff to answer queries quickly and efficiently can damage an organisation's reputation through poor service. AI is being deployed across a number of call centres in the form of 'intelligent' chat and voice bots. These offer the advantage of operating around the clock and are often able to answer queries faster than human operators. AI solutions are also more scalable for particularly busy times, such as for airlines when travel disruptions occur, and can operate in multiple languages. One of their greatest advantages is their ability to learn over time which responses are particularly useful in specific circumstances, making them more accurate than many human-based systems.

However, there is a tension between companies wanting to deploy AI-based customer service solutions and many of the customers themselves. A 2023 survey of 5,728 customers in the US found that 64% of them would prefer companies not to adopt such systems, with 53% stating they would consider switching to a competitor if this was the case (Gartner, 2024b). Despite this, the potential cost savings of incorporating AI into a call centre may be too tempting for many companies to ignore. Financial services firm, Klarna, has revealed that 90% of its staff are using AI on a daily basis with its Klarna AI assistant handling two-thirds of customer service chats in its first month of operation, the equivalent work of 700 full-time agents (Klarna, 2024). It might be expected that as these systems improve and are able to effectively hook into an organisation's customer relationship management (CRM) system, such deployments will become more widespread. Like self-checkouts at a supermarket, they may not always be appreciated by customers, but harsh economics coupled with improved technology will make it an inevitability.

Content creation

The key feature of Open AI's GenAI product, ChatGPT, that caught the public imagination on its launch in 2022 was its ability to create new information and, with its Dall-E offering, conjure images from just a simple text prompt. The potential for a number of use-cases was immediately apparent, from writing student essays to brainstorming ideas for a marketing strategy and creating graphics for presentations. However, the tendency for these models to hallucinate when writing text-based answers soon became apparent.

Hallucinations are welcome when it comes to image generation as the model is creating pictures that look like the images it was trained on based on user prompts. However, when this happens with text outputs it can lead to serious problems, particularly when the user has no easy way of checking if the answers are correct. An early high-profile example of this occurred in New York in 2023 when a lawyer submitted several prior legal cases as precedent to demonstrate the validity of his client's claim for damages against an airline. Unfortunately, the lawyer had used ChatGPT to support his research and it had made up the cases he submitted. When it was discovered that the cases were works of fiction, the lawyer claimed he had asked ChatGPT to confirm that they were genuine and it had confirmed they were (Scott, 2023; Dahl et al., 2024, 64). While regrettable, the case has been useful in that its wide reporting across news media has highlighted the issue of hallucinations and how hard it can be to spot them. This has encouraged organisations to develop and use more finely tuned LLMs using approaches such as RAG rather than rely on general purpose models.

The marketing industry has been an early adopter of AI tools and technologies as its workflows rely on the regular production of creative ideas and outputs such as web copy, images and videos. Consulting firm, McKinsey, have estimated that GenAI could improve the productivity of the global marketing sector to the value of US$463 annually (Harkness, 2023). The applications of AI within marketing include extracting insights from web analytics and customer data, automating sales processes, advertising campaign ideation and creating advertisement copy and images. A survey of 200 digital advertising agency leaders found that 89% of them expected AI to help them grow their businesses faster, with 87% believing AI would streamline their workflows, including content creation (Clarke, 2023). Smaller agencies and companies are using AI to increase their marketing outputs by automating some of their processes. Marketing software provider, HubSpot, has been using GPT-3 to generate blog post drafts, while social media software vendors, Hootsuite and Buffer, offer their customers AI-generated content suggestions to speed up their social media marketing (Agnew, 2023; Richardson Ellis, 2024; West, 2024).

Case study 3.2 – WPP Open

One of the world's largest marketing services providers, WPP, launched WPP Open in 2023, which it describes as a 'common technology platform, powered by proprietary AI models' (Harrington, 2024). The company has committed £250 million annually to the platform, which comprises a suite of technologies to process and extract value from internal and client data, predict market trends and consumer behaviour, interpret complex client briefs and create marketing content. The company describes WPP Open as technology agnostic in that it can plug into different technologies and LLMs as appropriate. It has announced collaborations with Anthropic, Nvidia, Google, Amazon AWS and OpenAI. One of the platform's features, Production Studio, launched in 2024, uses AI to streamline and automate the creation of text, images and video and has been used in campaigns by Ford and L'Oréal. Addressing concerns that AI might replace skilled, creative staff within the agency, Mark Read, WPP's CEO, stated, 'We firmly believe that AI will enhance, not replace, human creativity. We are already empowering our people with AI-based tools to augment their skills, produce work more efficiently and improve media performance, all of which will increase the effectiveness of our work' (WPP, 2024).

One of the key concerns resulting from the rise of GenAI applications has been the negative impact it might have on employment rates, particularly among creative professionals. Being able to produce 3,000-word articles or complex images in seconds from just a few prompts raises some obvious questions as to where humans have a place in AI-powered creative workflows. History offers a number of precedents that might be interpreted in different ways. The industrial revolution led to the rise of factories and a mass movement of populations from rural to urban settings. Many of these new working practices and the living conditions in the rapidly growing cities were detrimental to the health of the working class. However, they also created new skilled classes of workers and a middle class that enjoyed better living conditions and higher incomes than their ancestors. While rural life may have been romanticised by the Victorians as it became apparent that the UK was rapidly changing over the 19th century, living off the land had also been a precarious way of life for most farm labourers and smallholders. In 1800, average life expectancy in a world of one billion people was less than 30 years, but by 2000, with more than six billion people alive, it had risen to almost 67 years (Riley, 2001, 1). In most developed countries that had gone through industrialisation, life expectancy was even higher.

More recently, the rise of computers in the second half of the 20th century was expected to reduce the need for classes of office workers involved in tabulation, information processing and document creation. While this was true for some office-based occupations, the computing revolution also created new roles that had not previously existed. Between 1950 and 2023, the proportion of the total US workforce in white collar occupations rose from 38% to 62% (The Economist, 2023). At the same time, average wages rose as more advanced skills were required to work with computers (Dillender and Forsythe, 2022). A closer analogy to the possible displacement of creative jobs by AI can be found with the rise of desktop publishing software such as Quark and PageMaker in the 1980s and 1990s. At the time, many graphic designers feared their jobs were at risk as these new tools could be used by anyone to produce print-ready brochures and advertising materials. However, the reality was very different, with the number of graphic designer jobs in the US increasing since the 1990s to reach a total of 270,900 in 2022 (Bureau of Labor Statistics, 2024). When everyone has access to the same technology, people and businesses find new ways to use these tools to enhance creativity as well as work more efficiently.

Healthcare and medical research

While many AI stories in the media are dominated by fears of technology becoming self-aware and making decisions autonomously to the detriment of its human creators, the healthcare and medical sector demonstrates how AI offers enormous societal benefits. The National Health Service (NHS) is a particular case in point as it holds over 65 million medical records on UK citizens. In 2019, consultants Ernst and Young estimated that NHS data could be worth almost £5 billion to the British economy if better managed (Kollewe, 2019). Since then, there have been several initiatives to better use this data to improve treatments and patient outcomes, including OpenSAFELY and Health Data Research UK. OpenSAFELY is an open-source software platform that allows medical researchers to analyse 58 million NHS patient records, which have been anonymised to protect personal privacy (OpenSAFELY, 2024). One of its early successes was in identifying key risk factors associated with COVID-19, which helped doctors better understand those most at risk from the disease (NHS Transformation Directorate, 2024).

AI is playing a bigger role across all aspects of medical research and healthcare, from discovering and designing drugs to treat new and existing conditions to helping patients recover more quickly at home through remote monitoring. Figure 3.2 on the next page illustrates some of these key applications, all of which are already being deployed. AI has been used in drug discovery for a number of years to simulate how diseases and patients will react to new treatments and optimise drug formulations. In some cases, the time from initial research to launch has been reduced from 12 to 15 years down to 1 or 2 years, with associated cost savings of 30% to 50% (Lingolu, Kumari and Kumar, 2024, 68). AI analysis of medical images is another important application of the technology as it allows faster and, in some cases, more accurate identification of anomalies in X-rays, MRI and CAT scans (Rajpurkar et al., 2022, 32–4). In operating theatres, AI is helping surgeons by enhancing real-time images from cameras inserted into patients during

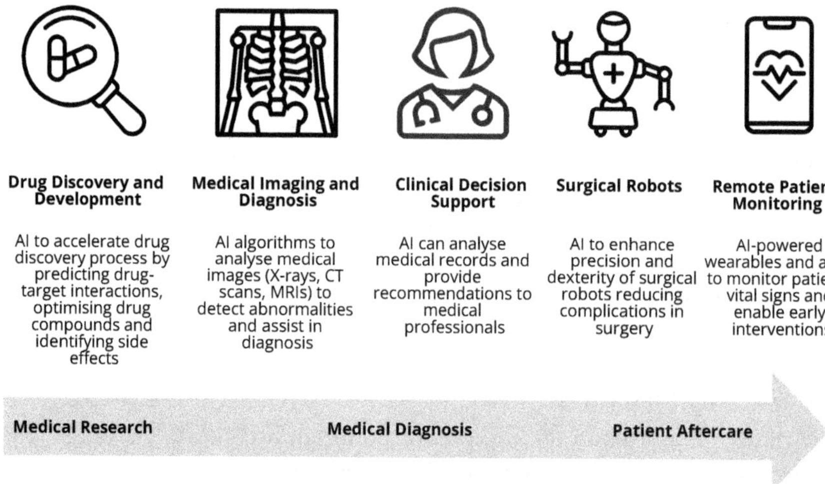

Figure 3.2 *AI healthcare and medical research applications*

surgery as well as streamlining some of the processes involved in complex operations (Knudsen et al., 2024, 102). Finally, the use of AI in remote patient monitoring (RPM) is transforming the treatment of patients after medical procedures and during their recovery by detecting early deteriorations in patient health through analysis of data from wearables (Shaik et al., 2023, 17).

Case study 3.3 – The NHS AI Lab

The NHS AI Lab was set up in 2019 as part of the UK government's £250 million investment in AI for the NHS. The key objectives and vision of the NHS AI Lab are: accelerating the safe adoption of AI in health and care; fostering cross-government, industry and academic collaborations in AI; developing AI governance frameworks to enable safe, ethical and effective development and use of AI; building a sustainable AI ecosystem for the NHS and UK health system; and improving patient outcomes, increasing service efficiency and reducing clinical workload through AI. Since 2019, the AI Lab has published guidelines on best practice for deploying AI systems in the NHS, set up the NHS AI Lab Skunkworks as a collaborative space to develop and test AI prototypes and delivered a portfolio of real-world AI projects in areas like medical imaging and screening (Morley, 2019; NHS AI Lab, 2024). While the Lab has helped NHS trusts and their staff better navigate the opportunities and dangers posed by AI, there are concerns its bureaucratic public sector heritage is holding it back from working effectively with private sector AI startups. A number of companies have expressed frustration at the speed with which agreements and contracts are approved (Nicol-Schwarz, 2024).

Medical research and healthcare is one of the most complex arenas for developing solutions due to diseases constantly evolving and becoming resistant to treatment, the complex relationship between genetics and patient lifestyles in terms of pathology, legal restrictions on drug testing and prescribing and the costs involved in developing and marketing drugs. In this respect, the application of data and AI to address these issues promises great returns to both the research community, their corporate sponsors and, ultimately, to patients. However, there are often tensions between these stakeholders as medical insurers and governments want to reduce healthcare provision costs, pharmaceutical companies want to generate returns on their significant drug development investments and healthcare want to provide the best care for their patients within their budget limitations. At the end of this are patients simply wanting to be made better.

Better use of the data that is generated by all these processes and interactions is part of the solution to satisfying these often conflicting demands. As we have seen with other applications of AI to solve organisational and societal issues, data underpins everything from model training, user prompts and then the final outputs and how they are integrated into other elements of organisational workflows. In the context of the NHS, as well as many other local and national healthcare systems, getting the most from its data assets is crucial if AI is to have the impact many hope it will. This is made particularly complicated as there are 189 NHS trusts that collect patient data and use different electronic systems to do so. According to Nigel Shadbolt, executive chair and co-founder of the Open Data Institute (ODI):

> Well-curated data infrastructure is essential for delivering AI's value effectively and responsibly. This includes interoperable open standards, secure data storage, efficient data processing and strict data protection regulations.
>
> (Shadbolt, 2024)

Shadbolt, an advocate for freeing up public data assets for the public good, believes the storing of NHS data in disparate data silos makes it almost impossible for public sector investments in AI to improve healthcare to deliver the expected benefits. We will explore these concerns about lack of access to data inhibiting AI deployments in more detail in Chapter 4.

Competitive advantage through data and AI

A key driver of many business initiatives is the pursuance of activities that give the firm a competitive advantage over its peers. This might be achieved through lowering costs to improve profits and/or reduce prices to customers, developing innovative new products and services that competitors find difficult to imitate or realigning business processes to make the company run more efficiently. Integrating data assets, either internally or externally sourced, with the capabilities of AI technologies has the potential to impact each of the above. The extent to which any business can achieve these benefits with data and AI will depend on the sector they operate in, their human and financial resources and their willingness to experiment with new technologies.

Davenport and Ronanki (2018) argue that AI can be deployed to support three key business needs: automating business processes; gaining insights through data analysis; and engaging more effectively with customers and employees. In terms of process automation, the authors looked at 152 projects and identified the automation of physical and digital tasks as the most common. This might include extracting useful information from e-mails and automatically inputting it into a CRM or reading large and complex contractual documents and extracting key information using natural language processing. They see such initiatives as the easiest for a firm to adopt and realise financial and operating gains. The second most common type of AI/data project they have observed, cognitive insight, is what they call 'analytics on steroids' (Davenport and Ronanki, 2018, 110) and typically involves predicting what customers will buy, identifying financial fraud in real time, automating digital advertising placement and helping insurers more accurately model risk. Finally, Davenport and Ronanki identify a class of projects that rely on natural language processing (NLP) chatbots and intelligent agents to better engage customers and employees. This might be through online chatbots that answer customer queries or internal systems that help new and existing employees find answers to questions about company procedures and processes.

Following the rapid evolution of AI systems and technologies since Davenport and Ronanki's paper was written in 2018, particularly the rise of GenAI offerings, Li et al. (2023) identify three main firm categories in the context of AI development and use. Firstly, they describe companies such as OpenAI and Anthropic that specialise in offering AI services for use by third parties. Second are firms that are not AI specialists but have the internal capabilities to develop and customise AI models for their own or others' use. They give the example of financial data provider, Bloomberg, and its BloombergGPT product, which helps financial analysts use NLP to undertake specific tasks. Then there is the final category of business – and the most prevalent – that does not undertake its own AI developments but relies on buying in those products from third-party specialists. These companies are typically the customers of industry-focused AI solution providers where products are developed to deal with very specific tasks.

Case study 3.4 – A&O Shearman

A&O Shearman is one of the world's largest legal firms , employing almost 4,000 lawyers globally and generating revenues of more than £2 billion (A&O Shearman, 2024). In 2023, the company launched its AI tool, ContractMatrix, in conjunction with Microsoft and legal AI startup, Harvey. A&O Shearman promotes the tool as an augmentation to the work its lawyers do with the strapline, 'Harness AI. Free the lawyer'. It is primarily a contract negotiation tool that uses AI to save the time of its lawyers when drawing up contracts, non-disclosure agreements and mergers and acquisitions (M&A) terms. The company estimates it can save up to seven hours in contract negotiations. It is being used in-house as well as being offered to clients. In an acknowledgement that AI has the potential to disrupt much of the expensive and highly profitable work done by legal firms, A&O Shearman partner, David Wakeling, said the firms goal was to 'disrupt the legal market before someone disrupts us. If we look at the impact of AI in law, it is happening and is likely to happen in a pretty big way in the next few years, and we are seeing it as an opportunity' (Criddle and Ring, 2023).

Research into how data and AI may provide sustainable competitive advantage to firms tends to focus either on ways AI will be a substitute for human activity or how it can complement the work of employees. The advantage with the former may lie with cost saving benefits while the latter may improve business operations through the enhancement of human capabilities. While reliable evidence to support either of the hypotheses will remain scarce until the technologies involved have been more widely adopted, Krakowski et al. (2023) believe that the ability to augment human activities rather than replace them will be the main competitive advantage that AI offers. They argue that more than just helping employees work more efficiently, AI substantially changes how they can make a difference. In this respect, they see AI having a considerable impact on the ways firms can outcompete their peers. This view is supported by Kenny et al. (2024) who believe AI allows small and medium-sized enterprises (SMEs) to compete with much larger enterprises in ways not possible before. This, they argue, is particularly true when it comes to strategic planning and modelling, activities that most small business owners do not have the time or resources to do effectively. By using AI assistants such as you.com and ChatGPT, they are able to more easily generate creative approaches to business problems and then model the likely consequences of different solutions. In Chapter 5, when we explore possible future scenarios for the AI and data revolution, we will consider how business models may evolve to cope with and, in some cases, take advantage of this emerging landscape.

Writing code with AI

It is not surprising that computer programmers have been among the first group of professionals to use AI to help with coding. Their familiarity with the software tools used to write code and create programmes has, perhaps inevitably, made them early adopters of AI tools. A 2019 study by Svyatkovskiy et al. (2019) found that developers using Microsoft's AI-assisted code completion tool, Intellicode, could save an average of 25% of the keystrokes they normally use to write code. According to Maxfield (2023), software developers spend about 50% of their time debugging code they have written. He goes on to argue that code written with assistance from the AI tool, Copilot, contains more bugs than a good programmer would normally have included in a traditional workflow, therefore negating many of the benefits such tools offer. However, there are now tools such as Metabob that can automatically detect bugs and, in theory at least, still offer net benefits. This is important due to the growing concern about organisations amassing 'technical debt' as they rapidly increase the volume of code being written by their developers at the expense of quality. This technical debt will need to be repaid later on as the bugs and errors start to surface. According to MIT professor, Armando Solar-Lezama:

> There is a risk of accumulating lots of very shoddy code written by a machine. People have talked about technical debt for a long time, and now we have a brand-new credit card here that is going to allow us to accumulate technical debt in ways we were never able to do before. Companies will have to rethink methodologies around how they can work in tandem with the new tools' capabilities to avoid that.
>
> (Bousquette, 2023)

Research from consultants McKinsey shows that programmers can complete coding tasks up to twice as fast using GenAI tools but, like Solar-Lezama, they point to the risks of adopting such tools without careful oversight. Aside from time-saving gains, the research also found developers using AI tools were generally happier at work as it allowed them to focus on the more interesting aspects of coding rather than the more routine and boring tasks (Karaci Deniz and Gnanasambandam, 2023). The McKinsey researchers point to issues aside from technical debt that managers need to be aware of. These include ensuring the AI tools do not compromise data privacy and are compliant with regulatory changes on the use of AI and making sure malicious code has not been planted in the training models that could lead to security vulnerabilities.

Whatever the risks might be from the greater use of AI to write code and create software, it seems inevitable that their use will continue. A 2023 survey of 500 US developers found that 92% of them were already using AI coding tools in their workflows, with 70% believing the tools gave them an advantage at work (Dey, 2023). However, like the McKinsey research, the survey also identified concerns among developers over ethical and security issues that might arise from an over-reliance on AI.

AI challenges

In the previous section, we touched on some of the challenges of data-driven AI solutions as corollaries to the opportunities they present. This section focuses on the challenges that organisations face as they seek to incorporate AI into their workflows. In terms of organisational challenges, we will look at the complexity of automating business processes with new and largely untested technologies. This section also considers the difficulties posed by hallucinating LLMs and how more traditional approaches to managing information play a vital role in rolling out AI solutions. Chapters 4 and 5 will consider some of the challenges that AI poses in a broader societal context.

Risks of automation

Business practices evolve over time to suit the demands of the market as well as the capabilities of the organisation in terms of expertise and financial resources. Tried and tested methods become the norm as they are found to be reliable and employees become comfortable with them. Data is often at the centre of these processes, whether generated internally or sourced from third parties. Establishing secure and safe methods for data sharing, particularly where it relates to individuals, is essential to ensure regulatory compliance and avoid scandals that might damage a firm's reputation. For these reasons, many organisations are rightly hesitant to incorporate new AI technologies into their workflows, whatever gains they might promise. Many Chief Data Officers (CDOs) and Chief Information Officers (CIOs) are concerned about the unauthorised use of AI by employees via consumer-facing products such as ChatGPT and Claude. This reflects similar concerns over the rise of personal smartphones and cloud computing a decade before when employees began using these technologies without authorisation from managers. CIOs feared confidential data might leak as staff shared corporate information via their phones and put it on their personal cloud storage from vendors such as Dropbox and Google (Miller, 2024). A 2023 survey of business managers found that 68% of them believed employees should not use AI tools with permission (Drapkin, 2023).

However, as with phones and cloud computing services, if employees find these tools useful then they are likely to continue using them. This is why organisational policies on how AI should be used at work have become more popular. These may cover issues such as what training is offered to employees on AI use, which tools are prescribed and the types of processes where they can be used (CIPD, 2024). While such policies are only effective if adhered to, they may help avoid high-profile cases of GenAI being used inappropriately at work. In 2023, for example, an engineer at the semiconductor division of Samsung inadvertently leaked confidential information about chip designs by uploading source code and meeting notes to ChatGPT to help solve a technical problem. As a result, these trade secrets are now in the databases of OpenAI, ChatGPT's creator. In this instance, Samsung's response was to develop an in-house AI solution for employees to use where data could not leak out to any third parties (Maddison, 2023).

The Samsung case was perhaps a precursor to more widespread concerns surrounding AI adoption in the enterprise. Microsoft's products, from Windows to Office 365, are pervasive across most businesses and so the company's Copilot product, which aims to help employees be more creative and productive, is also becoming widely used. Copilot is a GenAI chat bot based on an LLM and can generate text and images as well as summarise documents and web pages. However, Copilot's integration with other mainstream Microsoft products, including SharePoint, allows it to access an organisation's data assets unless permissions are set up correctly. This might include sensitive data such as colleague's pay information, company plans and the minutes of meetings. At a recent conference, the CDO of security and data governance specialists Securiti, Jack Berkowitz, expressed his concerns with the hooks that Copilot has into company data:

> Now, maybe if you set up a totally clean Microsoft environment from day one, these issues would be alleviated. But nobody has that. People have implemented these systems over time, particularly really big companies. And you get these conflicting authorisations or conflicting access to data.
>
> (Claburn, 2024)

He went on to make the point that this was very similar to issues 15 years ago when Google launched its Search Appliance to index corporate documents. The solution then, and now, is setting the right authorisations and having a firm policy for making changes.

Structured data is essential

One of the selling points of LLMs is their ability to ingest massive amounts of data sourced from multiple places, including web pages, e-mails, corporate documents and video transcripts. However, in an organisational setting where the accuracy of LLM outputs is essential, simply absorbing vast tracts of unstructured data can lead to problems. We've seen that RAG helps focus the answers given by LLMs by feeding in specific data rather than relying on the outputs of general purpose GenAI products. Someone wanting to know the process for booking annual leave in their company is not going to find the answer from ChatGPT. However, the utility of LLMs in the enterprise can be enhanced further by using more structured data that helps the LLM make better sense of what it has been trained on. Training primarily on unstructured data makes it difficult, if not impossible, to know how an answer was arrived at.

Knowledge graphs are an important part of the solution to producing better results from an LLM. A knowledge graph, sometimes referred to as a 'semantic network', represents a network of real-world entities. These include events, objects, situations and concepts and maps the relationships between them. The resulting information is generally stored in a graph database and can be visualised by users as a graph structure, hence the term knowledge graph (IBM, 2023a).

Knowledge graphs can be integrated within an information management system so it can interact with an LLM via database query templates. These templates help the LLM by removing the need for it to perform complex logic in interpreting user prompts. The query templates can be designed to suit specific use cases and domains, such as retail supply chains or oil exploration (Nilsson, 2024).

Knowledge graphs have a wide range of applications when used in conjunction with LLMs, from education and medical research to improving search engines and removing fake information from social networking sites. In terms of building confidence in the deployment of AI within organisations, knowledge graphs go some way to achieving this. By producing more accurate results and allowing a greater degree of transparency in how outputs were produced, users are more likely to use systems utilising the technology (Jarrahi et al., 2023, 96). AstraZeneca was an early adopter of knowledge graphs to help with drug discovery by mapping relationships between chemical compounds, molecules, diseases and biological entities. The company's AI engineering lead attributed Netflix's use of the technology to make film recommendations as part of AstraZeneca's inspiration to incorporate them into its AI initiatives: 'Sometimes, selecting the next best drug target can be compared to choosing the next best movie – just with much more serious implications if you get it wrong. Thanks to Netflix, we now know how to tackle these types of problems' (Dhuri, 2020).

The effective deployment of AI systems within organisations, like most new technologies, requires careful planning and oversight. An LLM cannot simply be pointed at a company's data assets and be expected to make sense of what it sees so instant answers can be given to employees. Data needs to be organised and structured to prevent sensitive data leaking into the system as well as offer the best chance of useful insights and answers coming out the other end. The danger for many organisations is that enthusiasm for the potential benefits of AI leads some to rush into deploying systems without due regard to the risks of not properly preparing the data that will feed the LLM. In their consulting work with businesses, IBM has noticed data is often an afterthought when designing and deploying GenAI solutions. This, they argue, results in inefficiencies and inconsistencies, which can lead to disillusionment among managers and users, potentially killing off further investments (Baird, 2024).

Prompt engineers: the new librarians?

Navigating information resources, whether analogue or digital, to find the insights and answers a user needs has been at the heart of the library and information profession. This has evolved over the last 30 years as many sources switched from paper to digital, but the core principles of organising knowledge into accessible systems and then being able to interrogate them has been central to an information professional's work. As these systems become smarter through AI and users come to expect answers rather than just being pointed to the appropriate resources, how might the work of information professionals change? At the back end, the work is becoming more technical and requires additional skills to incorporate LLMs and associated technologies appropriately into information management systems. However, at the front end where AI meets the end-user, there may be an interesting new range of skills required if LLMs are to deliver the most value. Knowing how to structure questions or prompts is a skill, as anyone versed with interrogating online databases effectively will attest. Even getting the most from common search engines, such as Google, requires knowledge of query syntax and being able to combine keywords, Boolean operators, phrase searching, wildcards and field-specific parameters.

IBM defines prompt engineering as 'the process of writing, refining and optimising inputs to encourage generative AI systems to create specific, high-quality outputs' (IBM, 2023b). Knowing how to optimally structure prompts is essential if organisations are to get a return on their GenAI investments.

Effective prompts may run into the hundreds of words with context windows becoming larger with successive generations of LLMs. Striking the balance between brevity and verbosity is a skill in structuring prompts: they need to be long enough to clarify the task, outline expectations and provide context while concise enough so as not to confuse the model or slow it down (OpenAI, 2024b).

Microsoft principal engineer, Jennifer Marsman, sees writing good prompts as essential to unlocking the potential of AI:

> I compare it to the early days of search engines – there was an art to choosing the right keywords to get good results and, over time, both the users and the search engine got better at understanding each other. This is the same paradigm. Over time, both we as users and the machine learning models will understand each other better.
>
> (Siegel, 2024)

According to McKinsey, developing prompt engineering skills is more a process of trial and error than a precise science. Models will respond differently to the same prompts depending on their design and the data that has trained the LLM or has been added via RAG (McKinsey & Co., 2024). This experimental and iterative approach seems to be supported by the demands of employers when recruiting prompt engineering roles. A London-based technology firm outlined one of the core activities for a prompt engineer role as:

> Creating and testing prompts: developing new prompts and iteratively improving existing ones using feedback from our users, internal reviews and performance metrics. You'll be thinking about the content of the output, alongside tone of voice, specialised vocabulary, and drawing out the highest priority information.
>
> (Beam, 2024)

Rob Green, Editor in Chief at the Chartered Institute of Library and Information Professionals (CILIP), believes the traditional information retrieval skills held by librarians can potentially play a significant role in this new landscape as they have the ability to structure complex search queries (Green, 2023). However, not everyone agrees that prompt engineering has a sustainable future as a role for humans. GenAI systems themselves are becoming better at understanding natural language and may not require such complex prompts in the future. Also, the same systems are developing the ability to help users craft effective prompts that play to the features of the model being used (Acar, 2023). In Chapter 5, we will consider how the role of information professionals may change because of AI and why human inputs will always be required in leveraging information assets, albeit in different ways.

Is AI dehumanising workers?

Since technology first started to change working practices, there have been concerns about its impact on the health and welfare of workers. While 'Luddite' has become a derogatory term for people irrationally opposed to a new technology, 19th-century Luddites were right to be concerned about the impact of the new weaving machines on their livelihoods. While they ultimately lost to the factory owners and their machines, their concerns about the deskilling impact of industrialisation on their ways of working and income were perfectly rational. There is a danger that the rush to automate workflows and make workers more efficient through AI triggers a similar response as the Luddites. Research across a number of industries in different countries on the views of workers dealing with the introduction of AI into the workplace discovered some worrying trends (Cremer and Koopman, 2024). Engineers adapting to AI systems at a Taiwanese biomedical company reported greater feelings of loneliness, leading to increased alcohol consumption and insomnia. Estate agents at an Indonesian property management firm felt that their use of AI made them seek greater connection with fellow employees to deal with the loneliness they experienced. The authors of this study believe that firms introducing AI need to carefully monitor the wellbeing of their employees while redesigning workflows so that the respective strengths of machines and humans are optimised.

Research across seven countries by the OECD on attitudes to AI in the workplace is more positive, with most workers and employers generally enthusiastic about its deployment. However, concerns were expressed about its impact on job losses, pay rates and the need for better training (Lane, Williams and Broecke, 2023, 12). This may reflect a belief that technology-driven change is an inevitability based on the experience of 30 years of the computing and internet revolution. A pragmatic approach that emerges from the OECD research seems to centre on workers wanting to build their skills for a changing workplace and expecting employers to play their part in this. The need for training to help workers adapt to AI-driven change is supported by other studies, with AI itself being able to help devise training programmes appropriate to the specific needs of employees and the businesses they work in (Cramarenco, Burcă-Voicu and Dabija, 2023; Morandini et al., 2023; Zirar, Ali and Islam, 2023).

This chapter has focused on the ways that data-driven AI is impacting on organisations, the way they work and the products and services they offer. Chapter 4 will now explore some of the legal, policy and ethical issues that are arising from these changes both at the organisational and the wider societal level.

CHAPTER 4

Ethical, Policy and Legal Issues of Data-Driven AI

This chapter explores the rapidly developing policies of national and international governmental bodies relating to data and AI, the emerging resulting legislation and the ethical concerns leading to these initiatives. As policies, laws and rulings are evolving to deal with the new challenges posed by AI and the data it feeds off, this chapter presents a snapshot of the legal situation in late 2024; however, the issues underpinning policy and legislative changes are ongoing. These centre on concerns with privacy and data protection, copyright, monopolistic practices and trust as well as efforts to stimulate economic growth and international competitiveness. The chapter focuses on developments in the UK and the US as well as across the EU, which allows for policies and legislation to be compared and highlights different national concerns and priorities.

Ethical concerns

Scientific breakthroughs and new technologies have long been a source of alarm for philosophers, writers and politicians. This is particularly true where questions of what it is to be human and how far machines can replace human activities emerge. Mary Shelley's 1818 creation of the Frankenstein monster highlighted concerns emerging from the enlightenment and the move from a society based on superstition to one more founded on the principles of science (Gunkel, 2024, 3). Science fiction novels and films – from *Metropolis* in 1927 and *Brave New World* in 1932 to *2001: A Space Odyssey* in 1968 and *Bladerunner* in 1982 – developed these ideas in different and unsettling ways. While public policies and laws change fairly frequently in response to events and differing priorities, the values and ethics that underpin them are more constant. That is not to say they do not change. Activities considered acceptable by many people in the past, such as slavery or child labour, are now, thankfully, confined to history across most of the developed world. However, these changes in values and behaviours can take years before they are translated into law.

Broadly, a society's system of values and the ethical norms that guide human behaviour that emerge from them can be seen to influence the policies and laws that public bodies create. This is not a completely linear relationship and there are a number of examples where values are not in line with the laws of the land. The civil rights movement in the US in the 1950s and 1960s used civil disobedience and peaceful law breaking to overturn centuries of racial segregation and discrimination, with many state and federal laws having to catch up with a major shift in the public mood. Ways to avoid or minimise tax payments may be legal but are often considered unethical, particularly when public funding cuts are government policy. Figure 3.3 presents a high-level overview of the relationship between ethics, public policy and legislation and, while much simplified, shows the path from what society may consider important to government actions.

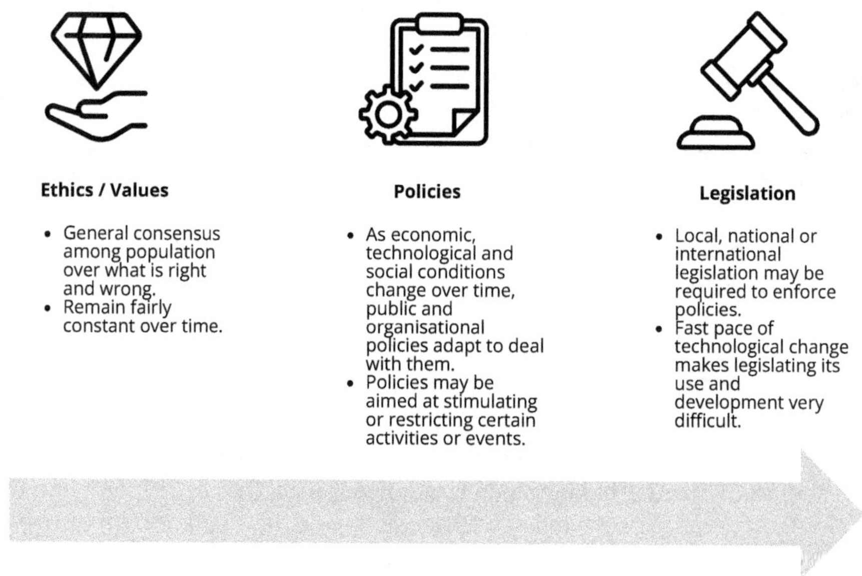

Figure 3.3 *Translating ethics into legislation*

In the context of AI, Sartor (2020, 706) argues that ethical concerns and legislation can exert influence over each other but may also diverge, with some ethical rights not being legally enforced while some legal rights may lack ethical justification. The complexity and rapid evolution of AI technologies is a problem for law makers at a technical level as well as on an international dimension. Robles Carrillo (2020) believes a less formal scientific methodology is needed to properly regulate the many complexities of AI, with international law having an important role to play in ensuring effective compliance. The importance of an international dimension to AI governance is acknowledged by Saheb and Saheb (2024) whose analysis of the ethical priorities of 24 countries highlighted national differences that need to be taken into account when devising guidance and legislation.

Ultimately, it is down to how individuals behave in the context of data and AI use. Ethical frameworks and guidelines are just that – recommendations for how these assets and tools should be used. In their survey of data professionals in the Netherlands and how they respond to professional guidelines, Fest et al. (2022, 11) found that there was a significant gap between the two. They suggest better training in data literacy is required, alongside tools being developed to offer prescriptive guidance tailored to specific contexts.

The law of unintended consequences

Societies are highly complex systems of interrelated and often conflicting stakeholders and interests. Making a change in one part of the system, particularly when it is at a national policy or legislative level, can lead to unexpected outcomes, sometimes positive but often negative. Dörner (1997) has written extensively about the problem of unintended consequences resulting from political and legal attempts to make the world a better place. He attributes this to several factors: a lack of understanding about the interconnections within a system and the ripple effects that a simple change can have; an oversimplification of the systems involved and overconfidence among policy makers as to their ability to control outcomes; a tendency to think linearly and ignore feedback loops; and a neglect of longer-term consequences that emerge over time. The impact of unintended consequences can be severe, particularly where public health is concerned. For example, the offer of free HIV testing during antenatal care in Botswana created opportunities for treatment for infected women but the policy also resulted in women being blamed and stigmatised for being HIV positive (Yang et al., 2021). In 2018, US limits on the quantities of steel that could be imported were designed to protect the domestic steel industry. However, the side effect has been that the cost of steel used by the US automotive industry went up as they had less access to cheaper imports, making it more difficult for vehicle makers to compete (Norton, 2018).

Dörner (1997, 198–9) suggests that to avoid such pitfalls, policy makers need to adopt a systems thinking approach that considers the interconnections within a system and then monitor the effects of their policies and make adjustments as necessary. Unfortunately, the political arena within which many high-level policies are made means that incoming governments are often too focused on implementing their own agendas rather than carefully evaluating what their predecessors left behind. We shall revisit this issue and the complexities of socio-technical systems in the next chapter when we explore possible future directions for the data-driven AI revolution.

Another approach for avoiding unintended consequences is to adopt the precautionary principle. The EU defines this as:

> . . . an approach to risk management, where, if it is possible that a given policy or action might cause harm to the public or the environment and if there is still no scientific agreement on the issue, the policy or action in question should not be carried out. However, the policy or action may be reviewed when more scientific information becomes available.
>
> (EUR-Lex, 2020)

The EU has made the precautionary principle a statutory requirement in some areas of law, including food safety, chemical use, environmental standards and consumer policy. While it seems a logical way to try and minimise risk, it is not without its critics. In the area of technology regulation, Miller and Engemann (2019) argue that its application may also have unintended consequences. Other critics point to its vagueness and ambiguity as a guide for policy makers, how it might hinder technological innovation by slowing down progress in scientific areas, a lack of scientific evidence for its effectiveness and the onus it places on those advocating change to prove something is completely safe (Holm and Harris, 1999; Marchant, 2003; Peterson, 2006).

As we shall see with the EU's GDPR Directive passed in 2016, the way it has been interpreted by businesses and the resulting practices has had unforeseen effects on the way digital marketing is performed and, for many internet users, been an annoyance as they navigate between websites.

AI and data policies

The policy initiatives on AI and data discussed in this section are broadly focused on encouraging certain behaviours in the context of economic growth, investment decisions, social change and technological innovation. This contrasts with the following section on legislative initiatives, which could be seen as trying to restrict or prevent certain behaviours. Although this is a little simplistic, it helps frame the discussions around the often competing interests of different stakeholders as well as the potential and limitations of AI. Public policy makers need to balance the economic benefits that technologies can offer in terms of inward investment and job creation with the social impact they may have. In the context of data and AI, the economic benefits may be increased productivity and exports of new products and services, while social concerns may arise from data breaches, job losses and the spread of fake information.

Data sharing

In Chapter 2, we explored the role of public sector information (PSI) in providing better public services and encouraging innovation through the commercial reuse of PSI to create new digital products. In the UK and Europe going back to the 1990s there have been a range of initiatives and policies to encourage this activity, particularly as it has the potential to stimulate economic activity and growth. The chair of the UK's statistics watchdog recently called for government ministers in the newly formed Labour government to boost the economy and improve public services by better sharing of data between departments (Tapper, 2024). He claimed that government data was too frequently siloed due to fears about possible criticisms of the quality of the data or just through inaction. Recent guidance from the Ministry of Justice found that better data sharing could have positive impacts on law enforcement as well as reduce reoffending rates (Ministry of Justice, 2024). Aside from general inertia and organisational tendencies to hoard data for political or cultural reasons, there are technical reasons for the lack of data sharing across and between public and private bodies. These may relate to it not being compatible with sharing across different technology systems or data being stored in non-machine-readable formats. There is also the issue of ease of accessibility: APIs that present streams of data for ingesting into other systems are more attractive to developers than less portable formats such as downloading onto hard drives. The New South Wales government in Australia advocates its departments make data available via APIs and argue it allows for more up-to-date data, allows users more flexibility, creates better opportunities for adding value and is better for combining different data sources (Data.NSW, 2024). This is particularly useful for services requiring real-time inputs such as transportation apps. Secondly, Data.NSW advocates machine-readable formats such as CSV, with care given to ensuring consistency across files.

An important characteristic of data is its non-rivalrous nature: its use by one person does not prevent another from also using it. This is particularly true when it is digitised as perfect copies can be made and distributed in seconds. As US President Thomas Jefferson said in 1813 when writing about patents, innovation and the sharing of ideas:

> As he who lights his taper at mine, receives light without darkening me. That ideas should freely spread from one to another over the globe, for the moral and mutual instruction of man, and improvement of his condition.
>
> (Jefferson, 1813)

From the broader economic and social perspective, data sharing makes enormous sense. We now have the tools and networks to achieve this more efficiently and in ways Jefferson could never have imagined. However, despite government initiatives in the UK, Europe and the US, there is still a long way to go before the true value of public sector data is realised. One of the factors holding back better sharing is a widespread mindset that data can have a value placed on it at source. However, this ignores the issue of externalities where value is added by allowing others to repurpose it in ways the originator had not thought of. Research from data sharing advocates ODI makes this point and argues that organisations should move away from seeing their data as a store of value for themselves and instead focus on letting others use it and create value:

> . . . it is more productive to think of data as an infrastructural good or resource, instead of as an asset that is 'owned' by private actors. Doing so helps emphasise the value that data can create for society rather than taking a narrow approach that focuses solely on the value that it can bring to those who collect or hold it.
>
> (Stiglich, 2023, 5)

In Chapter 2, we looked at some of the recent initiatives around the world to encourage greater sharing of public sector data. It is the EU that seems the most focused on realising the benefits of making data from a variety of sources widely available for multiple purposes. In 2020, the European Commission (EC) launched its European strategy for data (European Commission, 2020a). This was an ambitious statement of intent to create a single European data space that would allow data to flow freely within the EU and across different sectors while complying with existing rules around data protection and information security. Its key objectives were:

1 To establish a clear governance framework for data access and use, including legislation on data spaces and data usage rights.
2 To invest in data infrastructure, tools, and skills to strengthen Europe's capabilities in the data economy. This included a €4–6 billion investment in a High Impact Project on European data spaces and cloud infrastructure.

3 To empower individuals to exercise control over their data and to improve data literacy across the EU population and workforce.
4 To create common European data spaces in strategic sectors like industry, Green Deal, mobility, health, finance, energy, agriculture, public administration and skills.
5 To promote an open but assertive international approach to data flows, protecting EU interests and values while engaging with global partners.

The EC's plan was for these objectives to: make data more available for businesses, governments and individuals; create a competitive EU data economy that would benefit from the single market; improve public sector decision-making; and drive innovation across the EU's technology sector.

Critics of the strategy pointed to a lack of concrete details on the specifics of how these objectives could realistically be achieved, with others saying it amounted to a data grab by the EU as it could restrict data flows out of the bloc (Manancourt, 2020). Concerns were also expressed over the dangers of over-regulation that might emerge from the strategy acting to stifle innovation (Cennamo and Sokol, 2021). However, the strategy was a bold statement of intent that built on previous EU initiatives around data sharing and innovation. A key motivating factor behind the strategy was a recognition that Europe had fallen behind the US and some Asian countries in having a successful and growing technology sector despite significant investments in groundbreaking research. Like the UK, the EU has struggled to translate world-leading research outputs into viable commercial ventures. In early 2024, the seven largest US technology companies (Alphabet, Amazon, Apple, Meta, Microsoft, Nvidia and Tesla) were 20 times the size of the EU's seven largest and generated more than ten times the revenue (Foucart, 2024). Language and cultural differences between member states are two of the barriers to catching up with the US but it is possible that a more co-ordinated sharing of data, and incentives to encourage this, while putting restrictions on what US companies can do with EU citizens' data may help narrow the gap.

AI research and investment

AI, along with quantum computing, 5G and cybersecurity, has been a key focus of technology policy for governments around the world over the last decade. In 2018, the UK government announced the AI Sector Deal, which comprised a £1 billion package of support from government and industry to boost the UK as leader in developing AI and its related technologies. The policy was founded on what it called the 'five foundations of productivity': (i) ideas; (ii) people; (iii) infrastructure; (iv) business environment; and (v) places. These aimed to stimulate investment and innovation in core research and applied research and development (R&D), building appropriate infrastructure for harnessing data-driven AI, creating a business environment conducive to AI development, providing people with the skills to work in this sector and, finally, create geographic clusters around the UK for these activities. Much of the focus of this initiative was centred around four new institutions: the Alan Turing Institute; the Office for Artificial Intelligence; the Centre for Data Ethics and Innovation; and the AI Council. However, as with many government initiatives, they are announced with great enthusiasm and publicity only to rapidly change due to changing priorities and new administrations or even disappear completely. Of the four institutions mentioned above, only the Alan Turing Institute remains in its original form. The others have either been disbanded or quietly absorbed into other departments and initiatives. This is not unique to the UK, but it highlights a problem with much public policy where the outcomes often fall far short of the original objectives.

A good example is the 2023 AI Regulation Bill introduced into the UK Parliament and which proposed a relatively laissez-faire approach to regulating AI and associated technologies. The 2024 change of government from a Conservative to a Labour administration saw this bill dropped, with statements from the new government indicating a different approach. In February 2024, before the general election, the Labour leadership indicated:

> 'It would not rush to regulate' at that stage, because introducing binding measures too soon, even if highly targeted, could fail to effectively address risks, quickly become out of date, or stifle innovation.
>
> (Norton Rose Fulbright, 2024)

Uncertainty over how governments will react, positively or negatively, in terms of policy and regulation is an issue for businesses that need to plan their investment priorities often years in advance. For example, Google announced the building of its new £1 billion UK headquarters in London in 2016 with a view to moving in by 2025 (Partridge, 2022; Accoya, 2024). Since then, there have been six prime ministers, two general elections, Brexit and multiple, and often conflicting, technology policy changes. The environment for technology regulation has changed considerably, accelerated by the rise of AI and the possible upending of business models that have dominated the digital sector for two decades. We will consider what this means for Google and its peers in the following chapter, but these shifting sands make policy formulation extremely difficult. In this context, the EU's approach to AI policy making is particularly ambitious.

As with its approach to a pan-European data strategy, a key driver in the EU's policies around AI has been to catch up with the US and Asia. According to Ulnicane (2022), a 2017 McKinsey report commissioned for the EU Heads of State Tallinn Digital Summit was particularly influential in promoting this line of thinking. The report pointed out that European investments in AI in 2016 had totalled US$3–4 billion in 2016, compared with US$8–12 billion in Asia and US$15–23 billion in the US (Manyika, 2017). One of the report's recommendations was for the EU to accelerate the completion of a digital single market where there was free movement of data, like the single market for trade where goods and EU citizens could move freely between member states. The rationale was that a single market for data and digital services would create a far more scalable environment for innovation and technology investments.

This report and the discussions at the Tallinn Digital Summit led to the 2018 EU AI Strategy based on the argument that AI was 'one of the most strategic industries of the 21st century . . . . like the steam engine or electricity in the past, AI is transforming our world, society and our industry' (European Commission, 2018). The strategy emphasises the economic and social opportunities offered by AI but also recognises the need for caution and efforts to mitigate risks posed by job displacement and privacy. It sets out three broad aims that underpin the strategy. Firstly, it aims to create a technological environment in which the necessary research and investments can take place, including making more data available. Second, it addresses some of the socio-economic concerns around AI, including automation and its impact on employment. Measures suggested include modernising education and creating new training opportunities. Finally, the strategy argues the need for an appropriate ethical and legal framework that fits with the EU's values and is in line with the Charter for Fundamental Rights, a legally binding set of political, social and economic rights that came into force across the EU in 2009 (European Commission, 2010).

Following this strategy, in 2021 the EU published its proposal for AI regulation resulting in the AI Act, which came into force on 1 August 2024. This will be discussed in the following chapter and compared to legislative efforts in other countries. In the case of the EU and US, legislation, albeit in its early stages, and the focus of legislation has differed significantly and this is a reflection of the policy priorities that underpin them. It could be argued that federal US AI policy has emphasised the need to maintain its technological and commercial advances, with AI governance being largely placed in the realm of the private sector. The EU, conversely, sees a much larger role for public bodies to oversee AI developments, particularly in regard to how AI is deployed and its impact on EU citizens. For these reasons, it has been argued that the EU's frameworks and priorities for developing AI policy is more ethical (Roberts et al., 2021, 68).

This concern with protecting US commercial and technology interests is evident from the title of the 2019 Executive Order: Maintaining American Leadership in Artificial Intelligence. The first paragraph of the order emphasises this priority:

> The United States is the world leader in AI research and development (R&D) and deployment. Continued American leadership in AI is of paramount importance to maintaining the economic and national security of the United States and to shaping the global evolution of AI in a manner consistent with our Nation's values, policies, and priorities.
>
> (Executive Office of the President, 2019, 3967)

Of the five core principles guiding the order, only one is concerned with trust and civil liberties, while the other four focus on technological research, economic competitiveness, employment and protecting US businesses abroad. Two further executive orders in 2020 and 2023 centred on how AI should be used within federal government bodies, security and trust. An executive order is a directive by the President of the United States and relates to the operations of government at a national level. They do not require approval by Congress and remain in force unless ruled unlawful, cancelled or revoked by a later president. Perhaps the most significant executive order was the 1863 Emancipation Proclamation issued by Abraham Lincoln and which changed the legal status of over 3.5 million African American slaves (Guelzo, 2005).

It is the 2023 order titled Executive Order on the Safe, Secure, and Trustworthy Development and Use of Artificial Intelligence, passed by President Joe Biden, that draws the US closer to the European position on AI than the previous two orders. This is evident in the opening paragraph that states:

> Artificial intelligence (AI) holds extraordinary potential for both promise and peril. Responsible AI use has the potential to help solve urgent challenges while making our world more prosperous, productive, innovative, and secure. At the same time, irresponsible use could exacerbate societal harms such as fraud, discrimination, bias, and disinformation; displace and disempower workers; stifle competition; and pose risks to national security.
>
> (The White House, 2023)

While the order acknowledges the risks of unfettered AI developments and puts forward remedies to mitigate them, the criticism of some of these measures by US commercial interests points to tensions that are, perhaps, less evident in Europe. One of the order's provisions requires technology companies to provide information to the US Commerce Department about their advanced AI projects that use significant computing power on the grounds of national security. This has led to lobbying by industry advocates with threats of possible lawsuits (Chatterjee and Bordelon, 2024). Whatever the outcome of such lobbying, the order heralds a possible divergence of policy and legislation between the US and EU, which we shall see later in this chapter when the EU AI Act is considered in more detail.

Information and data literacy

It is generally accepted that the term 'information literacy' was coined in 1974 by Paul G. Zurkowski in a report to the US National Commission on Libraries and Information Science. He wrote:

> Information is not knowledge; it is concepts or ideas which enter a person's field of perception, are evaluated and assimilated reinforcing or changing the individual's concept of reality and/or ability to act. As beauty is in the eye of the beholder, so information is in the mind of the user.
>
> (Badke, 2010, 48)

Zurkowski was concerned that the study of information did not focus sufficiently on how people found it in the first place, made sense of it and then applied it into their professional and personal lives. He argued that those trained in these methods could be called 'information literate'. He believed that while individuals may be considered literate because they could read and write, they were not necessarily information literate as they, 'do not have the ability to mould information to their needs, and realistically must be considered information illiterates' (Badke, 2010, 48).

He estimated that only one-sixth of the US population were information literate and called for a national programme to bring the remaining population up to the same standard. While such an initiative never materialised, colleges and universities have increased their efforts to train students in using their information resources more efficiently. The subject is also an important element of many library and information courses. A related area of study is media literacy, which seeks to educate students in filtering messages broadcast from mass media outlets and, more recently, across social platforms. In 1999, The Society of College, National and University Libraries (SCONUL) in the UK published their Seven Pillars of Information Literacy, which was updated in 2011 (SCONUL, 2024). The model has been adopted by teachers and librarians around the world as a framework for teaching information skills. It describes a set of generic skills and understandings that information users can develop whatever their backgrounds or needs. The seven pillars (identify, scope, plan, gather, evaluate, manage and present) cover the skills needed to make best use of information resources in most research scenarios. It has been adapted for use in specific situations and sectors, including healthcare, small businesses and engineering, and in different countries (Wertz et al., 2013; Kelham, 2014; Swapna and Biradar, 2017; Lockerbie and Williams, 2019).

Although elements of information literacy are taught across many educational establishments, outside of library and information courses themselves it is often part of a student's training in how to use the resources of the library rather than underpinning all their academic work. A 2008 survey of over 100 colleges and universities in Canada and the US found that most information literacy training was done in a single session, with fewer than 6% of respondents being required to complete a one or two credit course (Badke, 2011). Badke concludes that 'information literacy is invisible because so few people recognise there is a problem to address' (Badke, 2011, 139). There are parallels with much of the training in the early days of personal computing where programmes were focused on helping users with word processing software, storing files and printing documents rather than giving them a better understanding of what was going on in the background. While it is unrealistic to expect computer users to be able to write code and create programmes themselves, a better understanding of why things work the way they do would help them better solve problems they might encounter. Similarly, we do not need to be able to do the work of a journalist, but knowing how the media industry operates and the interests certain outlets might be serving would prevent a lot of dangerous misinformation from being believed verbatim.

Alongside information and media, data literacy programmes have emerged in both academia and within organisations. There is an overlap between all three types of training as definitions are fluid and, at a basic level, data is a building block of information and media is simply information in different formats. Hence the rise of courses in data journalism as publications seek to tell stories and explain events with data. While information literacy, as a concept and in practice, has been largely confined to the library and information world and academia, data literacy has gained more widespread attention across a number of professions and industry sectors. Depending on the background and focus of its proponents, definitions vary in terms of specific details and the relationship to technology. According to an enterprise data architect, data literacy is:

> . . . the ability to derive meaningful information from data, just as literacy in general is the ability to derive information from the written word. The complexity of data analysis, especially in the context of big data, means that data literacy requires some knowledge of mathematics and statistics.
>
> (S. Robinson, 2024)

Technology consulting firm Gartner defines data literacy as:

> . . . the ability to read, write and communicate data in context, with an understanding of data sources and constructs, analytical methods and AI techniques. Data literacy helps people identify, understand, interpret and act on data within a business context to influence business value or outcomes.
>
> (Gartner, 2024a)

This ability to understand, interpret and then act on data is, according to S. Brown (2024), an essential skill for business leaders. Evidence-based decision-making can only work effectively if those making the decisions understand the data they are using. Wixom and Beath (2023) argue that employees at all levels of an organisation need to be data literate and extend the scope of data literacy in a commercial setting to being able to treat data as a strategic asset. This may involve finding ways to monetise internal data assets either through selling it directly or incorporating it into new products and services.

Data literacy should not be confused with 'digital literacy'. Digital literacy programmes have been initiated across many countries at local and national levels to help citizens, particularly some disadvantaged and vulnerable groups, use computers at a basic level. These have often focused on helping people access online public services via government websites and portals. In the US, for example, the Chicago Housing Authority runs a digital inclusion programme so residents can get access to and use broadband services and digital devices for finding employment, using online banking and accessing education resources (Chicago Housing Authority, 2024). In the UK, the charity Age UK offers computer training for older people, while Barclays, the retail bank, has offered similar services since 2013 (Barclays, 2020; Age UK, 2024).

It is interesting that while information literacy programmes have rarely crossed from libraries and academia into more mainstream public policy, data literacy has attracted more attention from governments. This, in part, is because data and the way it is used within industry is seen by many policy makers as a more tangible part of the economy and a driver of growth. In the UK, this was reflected in the 2020 National Data Strategy (discussed in Chapter 2), two core pillars of which were to 'unlock the value of data across the economy' and making sure 'people can continue to develop the data skills they need throughout their lives' (DCMS, 2020). Explaining why such a strategy is necessary, the supporting evidence outlines how the data economy grew twice as quickly as the rest of the economy during the 2010s and, in 2020, made up approximately 4% of UK GDP (DCMS, 2020). At its launch, the UK government positioned the strategy as part of its efforts to position the country as a world leader in data-driven innovation. These all sound like sensible aims that play to the UK's strengths in research and innovation but, as we saw in a previous section of this chapter, translating these aspirations into tangible steps and sustaining the public investments in rolling them out does not always happen. Priorities change, budgets shrink, global events such as COVID-19 and recessions occur, and governments change. A 2022 review of The National Data Strategy by the ODI concluded that while its objectives were laudable, it lacked focus in some key areas. On the issue of training and education, the ODI argued there was too much emphasis on training workers in technical data manipulation skills at the expense of also helping citizens better understand how data could help in their daily lives (Zimeta, 2022). This partly stemmed from there being no consistent definition of data literacy across government. The review also pointed to the danger of fragmentation and duplication in the government's own work on data literacy due to overlapping concepts of media and digital literacy. The review concluded by recommending the development of clearer definitions and frameworks around data literacy, better co-ordination across government to prevent overlaps, greater internal governmental resources being made available and extending the focus of training to include citizens.

During the consultation period of the National Data Strategy, a number of stakeholders and interested parties contributed their views. The digital rights campaigning organisation, Open Rights Group (ORG), raised concerns about the strategy, particularly what they saw as a core issue:

> The fundamental problem with the National Data Strategy is that it is a political strategy about data which works from the position that data is not political.
>
> (ORG, 2020)

They argued that the strategy viewed data as unbiased and factual strings that exist in a vacuum. However, based on historical precedents, the ORG sees data governance systems as central to how we live and work, which, in the wrong hands, can be used by authorities against citizens. The organisation cites the Covid OneView system introduced by the UK government in 2020, which pulled in personal data from multiple sources without the knowledge or consent of individuals. This, they argue, shows a disregard for existing data protection and privacy rules, most of which have emanated from the EU.

A more positive response from the UK's Information Commissioner's Office (ICO), responsible for enforcing data protection and freedom of information legislation, saw evidence in the strategy that data protection was recognised as important (ICO, 2020). While it recognised this as a positive sign, the ICO highlighted the importance of making sure that data flows of the country are managed within existing international safe harbour agreements. This is becoming a pressing issue, particularly for EU member states, where a number of US companies have been fined under the GDPR for not following rules on managing data related to EU citizens.

US data policies

European and US government policies towards the collection and use of data, particularly personal data, have seen a growing divergence over the last 20 years. We saw above how this is playing out in the sphere of AI policy, with the EU emphasising privacy and the rights of citizens while US policy, although acknowledging these issues, focuses more on stimulating research and commercial activities. To what extent this approach in the US has contributed to the country's enormous success in creating some of the world's most successful digital companies or whether it is a side effect of this success is debatable. There is evidence that restrictive data practices may act as a trade barrier to those countries enforcing strict rules on how organisations can use and share information (Van Der Marel and Ferracane, 2021). Research has also shown that such practices can negatively impact the performance of firms within those countries (Ferracane, Kren and Van Der Marel, 2020).

The difference between the US and European approaches to data policy can, perhaps, best be seen in the context of data protection. While the first EU data protection directive was passed in 1981, based on a belief that privacy is a fundamental right, the US has no single federal piece of legislation focused on this issue. Laws on privacy and the protection of personal data do exist but they are a combination of sector-specific federal and state legislation (Boyne, 2020). History no doubt plays an important part in how these differences have emerged. It might be argued that the policy in the US has been guided by a greater concern over the power of the state than of business in terms of impacting on individual liberties. In Europe, the devastation wreaked by the authoritarianism of fascism and its classification of individuals by their race and religion has shown the dangers of misusing personal data.

Despite the differences, it is interesting to note the impact that EU data protection regulations have had on US businesses. Despite recent trade conflicts, we live in a world of global trade and the EU market of 449 million people is not one that digital giants such as Alphabet, Meta, Apple and Amazon can ignore. For example, 30% of Alphabet's total 2023 revenue came from Europe, the Middle East and Africa, with Europe making up a significant proportion of that (Alphabet, 2024). Meta's European revenues for 2023 were almost US$9.5 billion, making up 25% of total turnover (Meta, 2024). It is worth noting that of the 107 mentions of Europe in Meta's 10K annual financial filing to the US Securities and Exchange Commission (SEC), 85 of them were in the context of European regulations around data protection, privacy and competition.

The tensions created by the practices of US technology companies in relation to European data protection regulations were brought to the fore by the *Schrems I* and *Schrems II* legal cases. These were brought by Austrian privacy activist and lawyer, Max Schrems, with the first complaint being filed in 2013 against Facebook Ireland Ltd with the Irish Data Protection Commissioner (DPC) (Baker McKenzie, 2019). At the time, Facebook's European headquarters were in Ireland and Schrems' complaint centred on the personal data of Facebook users in Europe being accessed by US state security agencies. This emerged from disclosures by whistleblower Edward Snowden, who highlighted a data-mining program called PRISM operated by the US National Security Agency. Schrems argued that this was outside of the already agreed Safe Harbour agreement between the US and Europe that allowed data transfers across their borders. Although the DPC declined to investigate the complaint, it eventually went to the European Court of Justice (ECJ) in 2015, which ruled the Safe Harbour agreement invalid (European Union, 2015). As a result, a new agreement known as the Privacy Shield was put in place in 2016 to allow data flows to continue but this too was declared inadequate in 2020 by the ECJ following another complaint brought by Schrems (Pinsent Masons, 2024). Following this, the EU-US Data Privacy Framework was agreed which, it is hoped, will satisfy EU privacy rights while allowing US companies to collect data from European citizens.

These complaints and the resulting legal cases have demonstrated the growing willingness of the EU to confront US business practices with respect to the collection and use of personal data. It has been argued that this concern with individual privacy rights is a factor in explaining the relative lack of global success of EU technology companies (Coatanlem, 2024). However, there is strong evidence that these and other cases have forced US regulators and companies to change their approach to data protection and strengthen many of their laws (Calia, 2022, 271–2).

AI and data legislation

The discussion above on data and AI policies has set the scene for an exploration of specific pieces of legislation in these areas and the impact they are having on the ways organisations use data. Some of this legislation has already been touched upon in the context of the policies and philosophies that underpin them in the US, UK and EU, particularly with regard to privacy and data protection. This section will consider the EU AI Act as an ambitious and pioneering attempt to regulate and shape the evolution of a rapidly developing technology and discuss what it might mean for data-driven innovation in the EU and elsewhere. We will also look at some of the challenges that AI is posing to content creators in terms of copyright infringements and how they are responding. The EU Digital Markets Act will be discussed and how US companies are responding to it. This section will also discuss the evolution of Net Neutrality legislation to explore the shifting power balances in the technology industry brought about by the rise of the internet. As we shall see, the recent rapid developments in AI and its reliance on data of all sorts to feed the large language models (LLMs) is forcing both developers and data owners to rethink their strategies and business models.

The EU AI Act

The EU Act came into force on 1 August 2024 and is due to be effective from 2 August 2026. This means that, although the Act legally existed from August 2024, it is not enforceable until August 2026. It is important to note this is an Act and not a Directive, the difference being that an Act has binding legal force in every EU member state while a Directive sets objectives that members must incorporate in their national laws by a certain date (European Parliament, 2024). Article 1 of the Act summarises its key objectives and rationale at a macro level:

> The purpose of this Regulation is to improve the functioning of the internal market by laying down a uniform legal framework in particular for the development, the placing on the market, the putting into service and the use of artificial intelligence systems (AI systems) in the Union, in accordance with Union values, to promote the uptake of human centric and trustworthy artificial intelligence (AI) while ensuring a high level of protection of health, safety, fundamental rights as enshrined in the Charter of Fundamental Rights of the European Union (the 'Charter'), including democracy, the rule of law and environmental protection, to protect against the harmful effects of AI systems in the Union, and to support innovation.
>
> (Official Journal of the European Union, 2024, 1)

The Act is the first wide-ranging and detailed piece of legislation globally that addresses the specific issues raised by AI technologies and their use. It provides definitions of three key elements of AI:

- 'AI system' – defined as a machine-based system that can operate with some degree of autonomy and which can adapt depending on the inputs it receives. It can generate outputs such as recommendations, predictions and digital content.
- 'General-purpose AI model' – this is an AI model trained on large amounts of data, and which is able to self-supervise at scale and be integrated into downstream systems or applications.
- 'General-purpose AI system' – defined as an AI system based on a general-purpose model and which can be used for a variety of purposes, both directly and integrated into other AI systems.

(Official Journal of the European Union, 2024, 50)

As well as applying to organisations based in the EU, it also applies to any provider deploying an AI system within the bloc regardless of where the provider is located or what sector they operate in. There is a duty of compliance to the Act by any individual or organisation, public or private, developing, deploying or using an AI system. An AI Liability Directive is due to follow the Act that would increase the likelihood of a successful claim against an AI system developer or the user of an AI system that relied on its output (White and Case, 2024).

The comprehensive nature of the Act is evident in the way it classifies AI systems according to risk and imposes different requirements on users and providers depending on those levels. These range from 'low or minimal risk' where little or no danger is anticipated from the system to 'unacceptable risk', which is prohibited and includes where a system might engage in social scoring or distort a person's behaviour in a manner that might cause harm (White and Case, 2024). Social scoring relates to the potential for governments to use AI to give citizens scores based on surveillance of their behaviour to create risk profiles (Grady, 2023). Between these extremes are 'limited risk' and 'high risk', with 'limited' applying to interactive systems such as customer chatbots and image generators and 'high-risk' systems being those employed in specific sectors such as education, law enforcement and the justice system where the potential for errors and misuse could have serious consequences.

Penalties for non-compliance range from forcing the AI system to be taken off the market to fines of up to €35 million or 7% of a company's total annual worldwide turnover (Official Journal of the European Union, 2024, 115). This range is important as a startup with little revenue may not be concerned with a fine of 7% of its revenue, while a €35 million fine would be a much larger deterrent. Conversely, €35 million to a company like Alphabet would be trivial but 7% of its 2023 global turnover would amount to US$21.5 billion (Alphabet, 2024).

Responses to the EU AI Act have been varied with some welcoming its broad reach and emphasis on the rights of individuals and others, primarily from the business and developer communities, expressing concerns about possible chilling impacts on innovation and the costs of compliance. As the law was first proposed in 2021, the sudden emergence of ChatGPT onto the market in late 2022 forced the regulators drafting the Act to rethink some of its provisions. It has been argued that this urgency to specifically address LLMs such as ChatGPT has weakened aspects of the Act, with regulators leaving out the essential details needed for clarity. This vagueness, it has been estimated, may require 60 or 70 pieces of secondary legislation to support the Act's implementation (Espinoza, 2023). DigitalEurope, an industry interest group representing the European digital sector, has argued the law will make it more difficult for EU-based technology companies to compete with their US counterparts, with their director-general claiming: 'The extra cost of compliance on EU companies is bringing us further down. We will be hiring lawyers while the rest of the world is hiring coders' (Espinoza, 2024).

Although the EU AI Act has been passed, it will take a number of years for its impact to become apparent. Clarifying aspects of the Act in terms of how they apply in very specific circumstances and to new and rapidly developing technologies will require amendments and secondary legislation, all of which will be subject to lobbying from vested interests. Whether it will have a chilling impact on European technology companies' investments in AI will be hard to determine as many other variables are also at play. These include limitations of the technology itself and not delivering on the promises of its developers, a public backlash against AI technologies following some high-profile cases and broader economic factors impacting business investments. Critics believe that European technology startups will be most negatively impact by the Act. They argue that large US companies, such as Alphabet and Microsoft, can afford to pay the costs of compliance or employ enough lawyers to fight challenges from the EU for breaches. Smaller businesses in the EU trying to develop new AI services may feel the level of uncertainty created by the Act and prohibitive legal costs may not be worth the risk (Laurent, 2024).

One of the most significant and immediate impacts of the wave of LLMs started by OpenAI's GPT family of models has been the concerns raised by content creators, from news publishers and bloggers to image and video sharing platforms such as YouTube and Instagram. Training many of these models, particularly the frontier ones from OpenAI, Anthropic and Alphabet, has required massive amounts of data to be ingested. Much of this has been scraped from public-facing sites and platforms without the knowledge of the content owners. Web crawling has been common since the early days of search engines and, in most cases, is allowed by site owners, particularly those wanting their content to appear in SERPs. Google even offers a tool, Search Console, allowing website operators to request a crawl from the company's web spider whenever they add or update web content. Site owners that do not want to be crawled by search engine bots can use a simple command on a text file telling bots not to index content on that page and most search engine operators will comply.

The rapid rise of LLMs since 2022 and the training that went into them caught many content owners by surprise. However, since then, the larger ones have started to restrict what AI developers can do with their content. The EU AI Act imposes transparency requirements and compliance with EU copyright law in the context of general-purpose AI models and US copyright law has already been used in cases against LLM developers. By May 2024, there were at least 24 pending cases against AI providers with copyright and privacy laws being used as the basis for the complaints (Coyer, 2024). The extent to which these LLMs rely on third-party content for their training was revealed in a 2020 research paper produced by academics and OpenAI developers that showed what the GPT-3 model had been trained on. It showed that 16% of the weighting in the training mix had come from books fed into the model, comprising 67 billion tokens or approximately 50 billion words (Mann et al., 2020). This is part of the evidence in a US case, *Author's Guild v OpenAI*, in which 17 authors including John Grisham and R.R. Martin claim: 'Defendants' decision to copy authors' works, done without offering any choices or providing any compensation, threatens the role and livelihood of writers as a whole' (Author's Guild, 2023).

In Europe, similar concerns have been raised by authors and their representative bodies. At the 2023 Frankfurt Book Fair, three bodies, The European Writers' Council, the Federation of European Publishers and the European and International Booksellers Federation, signed a statement urging regulators to use the new AI Act to prevent unauthorised use of copyrighted material by AI companies. The statement claimed that apart from infringing the rights of authors to control how their works are used, the unauthorised ingestion of content by LLMs had wider implications for society:

> Generative AI models have been developed in an opaque and unfair way, illegally making use of millions of copyright-protected books without permission

> from authors or publishers. This practice impacts negatively not only rightsholders, but also democracy itself, by facilitating the mass creation of misleading, biased, and even dangerous content which has the potential to undermine European democracy.
>
> (Creamer, 2023)

Anthropic, creator of the Claude LLMs, has also been the subject of complaints and lawsuits. In August 2024, three authors filed a copyright infringement case in California alleging Anthropic had used 'pirated' copies of their books to train its AI chatbot, Claude (Battersby, 2024). The case has particularly incensed authors as the use of pirated copies indicates the company probably knew its actions were an infringement of copyright.

Complaints and lawsuits against AI companies extend beyond the training of models on text-based content. Many artists have expressed concerns that their creations have been used in image-generating products such as Dall-E, Midjourney and Imagen. An interim ruling in a legal case against the creators of the Stable Diffusion image generator, which was trained on over 5 billion images, may have implications for any companies that have built their own products on the model (Cho, 2024).

These and other cases against OpenAI and Perplexity among others are forcing a change in how developers view training content and how to source it. One outcome is a growing number of financial deals between content owners and developers that, not surprisingly, favour well-funded companies with the resources to pay. As Alex Ratner, co-founder of Snorkel AI, put it: 'There's no more free lunch. You can't scrape a web-scale data set any more. You have to go and purchase it or produce it. That's the frontier we're at now.' (Hammond, 2024) AI search engine, Perplexity's response has been its 'Publishers' Program', which aims to share advertising revenue with publishing companies that sign up to it. Publishers in Europe and the US have signed up, with the renumeration being on a 'per-source' basis, meaning that content partners are paid for each article that is used in responses. Participating partners will be given tools to track how often their articles appear in search queries (Robison, 2024). Other deals between AI developers and publishers have been agreed with Condé Nast, News Corporation, NBC News and The Atlantic (Tobitt, 2024).

As with many legal disputes, some of these cases may take years to conclude and with a number reaching out-of-court settlements. In that time, the technology will have moved on and the business models of AI companies as well as publishers will have evolved and adapted to a rapidly changing environment. These changes will be considered in more detail in the following chapter where different scenarios for the evolution of the AI and data landscape will be explored. The intersection of the law, AI technologies, the commercial interests of business and the personal interests of individuals provides fertile ground for discussing what the future may hold.

The EU Digital Markets Act

The Digital Markets Act (DMA) came into force across the EU from November 2022 and became applicable from May 2023. Its aim is to 'make the markets in the digital sector fairer and more contestable' (European Commission, 2023). Primarily, it was designed to prevent large technology 'gatekeepers' operating in Europe – Alphabet, Meta, Apple, ByteDance, Microsoft and Amazon – from stifling innovation and smaller businesses from competing with them. Network effects have benefited these companies as their value to users increases the more they grow. Conversely, network effects, once harnessed, can make it more difficult for new entrants to gain a foothold. Persuading users to join a new social network when they don't know anyone on it is a major challenge to kickstarting growth. Similarly, Amazon benefits from its large user base making its marketplace for third-party sellers very attractive which, in turn, gives more choice to Amazon subscribers. Trying to replicate this with a competing marketplace takes time and substantial financial resources, as Chinese firm Temu has discovered in its attempts to take market share in Europe and the US.

There are ten core provisions in the Act that define its scope and powers:

1 Gatekeeper designation – companies that meet specific thresholds in terms of revenue, market capitalisation (total value of the company's shares) and number of users will be defined as gatekeepers and be subject to the Act.
2 Interoperability requirements – gatekeepers must allow third-party services to interoperate with their own services in certain circumstances. Particularly relevant to communication tools.
3 Data access and portability – users must be allowed to access and transfer their data to other services. Business users must be given access to data generated through their use of the platform.
4 Pre-installation and default app restrictions – users must be allowed to uninstall pre-installed apps (phone and computer operating systems such as Windows, Android and iOS) and change default settings easily.
5 Prohibition of self-preferencing – gatekeepers are banned from giving preferential treatment to their own services or products over those of competitors. For example, this would include Google prioritising its own products in search results.

6 Fair access to app stores – gatekeepers operating app stores must allow developers to use third-party systems and promote offers outside the gatekeeper's platform.
7 Advertising transparency – advertisers and publishers must be given access to performance measuring tools and information needed to carry out their own verification of ad inventory. This has parallels with independent companies that monitor television, radio and newspaper audiences.
8 Merger notifications – gatekeepers must inform the European Commission of all intended acquisitions of technology companies. This is to avoid large companies killing nascent competition by buying startups.
9 Penalties for non-compliance – fines may be up to 10% of the company's global total turnover or 20% for repeated infringements.
10 Structural remedies – in cases of systematic non-compliance, the Commission may force a gatekeeper to sell part of its business.

A 2020 impact assessment of the DMA highlighted the concerns that the Commission had in terms of the market power of the six gatekeepers. It showed Microsoft with a 78% market share of desktop operating systems, Google Chrome's 60% share of web browsers, Google Search with 95% and Amazon taking 60% of the European ecommerce market in terms of revenues (European Commission, 2020b)

In some respects, the objectives of the Act can be seen in the light of historical regulatory interventions in the US. In 1911, the US Supreme Court ruled that Standard Oil Trust be broken up and split into 34 companies (Saelee, 2020). This was following several previous cases and growing concerns that the company was abusing its dominant position in the drilling, refining, transportation and selling of petroleum products. By undercutting competitors in its pricing, Standard Oil forced many of them out of business and was then able to raise prices once competition abated (McGee, 1958). Similarly, in 1982, AT&T was ordered to give up control of the Bell Operating Companies that provided regional telephone services in the US, leaving AT&T with a dominant position in long distance telephone calls.

Closer to the concerns of the EU and the DMA, Microsoft was the subject of an antitrust case in the US brought under the same legislation that led to the breakup of Standard Oil 90 years previously. In 2001, the United States District Court for the District of Columbia ruled that Microsoft had acted unlawfully in bundling its web browser, Internet Explorer, with Windows and making it difficult for users to use competing products such as Netscape (Justia Law, 2001). Although the ruling was later modified, it highlighted the issues of dominant power in the new environment of digital services. The costs of bundling digital products together by dominant companies is much lower than doing the same with physical products. The cost of reproducing digital artefacts is next to zero, unlike in the physical world where the variable costs of materials and labour have to be factored in. The case against Microsoft took several years to go through the courts and by the time of final ruling, the market environment for web browsers and internet services had changed so much that it was largely irrelevant.

Following the Act coming into force in May 2023, several cases have been considered by the Commission. Most decisions in the first 18 months focused on defining whether certain services and products could be classed as gateways. For example, in May 2024, the Commission designated Apple's iPadOS as a gatekeeper. The iPhone's iOS had been similarly classified a few months previously. These decisions were based on the number of users of the systems and the fact they were locked into them on iPads and iPhones as users could not realistically install different operating systems on them. Also, the integration of iPadOS with other Apple products made it less likely users would want to switch to a device with a different, non-compatible operating system. In this sense, the Commission concluded they were important gateways for business users to reach end-users (European Commission, 2024a). The impact of network effects was considered a significant factor in the Commission's decision, as it has been with other cases:

> The Commission finds that iPadOS exhibits strong network effects. This is because it benefits from the positive feedback loop stemming from the increasing end user base drawn to the Apple OS ecosystem and the ensuing concentration of business users to reach this valuable customer population. This market dynamic is also evidenced by the lack of success of competing operating systems, other than Android OS, to successfully and sustainably establish themselves with users of tablets.
>
> (European Commission, 2024b, 18–19)

The implications of the ruling are that Apple must comply with the DMA in respect of iPadOS, which would involve allowing users in Europe to download apps from outside the Apple app store, uninstall preloaded apps and be presented with choice screens to select default services such as web browsers and e-mail. This brings it into line with the mobile phone operating system, iOS. Failure to comply within a specified timeframe could result in fines as described above. This and other rulings on Apple under the DMA led one commentator to claim it is 'yet another prominent crack in the walled garden of Apple's ecosystem' (Weatherbed, 2024).

It is important to note that DMA investigations and rulings have not been restricted to Apple. In the 12 months since coming into force, there have been more than 40 decisions made by the European Commission on X (formerly Twitter), Booking.com, ByteDance, Alphabet, Meta and Microsoft. It seems clear that the Commission is taking the Act seriously and changes to a number of the operating practices of designated gatekeepers have been made. The commissions charged to developers by app store owners, Alphabet and Apple, have been reduced from 30% to 27% with some flexibility in the billing process. However, these changes have been criticised by software developers as tokenistic and, after new charges are levied, not amounting to anything substantial. The Commission is also concerned that some companies are not taking the decisions seriously enough and opened several investigations into non-compliance by Amazon, Meta and Alphabet.

Legal advisors Winston argue that the DMA will only be truly effective if the Commission is willing to enforce it and levy fines for non-compliance or force companies to divest some operations as a last resort (Arguello, Crowther and Vyas, 2024). Winston's lawyers also believe that the DMA will be more effective if private actions from third parties are brought alongside those from the Commission, something which is allowed under the provisions of the Act. The Commission is also watching what other countries do in response to the DMA as Japan, Britain, Mexico and Australia are looking at similar legislation. It will take a number of years for a clearer picture of the impacts of the DMA to emerge, but the Act has the potential to substantially change the data and AI landscape. Some immediate changes have already become evident with Apple announcing it would not include its AI offering, Apple Intelligence, on the iPhone 16 in the EU due to 'regulatory uncertainties brought about by the Digital Markets Act' (Espinoza and Acton, 2024). These 'regulatory uncertainties' are at the heart of technology regulations, particularly the DMA. The Commission has set general principles for how and to whom the DMA will be applied but a lack of specificity raises uncertainty among the larger technology companies as to whether new services they introduce will fall foul of the law. However, being too precise when drafting such legislation also raises problems down the line as new technologies and ways to use them emerge that could not have been predicted. Either way, the law of unintended consequences may apply and problems that were never anticipated may cause regulators to rethink their approach. There is, however, one certainty: the DMA and its enforcement will keep lawyers, policy makers, regulators, developers and academics busy for years to come.

Network neutrality

In Chapter 1 we explored the importance of open technology standards as a way of promoting innovation. Allowing anyone access to non-proprietary tools to build products and services encourages innovators to experiment more freely. We have seen how opening technology platforms to third parties has helped grow the businesses of Alphabet, Microsoft and Apple. The internet is, perhaps, the ultimate example of how open and non-proprietary standards and protocols have created, outside of the control of large businesses, the world's largest network of over five billion users and generated trillions of pounds of value. None of this was planned, with the internet originally being developed for military and academic purposes to share information across a resilient network that could interconnect with computers of all sorts. Until the late 1990s, most telecommunication networks were run by state-controlled operators such as BT in the UK, France Telecom in France and Deutsche Telekom in Germany. The US telecommunication networks were privately run but had done little to innovate beyond providing voice services for a hundred years. Most of these operators had little interest in developing new products and services as they were either state-run with no profit incentive or quasi-private monopolies that were doing well financially by providing traditional telephone services. This started to change in the 1990s with the privatisation of most public operators in Europe, the rise of commercially aggressive mobile networks and the growth of online service providers such as AOL and CompuServe. Alongside this, the internet experienced rapid growth as it was opened to commercial activities in the US and e-mail and the World Wide Web provided services that business and private individuals wanted to use. As PCs began to proliferate during the 1990s, people increasingly had access at home and work to devices that could make use of online services.

It is interesting that many telecom operators were not enthusiastic about the internet. Many saw it as either a nuisance or a threat to their traditional ways of operating. In the UK, BT's reluctance to provide broadband internet to many rural areas was illustrated by the registration system it set up in the early 2000s. Local telephone exchanges would only be upgraded to offer broadband when enough inhabitants signed up, a system that was only scrapped in 2004 (Dodson, 2004). The frustration this caused in many rural areas led some communities to commission their own broadband networks, including Blewbury in Oxfordshire where the community paid to set up a network of local antenna around the village connected to a physical leased line from Invisible Networks (Select Committee on Environment, Food and Rural Affairs, 2003). This has clearly changed now with broadband subscriptions generating higher revenues for operators than their income from voice services.

While the commercial, technological and regulatory environment within which most telecom providers operate has changed significantly since the 1990s, there are still conflicting interests at play between these companies and those offering services across their networks. Providing internet connectivity, fixed and mobile, requires massive investments to upgrade and build the networks as well as maintain them. During the financial year 2023/24, BT's capital expenditure totalled almost £5 billion while the company generated £20.8 billion in revenue and £0.9 billion in post-tax profits (BT Group, 2024, 2). In the same period, Alphabet generated almost £14 billion in the UK alone from its search advertising business, which, based on Alphabet's estimated 75% profit margin for search advertising, means the company's profits in the UK alone were nearly £10 billion more than BT (Wellman, 2007; Ponsford, 2024). It is important to note that Alphabet has modest capital expenditure costs in the UK beyond office buildings and some computing infrastructure. This is a pattern repeated across most countries and their telecom providers and applies to Meta, Amazon and Apple as well as Alphabet. Therefore, a relatively small number of companies have the complex and expensive task of providing internet connectivity to individuals and businesses, while most profits generated from what people do on these networks goes to the third parties providing the applications that sit on top of them. Perhaps it is not surprising that these imbalances have raised complaints from the connectivity providers, many of which see an unfair commercial and regulatory playing field. This has led to the issue of 'network neutrality', which raises questions about the dynamics of innovation, the best interests of end-users and who should ultimately pay for advanced communication networks.

Network or net neutrality was first coined as a phrase in 2003 by legal scholar Tim Wu, who saw potential for a conflict of interest between broadband providers and the companies developing new services that required higher bandwidth, such as voice and video applications (Wu, 2003). A ruling in 2002 by the US communications regulator, the FCC, that internet service providers (ISPs) were providers of information services and not telecommunication providers meant they were not obliged to provide open access to other service providers and fell outside the regulatory powers of the FCC. This opened up ISPs in the US to discriminate against some third-party service providers either by slowing down the traffic flowing over their networks, charging different rates for it or even blocking it completely. However, the FCC recognised how discriminatory practices by ISPs might harm the experience of internet users and potentially stifle innovation in this rapidly developing environment. This led to the regulator issuing a set of non-discrimination principles called 'Preserving Network Freedom'.

Although not legal requirements, these principles encouraged ISPs to embed four freedoms in their operations and offerings to users (Powell, 2004):

1 Freedom to access content – consumers should have access to their choice of legal content.
2 Freedom to run applications – consumers should be able to run applications of their choice.
3 Freedom to attach devices – consumers should be permitted to attach any devices they choose to the connections in their homes.
4 Freedom to obtain service plan information – consumers should receive meaningful information regarding their service plans.

These principles, and the FCC's propensity to enforce them, were tested in 2005 when it opened an investigation into a local telephone carrier, Madison River Communications, that was blocking the voice-over-internet (VoIP) services of Vonage. Madison River Communications saw Vonage's VoIP offerings as a direct threat to the revenues from its own voice services. The case was settled without a ruling from the FCC, with Madison River agreeing to stop blocking Vonage's traffic and pay a US$15,000 fine. Although a legal precedent was not set, it sent a clear signal to the industry that the FCC would take action against any operators contravening the four principles (Beard et al., 2015).

For the next 16 years, FCC rulings and policies from different administrations saw the regulation of net neutrality swing back and forth. Under the Obama administration in the US, the principles of net neutrality were upheld; however, the Trump administration reversed this in 2017 with a new appointee to head the FCC who saw proponents of existing regulations as promoting 'hypothetical harms and hysterical prophecies of doom', while arguing: 'It's basic economics. The more heavily you regulate something, the less of it you're likely to get.' (Solon, 2017). The FCC presented its proposals to roll back net neutrality rules as progressive, calling them, 'Restoring Internet Freedom' rules. As part of this process, they opened a public consultation and invited individuals and companies to submit their comments on the proposals via an online portal. Almost 21.9 million comments were received but, after careful examination by third parties, it was revealed that many of these were duplicates as well as coming from automated bots, including 500,000 of them from Russia (Birnbaum, 2018). After taking out boilerplate duplicates and those that had been artificially generated, it appeared that 1.52 million comments were in favour of retaining net neutrality laws while only 23,000 argued for overturning them (Finley, 2017). Despite this, the FCC decided to reverse net neutrality rules, a decision that was reversed again in 2021 under the Biden administration.

In the EU, a less frenetic situation regarding network regulation has developed with the 2015 Net Neutrality Regulation setting a framework for ensuring net neutrality across the bloc (European Parliament, 2015). Despite concerns that the EU rules may have some loopholes that could allow operators to discriminate against some services, they have been broadly welcomed by consumer groups (Hern, 2015).

While this legal to-ing and fro-ing is of interest to lawyers and students of public policy, they present fascinating insights into the commercial and political tensions caused by transformative technologies such as the internet and AI. They also highlight the complexity of information systems and the services they provide. The main lobbyists arguing for the overturning of net neutrality rules were funded by the operators of the network infrastructure, the telecommunication companies such as AT&T, Verizon and Comcast. On the other side, those arguing to maintain net neutrality were largely a combination of individuals and groups concerned with freedom of information as well as the companies that have benefited most from the internet as a neutral carrier of bits and bytes. Google, Amazon, eBay and Meta would not exist were it not for the level playing field of the internet, its open standards and the lack of a single commercial owner. Larry Page and Sergey Brin did not need to ask a monolithic telecoms provider for permission to launch Google on the world. Neither did Mark Zuckerberg with Facebook or Jeff Bezos with Amazon. The infrastructure was there and, if their services complied with the technology stack of open protocols that made up the internet and the WWW, could be used by anyone.

While this undoubtedly led to a wave of innovation and new digital services that were popular with the public, it is important to also note the need for network operators to earn profits so they can invest in improving and upgrading their networks. Installing fibre optic connections to every home and providing 5G wireless coverage to a country requires massive investments. It is essential that the companies building these networks can generate profits from doing so as the digital services we use daily and the data that drives modern business rely on them. Recent moves such as the EU's DMA, discussed earlier, indicate that regulators see the power wielded by some of the internet giants that have benefited from a neutral internet as having become uncompetitive and against the interests of many consumers. While the answer is therefore probably not to grant more powers to network operators as a counterbalance to these developments, it does illustrate the need for regulators to constantly monitor the situation and regulate accordingly.

This chapter has considered some of the most significant policies and regulations impacting the environment for data-driven innovation and AI across the EU and the US. As well as presenting some of the key facets of the regulations and the debates surrounding their formulation, it has shown the complexities of attempting to anticipate the impacts of new technologies and balance the competing interests of commercial stakeholders as well as those of end-users. This is an ongoing process as technologies evolve, use cases emerge and economic circumstances change.

The 30 years from the early 1990s to the early 2020s saw the emergence of a transformative network, the internet, combined with the rise of increasingly cheap and accessible technologies, PCs and smartphones, to put access in the hands of billions. The innovations in communications and information sharing this has enabled have transformed many aspects of how we work and socialise. We are now at the beginning of a new era of social and economic transformation that is building on the last 30 years of innovation. AI will shape many of the ways we generate and use data and will have profound consequences for our personal and professional lives. The following chapter will discuss a number of these changes and consider how they may impact us.

CHAPTER 5

Looking Ahead

One of the aims of this book is to show how the evolution of the data industry and the organisations that use data in all its forms has facilitated the current wave of innovation in AI. The two sectors are inextricably linked, with data acting as the fuel powering the rapidly developing plethora of AI services.

In Chapter 1, we have seen how the first transcribing and storing of information had its roots in commerce, with technology evolving to better manage and share data within and between organisations. More recently, data-driven innovation has resulted in the creation of some of the world's largest and most profitable companies. During the second half of the 20th century, AI has moved from universities and research centres into commercial applications, with businesses' and the public's imaginations being captured by GenAI as a tangible and usable product. We have also examined some of the research and frameworks that explain the drivers of innovation with a focus on the impact of digital platforms. Finally, we looked at how the recent wave of data-powered platforms and concerns about the applications of AI are impacting political and legal initiatives around the world.

These developments are all in a state of flux and it will take several years before the economic and social implications of this data-driven AI revolution are fully understood. This chapter considers how this all might play out in the medium term in the context of how AI technologies will evolve (and what this means for the data sector and businesses) as well as the broader social and economic impacts.

Predicting the future is fraught with dangers and, for the most part, inaccurate. However, looking at recent precedents in the ways new technologies have diffused, the unchanging realities of business and the need to generate profits, and the current state of AI technologies, we can make some broad assumptions in this space.

Predicting the future

The problems with futurology were recognised by Nobel prize-winning physicist, Niels Bohr, when he stated, 'Prediction is very difficult, especially about the future' (Anker, 2017). This was especially true in the early days of the internet and the World Wide Web (WWW). Robert Metcalfe's doubts about the internet's future and his prediction in 1995 that it had a 12-month future came back to bite him. He literally ate his own words two years later at the 1997 WWW Conference when he blended a paper copy of his prediction with some water and drank the mixture down (Chai, 2020). As technology analyst Benedict Evans stated, it is not that we get predictions wrong but that we make predictions about the wrong things (Evans, 2017). We need to ask different questions and not assume innovation will simply be about making existing technologies better.

Without doubt, many consultants, analysts and 'business gurus' make very good livings on telling their clients what is going to happen in any given industry or economy. For the most part, these predictions will be wrong but there seems to be an innate need among many business leaders and strategists to be told what the future holds so they can plan accordingly. Sherden (1997) does an excellent job of debunking many of the claims made by futurologists with numerous examples going back hundreds of years. A core fallibility of the prediction business is the complexity of social systems and the unpredictable nature of predicting technological innovations. If we knew what was going to be invented in 30 years then we would be doing it now. This is well illustrated by the case of Thomas Malthus and his doom-laden predictions of population collapse and mass starvation in the late 18th century. His forecasts were based on the rapidly growing population of England and his observation that current rates of food production would not be able to feed everyone in the near future. Malthus's error was not being able to anticipate the rapid developments in agricultural methods, from the use of fertilisers to new types of machinery, which saw average wheat yields in England almost double in the first half of the 18th century (Overton, 1996). However, this does not mean we should not bother trying to anticipate what might be around the corner in terms of how existing technologies may evolve and their potential impact on society. Organisations need to plan where to invest their resources for future growth and to remain competitive, while investors need to optimise their investments by backing companies that have a chance of success. There are times in the evolution of new technologies when trajectories of development may be predicted with some degree of accuracy. Intel co-founder, Gordon Moore, predicted in 1965, with a revision in 1975, that the number of transistors on an integrated circuit would double every two years (Intel, 2023). Despite the technological challenges in keeping up with this prediction, the so-called Moore's Law has broadly held true to the 2020s, with some evidence of a slowing down due to some basic laws of physics (Connatser, 2023). Some of the most successful software and hardware companies have used Moore's Law as a guiding principle for product development, anticipating advances in processing power and planning new products and services around it. Similarly, the rise of smartphones saw the birth of mobile-native applications such as Instagram, WhatsApp and Strava, which anticipated the potential of these devices to allow new functionalities built around cameras, location-awareness, portability and data sharing. As Sherden notes of Moore's Law:

> . . . although predictions based on these persistent trends need to be taken seriously, we should be careful to consider that these trends will some day cease to continue . . . . [M]ost trends follow the S-shaped growth curve, going through three distinct periods of birth, rapid growth, and maturity.
>
> (Sherden, 1997, 261)

While predicting the S-curve timeframe for specific technologies is difficult, we can apply tried and tested theories and frameworks such as Moore's Law, network effects and diffusion curves to consider possible paths of development for AI and other data-driven innovations, at least in the short to medium terms. The following sections will attempt to do just that.

Social and economic implications of the AI and data revolution

Unemployment

In 1964, US President Lyndon Johnson was given a memo written by several Nobel prize-winning economists outlining the impact that the computer revolution was going to have on the economy and employment rates. In a warning to Johnson, they stated:

> A new era of production has begun. Its principles of organisation are as different from those of the industrial era as those of the industrial era were different from the agricultural. The cybernation revolution has been brought about by the combination of the computer and the automated self-regulating machine. This results in a system of almost unlimited productive capacity which requires progressively less human labor. Cybernation is already reorganising the economic and social system to meet its own needs.
>
> (Levy and Murnane, 2004, 21)

Fifty years later, researchers at the University of Oxford estimated that 47% of total US employment was at risk from computerisation and AI across a wide spectrum of industry sectors (Frey and Osborne, 2017). We saw in Chapter 3 how computers have made some occupations largely redundant while others have grown and how new types of jobs have been created. The 1964 warning to Johnson had a technologically deterministic theme to it with the claim that the 'cybernation' had 'its own needs', a simplistic view of technology that imbues it with organic characteristics. While the use of new technologies may certainly alter working practices, as the Luddites sadly discovered, they also create opportunities for organisations and countries that are able to harness their potential.

McAfee and Brynjolfsson received widespread attention for their warnings about technologically-driven unemployment but concluded that the answer is not for humans to try and compete against computer technologies but to use them to compete against other businesses (Brynjolfsson and McAfee, 2012). This recognises a truth that when a technology emerges that helps businesses operate more efficiently, save costs and, potentially, outcompete their rivals then it will be used. Of course, legislation may emerge to limit its use if there are proven health risks or dangers to society, but this has not previously happened with any computing-based innovations. If it offers benefits, then businesses will adopt it. Mollick (2024) picks up this theme and argues that, long-term worries about AI destroying humanity aside, AI can be a useful partner to individuals and businesses. He presents the case that human judgement is still needed in decision-making, but AI can help inform those decisions. After all, he argues, these systems were trained on human-created data so have not emerged from another planet, lacking any understanding of the modern world. Based on his consulting work with McKinsey and now as a Senior Vice President at Alphabet, James Manyika adopts a similar theme, arguing that businesses that focus on using AI to reduce costs at the expense of developing new products and services are going down the wrong path: 'You don't win by cutting costs. You win by creating more valuable outputs.' (Mance, 2024). There are parallels with the backlash against the 1990s trend for enterprises to downsize to increase their profitability and share price. In the short term, this might generate results but ultimately no company ever shrank their way to long-term success.

It is very likely that AI, in all its forms, will result in some roles becoming redundant. We no longer see rows of typists or office workers operating mechanical calculators. Word processing software and spreadsheets put paid to that and, no doubt, AI will do the same for many of the jobs that involve sitting at a PC entering data or writing reports. In this respect, it is important to focus on outcomes not on processes. Trying to build a faster calculator was not the answer to prevent those operating them from losing their jobs. In a world of spreadsheets, calculators had no place, just as spreadsheets probably won't in an AI world. Organisations want the answers that manipulating numerical data provides and will choose the most efficient way of doing that. In the process of doing this, new types of jobs will emerge. As AI-based technologies become commoditised, which many of them will, they will become ubiquitous like PCs and productivity software is today. They will fade into the background noise of working practices while human creativity and imagination continue to be competitive differentiators. It is possible that AI will allow smaller businesses to compete more effectively with larger ones as data processing and content creation requires fewer resources.

Trust

We should, perhaps, be more concerned about the ways AI can create and manipulate digital content at scale and great speed than its impact on employment. We have all seen how quickly GenAI services can create text, images and videos from just a few prompts. These services will only become faster and cheaper as the technologies underpinning them follow the same pattern as all computing-based products have over the last 50 years. It has been possible for several decades to manipulate images with software such as Photoshop and many publications have done so. However, this has required some level of skill and could take several hours to do so in a convincing way. The difference now is in scale and scope, with software available on app stores that can be used on the several billion smartphones in use today. We have already seen these being used by political campaigners to create fake images showing their opponents in compromising situations. They have also been used to create obscene images of ex-partners and celebrities that are then spread across social platforms. The adage 'the camera never lies' no longer holds true and it is becoming very difficult to know what and whom to trust when online. As George Orwell presciently wrote in 1948, fresh from experiencing the propaganda used by all sides in World War 2:

> Every record has been destroyed or falsified, every book has been rewritten, every picture has been repainted, every statue and street and building has been renamed, every date has been altered . . . . I know, of course, that the past is falsified, but it would never be possible for me to prove it, even when I did the falsification myself. After the thing is done, no evidence ever remains. The only evidence is inside my own mind, and I don't know with any certainty that any other human being shares my memories.
>
> (Orwell, 2021, 103)

When we can no longer trust what we see or hear, how will we differentiate between truth and fiction? When the tools and platforms are available to everyone to create and distribute fake media, how can any organisation, public or private, control the flow of disinformation? These are not hypothetical questions that may need addressing at some point in the future, they are the reality now, requiring practical solutions. In 2020, researchers at University College London (UCL) ranked deepfakes as the most serious AI crime threat, largely due to the ability of technologies to perform complex operations at speed and scale in ways not possible with conventional computing technologies (UCL, 2020). Deloitte estimates the global costs of deepfake-related losses to have been US$12.3 billion in 2023, rising to US$40 billion by 2027 (Lalchand et al., 2024). Classified as a form of adversarial AI, it is estimated there were 140,000 to 150,000 cases globally in 2024 (Columbus, 2024). Examples of their use include faking the voices of senior staff in online meetings, creating fraudulent documents such as contracts in near real-time and even creating fake video personas in meetings. A 2024 survey of 7,000 cybersecurity professionals found 74% of them were already seeing evidence of AI-powered threats including those from GenAI (Ivanti, 2024). The use of deepfakes is becoming part of the broader attack strategies of malicious hackers as they seek to exploit vulnerabilities in systems. In 2024, the UK engineering group Arup lost US$25 million when criminals used fake video of a senior manager to arrange financial transfers during a video conference (Leng and Ho-him, 2024). The CEO of WPP, the world's largest advertising group, was also the subject of a similar scam when a voice clone and YouTube footage were combined to attempt a financial fraud, which was spotted before any money had been transferred (Robins-Early, 2024b).

Law enforcement bodies, as well as cybersecurity teams within organisations, also see AI-generated deepfakes as a significant threat. The EU law enforcement agency, Europol, has been monitoring the dangers posed by deepfakes since 2022 and has expressed deep worries about the social threats they pose. In a 2022 survey of law enforcement professionals, Europol found that 'Participants were especially concerned about the weaponisation of social media and the impact of misinformation on public discourse and social cohesion' (Europol, 2024, 5). They cite evidence of Russia's use of deepfakes to destabilise Ukraine at the beginning of its invasion in 2022, with videos being circulated showing Ukraine's President Zelensky telling his troops to surrender (Europol, 2024). A 2024 experiment by a *Wall Street Journal* journalist demonstrated the ease with which fake information can be created and distributed at scale and at very low cost. Jack Brewster claims it took him two days, US$105 and no expertise to launch a fully automated, AI-generated news site capable of publishing thousands of articles a day (Brewster, 2024).

The content was created by using AI to scrape and rewrite content from legitimate news sites without any attribution and adding a partisan angle to favour a particular political party. He made use of freelancing site, Fiverr.com, to find a programmer who could write some simple code that made use of ChatGPT to rewrite and publish the articles. Brewster claimed 'Purchasing an AI content farm on Fiverr.com is as easy as ordering on Uber Eats' (Brewster, 2024).

Cybersecurity monitoring company Recorded Future discovered Russian interference in French politics that was using a similar approach to that described by Brewster. Legitimate news stories had been taken from traditional media sources and rewritten with a bias against French President Macron. This was made evident by the ChatGPT prompt still being visible on some of the fake stories: 'Please rewrite this article taking a conservative stance against the liberal policies of the Macron administration in favour of working-class French citizens.' (The Economist, 2024).

It is clear that deepfakes and the spread of misinformation is a major problem for societies to deal with whether to prevent financial fraud, malicious image sharing or the destabilisation of democracies. Measures are already in place to prevent or deter such activities but there is a sense that criminals and mischief makers are often one step ahead of such initiatives. In the UK, creating and sharing sexually explicit deepfake images of real people without their consent has been a criminal offence since the 2023 Online Safety Act and an amendment to the 2024 Criminal Justice Bill (Herbert Smith Freehills, 2024). Aside from criminalising certain deepfake uses, other measures to limit their spread involve platform owners blocking or labelling specific users and posts as fake or unreliable, tightening age and identity verification processes and supporting fact-checking organisations.

The non-profit organisation International Panel on the Information Environment (IPIE) is focused on analysing and providing solutions to threats to the global information environment. IPIE states its mission is 'to provide policymakers, industry, and civil society with independent scientific assessments on the global information environment by organising, evaluating, and elevating research, with the broad aim of improving the global information environment' (IPIE, 2024). A 2023 IPIE study on how social platforms are dealing with misinformation found that the labelling of untrustworthy internet content and media literacy were among the most effective ways to counter the rise of deepfakes and their impact on users (IPIE, 2023).

Compelling companies to accurately label their offerings has been very effective over the last 150 years with respect to food and medicinal products. As populations in industrialising countries moved from rural to urban environments during the 18th century, people became divorced from the production of food. At the same time, the mass production of food products in factories combined with the rise of marketing techniques to sell these packaged items to a growing middle class. Unscrupulous manufacturers and retailers took advantage of these changes to adulterate food with often poisonous additives to lower their costs. Numerous cases of food poisoning leading to multiple deaths sowed the seeds of mistrust among nervous populations in the US and across Europe. The adulteration was not restricted to food products. Mrs Winslow's Soothing Syrup, marketed as a cure-all for babies in the US and UK, contained morphine and alcohol in doses so high that many babies went to sleep after being given it and never woke again. More than 1.5 million bottles of the syrup were sold annually in the 1860s before its dangers were recognised. It is estimated that thousands of children had died from overdoses, addiction or withdrawal (Berger, 2019). The Food and Drug Act in the US outlawed false claims being made for medicines, while other legislation around the world began to force manufacturers to label products with their ingredients (De Saulles, 2024). Mandatory labelling has been effective in holding manufacturers to account as it provides a basis for third parties and regulators to bring actions where the contents do not match the claimed ingredients.

Another development that emerged from the poisoning scandals of the 19th century was the rise of branding as a marketing tool. While food had been generically sold for centuries in markets, rapid urbanisation and a growing middle class forced food manufacturers to look for ways to make their products stand out from competitors. Branding and distinct packaging, combined with advertising in the emerging media landscape of newspapers and magazines, were effective techniques for increasing sales. Brand loyalty among consumers for popular products led to the creation of many food products we still recognise today. In this regard, brands became trusted symbols that consumers felt they could rely on for safe and pleasurable food. Maintaining this trust was a profitable strategy for many companies as loyal customers were much more valuable than fickle ones who only chose the cheapest products (Room, 1987).

These lessons from more than 100 years ago chime with current thinking about how to deal with deepfakes. Labelling has been shown effective in both cases while the aim of any initiatives is to build and maintain trust. As the media landscape becomes ever-more fragmented from the rise of digital news and commentary outlets and pervasive social platforms, establishing trust is going to be increasingly important. Most news publishers and broadcasters have always had their biases, some more extreme than others, but it was transparent where these biases leaned. In the UK, the *Daily Telegraph* and *Daily Mail* have clearly supported politics and policies from right of centre, while the *Guardian* and *Daily Mirror* have tended to be on the left. They built loyal readerships over many decades among people who shared those views. In a world where US$105 can create a news publishing platform in a few hours capable of putting out thousands of articles a day, all with a particular political bent, how are individuals supposed to know what to trust? Part of the answer lies with the trusted information brands we already have. These will be able to command a premium as sources of information, not without bias but offering a degree of transparency in where those biases lie. Just as Heinz, Cadbury's, Colman's and Guiness have stood the test of time by offering consistent products that consumers know and trust, so, it might be hoped, will the BBC, ABC, *Guardian* and *New York Times* among others.

Education

As discussed above, aside from labelling, another effective way to deal with deepfakes, according to IPIE, was better information and media literacy. Again, there are parallels with government attempts in the previous century to deal with food poisoning. Unhygienic food preparation was identified as a frequent cause of poisoning and, particularly in the mid-20th century, education programmes to help commercial kitchen staff as well as individuals in their homes were developed to counter this (Mold, 2022). As with personal health, prevention, where possible, is better than cure. In the previous chapter, we saw how policy makers recognised the need for education programmes around data, information, digital and media literacy, but that differing views of what those programmes might look like, and a lack of resources dedicated to providing them, had held progress back. Most colleges and universities dedicate some time to helping students with information literacy but, as we saw, this is often inadequate and tends to focus on how to use the resources of the library more effectively.

The time is now overdue for action. It needs to reach people at a much earlier age and be focused on helping them better navigate the world of social media and other online information services. Teacher-training programmes should build this into their curricula so new teachers are equipped to deliver appropriate lessons, while existing teachers could be trained on the job by visiting instructors. This requires financial resources dedicated to such initiatives and will need to be planned carefully to avoid claims of bias in the way such courses are delivered. However, without something like this being implemented, we are sending young people out into a world of often angry, agenda-laden content they are not properly equipped to deal with.

In the UK, the National Literacy Trust (NLT), a charity, has developed and helped deliver such programmes in a selection of UK schools at primary and secondary levels. In the academic year 2022–23, the NLT with the Guardian Foundation, a charity affiliated with the *Guardian* newspaper and dedicated to promoting global press freedom, delivered a series of media literacy training workshops to 28 secondary schools. The objective was to train students as 'Media Literacy Ambassadors' who could then co-design and co-deliver media literacy sessions to fellow students. An evaluation of the results of these training sessions found the number of students able to correctly identify news items as fake or real increased from 40% to 69% (National Literacy Trust, 2024). These results are encouraging and demonstrate that such skills can be taught.

However, despite encouraging words from public bodies and politicians, there is a resourcing problem. The UK's Department for Digital, Culture, Media and Sport announced its 'Online Media Literacy Strategy' in 2021. This was aimed at addressing the issues raised above and has led to the formation of a Media Literacy Taskforce but, as of late 2024, seems to have only spent £250,000 of public funding to help schools deliver any training (Department for Digital, Culture, Media and Sport, 2024).

The UK media and telecommunications regulator, Ofcom, has a statutory duty to promote media literacy and in 2024 launched a consultation on its proposed three-year media literacy strategy. Part of this strategy involves a plan to work with teacher training providers and relevant government departments and regulators to support the development of media literacy practices in schools (Ofcom, 2024a). These aspirations, alongside government recognition of a need for media literacy training, are all welcome but have the feel of too little, too late. Just as the teaching of maths has become a focus of England's national curriculum for schools, so should media literacy and the development of critical thinking skills. This requires mandated time dedicated to it in the school day and financial resources provided for sufficient teacher training.

The state-level system of education in the US has seen a more fragmented implementation of media literacy programmes in schools with some interesting initiatives that could point the way for other schools around the world. In 2023, California, the state with the largest K-12 (5- to 16-year-old students) school population, passed a comprehensive media literacy law that will redirect priorities and funding to media literacy teaching and professional development. Pupils will be taught a range of skills including recognising falsified data and identifying fake news as well as creating responsible internet content. According to California assembly member Marc Berman, who sponsored the bill:

> What happens online can have the most terrifying of real-world impacts. This instruction will help students to be more responsible digital citizens, more intentional about what they put online, and better understand online safety and privacy.
>
> (Buller, 2023)

According to the grassroots campaigning organisation Media Literacy Now, this 'is a major advancement that will reverberate across the country' (Media Literacy Now, 2024, 4). With 6.7 million students in almost 10,000 state-funded schools and a US$130 billion education budget, the results of this legislation will provide important lessons for education policy makers and demonstrates there is a will for such programmes (California Department of Education, 2024).

However comprehensive any media literacy programmes and whatever funding is allocated to them, the challenge in changing people's attitudes to and understanding of the information and media landscape should not be underestimated. A key challenge is to raise awareness among the general population that this is an issue they should care about. There are obviously vested interests within society that are less keen on such programmes. Some media owners may not welcome the spotlight being shone on the biases in their outputs. Social media company owners, as we have seen, may have their own political agendas and use their platforms to amplify them as well as encouraging users to do the same. It is a little like persuading banks and credit card companies to support the education of children in financial matters when their commercial interests are in selling services to the masses that are not always in the interests of their customers. The difference with media literacy is that unenthusiastic media and social platform owners have the means to spread negative stories about any media literacy initiative they do not like.

Data and AI technologies to 2030

The key roles that data and the infrastructure that stores and transmits it play have become apparent in recent years. In the run-up to Russia's invasion of Ukraine in 2022, Ukraine suffered an estimated 288,000 cyberattacks in the first 10 months of 2021 and 397,000 in 2020 (OBR, 2022). As a result, other countries have stepped up their efforts to protect key infrastructure from online attacks. The NotPetya ransomware attacks in 2017, widely thought to have originated in Russia, almost brought commerce around the world to its knees, with the US government estimating it cost the countries, government bodies and corporations targeted US$10 billion (Greenberg, 2018). Shipping companies, port authorities and government bodies were a particular target, with the city government of Atlanta in the US suffering US$10 million of damages. Since these attacks, governments have prioritised preventative measures to limit the damage from future security breaches.

In 2024, the UK government announced data centres would be classified as critical national infrastructure (CNI), with a focus on sites storing NHS, financial and personal smartphone data (Gross and Fisher, 2024). Aside from reducing the damage from cyberattacks, the UK measures are part of a proactive strategy to make the UK a more attractive location for foreign technology companies to invest in. Being able to offer a safe environment for data-driven companies through the government backing of security measures is seen as differentiating the UK from other potential locations. The rewards in terms of job creation and inward investment are clear, with one of Europe's largest data centres scheduled to be built just north of London. This will comprise up to two million square feet of floor space, cost approximately £3.75 billion to build and create hundreds of jobs once complete (D. Robinson, 2024). More significant will be the jobs created by companies using the data centre to power their operations. This development and those already built or in the planning stages are linked to the rise of AI and its seemingly unquenchable thirst for data. Around the world, demand for data centres, fuelled by AI and high-performance computing, has been growing since the early 2020s, with new infrastructure growing annually between 15% and 40% across Europe, the US and Asia (CBRE, 2024).

Energy shortages

Aside from funding and planning permission, a lack of energy to power these new data centres is limiting the speed of their rollout. While AI enthusiasts may believe in its promise to help solve some of the greatest problems facing the human race, such as disease and climate change, the infrastructure needed to run these models may cause more damage than AI solves. Data centres and the computers that underpin AI require massive amounts of energy both to power the processors but also to cool them down. In 2022, data centres consumed 460 TWh of electricity, 2% of total global demand, with this figure expected to more than double by 2026 (International Energy Agency, 2024). According to the International Energy Agency (IEA), 40% of the power required goes to the computers in the centre, 40% for cooling and 20% for associated IT equipment. Of the 8,000 data centres around the world in 2024, 33% of these were in the US, 16% in Europe and 10% in China (International Energy Agency, 2024). For reasons of tax and local geography, some countries have a far greater concentration of centres than others. Ireland, for example, a country of five million people, has more than 80 large centres, which are estimated to consume over 30% of the country's electricity by 2025, more than the demands of its houses and population (Ambrose, 2024). Compounding the problem of rapidly increasing demands for electricity to run AI applications in these data centres is the energy intensive requirements of GenAI models. Research has shown that these systems may require approximately 33 times more energy than standard software applications (Luccioni, Jernite and Strubell, 2024). The head of the UK's National Grid, responsible for distributing electricity from generators to homes and businesses, stated that the country's need for electricity will rise six-fold by 2034, due largely to the demands of AI (Baraniuk, 2024). Generative capacity is not the only issue, with national grids around the world struggling to cope with new sources of green energy from solar and windfarms and shifting demand patterns due to electric vehicles and a shift from natural gas to electricity to heat homes.

The answers to these problems lie within several approaches and technologies. Governments and energy companies will need to make substantial investments to upgrade existing infrastructure and build new powerlines that connect offshore wind and solar farms to national and local grids. Alongside this, new systems are needed for storing energy that is produced in less controllable ways than was the case with power stations, which could be fired up and down to meet predictable demand patterns. The sun only shines during the day, and in many countries not reliably, while the wind may be relatively constant out at sea but less so onshore. Tidal generation is, perhaps, the most predictable form of generating electricity, particularly for island nations such as the UK, but these systems are still at the very early stages of development.

Methods for storing energy are developing rapidly. Batteries offer the most immediate solution but these are expensive to build and the raw ingredients needed to build them, such as nickel, manganese, cobalt and lithium, are becoming more difficult to source. International competition to buy these materials is fierce, with national governments around the world seeing access to them as critical to their economic security (Mardell, 2021).

Some data centre operators are addressing the challenge of sourcing sufficient electricity by building new sites next to existing power generating stations. These so-called 'behind-the-meter' (BTI) configurations bypass the need to connect to the grid at all. In the US, a number of data centres are connected to the 2.5 gigawatt station in Berwick, Pennsylvania, with other operators planning to do the same in other locations (FTI, 2024). This raises important issues around who in the future will have access to electricity and at what cost. If generators are able to sell directly to a small number of well-resourced technology companies then the incentive to sell electricity to domestic consumers and the costs of doing business with millions of users may shift toward the interests of commercial customers. Public policy and regulations will be key to ensure individuals are not left without sufficient power, particularly as the world shifts from fossil fuels to green energy. The extent to which electricity may be a limiting factor on the future of AI was made clear in late 2024 with announcements from Alphabet, Microsoft and Amazon that they are investing in and commissioning their own nuclear reactors (Moore, 2024; Smyth, 2024).

Innovations in the computing world may also provide part of the solution to a growing mismatch between energy generation capacity and demand. As GenAI models have far greater power requirements than conventional software applications, building more efficient processors could make a substantial difference. Nvidia graphics processors (GPUs) are a backbone technology for most AI training and deployments, with the company's sales more than doubling in 2024 and its GPUs controlling 88% of the market (Allan, 2024; Bradshaw and Acton, 2024). The company claims its Grace Blackwell chips, launched in 2024, require a quarter of the energy of its existing processors and, if widely deployed, could significantly ease demands on generative capacity (Baraniuk, 2024). Less demanding AI models and AI-optimised chips based on reduced instruction set computer (RISC) architectures, which typically consume less energy than those normally found in data centres, could also help match demand with supply in the coming years. However, the road to a more sustainable future for our data needs will be paved with increasing pressures and demands from the various stakeholders. If, as seems the case with many countries, AI and data infrastructure is seen by governments as key to building competitive and growing economies, the demands of technology companies may become more intense. Google, for example, has claimed the UK risks being left behind in this 'race' unless more data centres are built and other restrictions, such as copyright, are not relaxed in the case of AI model training. Google's UK managing director stated in 2024:

> [The UK government] sees the opportunity in AI but needs to introduce more policies boosting its deployment. We have a lot of advantages and a lot of history of leadership in this space, but if we do not take proactive action, there is a risk that we will be left behind.
>
> (Milmo, 2024)

This highlights the connections, sometimes conflicting, between the state and private interests in encouraging data-driven innovations. Balancing regulations that protect the environment and intellectual property with the demands of a rapidly developing new technology and its backers will be key. How successfully that balance is achieved will shape economic growth in much of the developed world to 2030 and beyond.

Data marketplaces

We've seen in previous chapters how data marketplaces and exchanges are key to providing the liquidity that many AI developers as well as other innovators require. Most companies do not have access to sufficient internal data to create commercial products and services and rely on buying data in from third parties. Even Meta, with its billions of users, has, for a number of years, bought data from third parties to supplement its targeting capabilities for advertisers. Access to external data sources has become even more important in the development of large language models (LLMs) and their training. As AI developers seek to build and improve models in an increasingly competitive market, data will become even more important as a differentiator.

Exclusive deals between some of the larger AI developers and content creators and owners have been taking place since 2023 and exclusivity of access to valuable and unique information may see the power balance between publishers and technology companies shift. The first 30 years of the internet have seen many publishers and content creators struggle to remain profitable, with the lion's share of profits from the digital revolution going to the gatekeepers controlling search and social platforms. Between 2003 and 2013, the total advertising revenue of US newspapers fell by 50% while Google's advertising revenue increased by 25 times (Dews and Bull, 2014). These figures will be even more polarised in 2025, with many national and most local papers either shutting down or going digital-only. In the UK, 293 local newspapers were shut down between 2005 and 2024, with journalists employed by the largest local news groups over the same period decreasing from 9,000 to 3,000 (Hunter, 2024). News content, both current and historic, will become increasingly important for GenAI providers building general purpose models that are designed to answer queries across a wide range of topics and geographies. Publishers will need to decide whether it is more profitable to sign exclusive deals with developers or offer their content via data marketplaces to a broader range of purchasers. Much will depend on the size of archives and the breadth of news offered by individual publishers who may find it more profitable to form co-operatives with other smaller outlets, strengthening their bargaining power. These co-operatives could take the form of data marketplaces where buyers could select slices of content depending on their needs, with the marketplace infrastructure managing licencing and payments.

As AI developers look for ever more data to train their models, the focus will shift from the low hanging fruit of web data that can be scraped relatively easily to more inaccessible sources. The gates are already closing to taking information from the public web, as we saw in Chapter 2, as content owners put blocks on the activity. A problem for data seekers is that much data is hidden in silos within organisations, with even its owners not knowing what they have. Even where data is well organised and accessible, there may be other restrictions such as data protection for personal information and commercial sensitivity for strategic corporate data. Companies looking to exploit their own information resources will appoint specialists for the task, referred to by consulting firm Gartner as 'data curators' (Schatsky, Camhi and Muraskin, 2019). Their job is to help organisations identify and access relevant data sources that match business requirements. Forrester Research has identified similar new types of employees it calls 'data hunters' and 'data scouts' whose task is to source information both internally and externally (Davis, 2019). These are defined by their proactive attitude to seeking information in often unusual places. Gaglione et al. (2017) argue that these hunters and scouts need to be able to navigate through complex and often unclear data descriptions as well as identify trustworthy sources and understand detailed licencing agreements. Technology consulting firm IDC argues this is an increasingly important set of tasks and, coupled with the role of data exchanges, terms it Data as a Service (DaaS) (IDC, 2021). As data becomes a key driver of innovation and competitive advantage within companies, this is a useful way of thinking about how organisations should approach exploiting information resources. According to IDC's research director:

> As enterprises continue their drive for more intelligent decision-making and greater knowledge, the data-as-a-service market provides an opportunity for data monetisation and data consumption.
>
> (Schneider, 2024)

As organisations become aware of the value of the data assets they hold as well as the potential for increasing their value by combining with external sources, data exchanges will become ever-more important. The term 'infonomics' has been coined by Gartner analyst Douglas B. Laney and his book of the same name outlines approaches and methodologies companies can follow to 'more fully wield information as a corporate asset' (Laney, 2017, 9). As AI applications designed to extract meaning and value from data assets become more widely deployed, we can expect to see more organisations find ways to repurpose and reuse information both to streamline internal operations but also to create new products and services. Data exchanges will need to evolve to meet these opportunities and challenges, and application programming interfaces (APIs), as we shall see in the next section, will be an important part in that process. Another path in their development may be towards more decentralised models that could reduce the barriers to smaller AI developers accessing the data they need. According to Boscovic et al. (2023), decentralised exchanges where data is transformed into tokens that can be bought and sold using blockchain-based smart contracts may help AI developers with limited resources build models. The authors claim this approach enables AI models to be trained without transferring raw data, helping to protect privacy where personal data may be involved. However, these are hypothetical suggestions and, bearing in mind the many unfulfilled promises of blockchain technologies, may not materialise.

The API economy

In Chapter 4 we saw that APIs are helping commercial companies access public sector data resources by providing reliable flows of data that can be, relatively seamlessly, incorporated into applications for processing. IBM defines APIs as 'a set of rules or protocols that enables software applications to communicate with each other to exchange data, features and functionality' (IBM, 2024b). Many of the applications and services we use every day rely on APIs that could be seen as a core part of the plumbing of the digital economy. APIs are not always used to transfer data but can also be deployed to access software where processing is required that is not available within a particular application. Twilio is an example of this type of API provider as it links applications with communication tools such as video, voice and text calls. Amazon has long been an advocate for the use of APIs to stimulate both internal productivity and externally facing service innovations. In 2002, Amazon founder and CEO Jeff Bezos published an internal edict stating that all product teams were required to share their data and functionality through APIs. According to Xingyu Wang and McLarty (2021), it took several years for this mandate to be fully implemented but ultimately led to highly profitable product and service innovations. The skills and infrastructure that emerged to realise this ambition resulted in the company launching its most profitable business unit, Amazon Web Services (AWS). In 2023, AWS generated US$91 billion in sales and US$25 billion in operating profits (Amazon, 2024).

While data exchanges and marketplaces provide the infrastructure for organisations to buy and sell data, APIs offer the mechanisms to transfer that data to where it is needed. The development and deployment of GenAI products and services will depend on APIs as developers hook into large LLMs such as GPT-4 and Claude 3.5. Many of the apps available for use on smartphones that help with identifying what the phone's camera is looking at, such as plants and products, are built around APIs that link to LLMs from Anthropic and OpenAI. Job listing site Indeed, for example, uses GPT-4 to help match job seekers with appropriate vacancies listed on the website. Alerting job hunters to roles the AI model deemed particularly suitable, Indeed saw a 20% increase in started job applications and a 13% increase in employers finding applicants to be a good fit (OpenAI, 2024a). A driving force behind the API economy is the ability of these connections to allow organisations and developers to focus on what they do best whether its collecting, collating and storing data or adding value to that data by integrating it into an application. In this respect, the whole is greater than the sum of its parts. We can expect to see their importance grow as new ways are found to combine the power of AI with the ever-increasing sources of data, many of which will be created by AI itself.

Network infrastructure

The early days of the internet saw a focus on designing and building the infrastructure and protocols to allow the free exchange of data between computers around the world. The aim was to share research information between universities and research centres within government bodies and corporations. Once the flexible and robust nature of this network was recognised, other applications and types of data started to flow across it. A defining characteristic of the infrastructure's evolution is pervasive growth from research laboratories into businesses, homes and, most recently, our pockets. The other area of change has been the steady rise in the speed with which data flows across it and a corresponding decline in the cost of sending and receiving that data. In 1990, the global average speed for a wired internet connection was 14 kilobits per second (Kbps) whereas by 2022 this had risen to 100 megabits per second (Mbps), a 7,000 fold increase (Fox, 2024). The changes in mobile data connections is even more dramatic, with average 5G speeds in the UK from the operator EE of 174 Mbps (Daws, 2024). The deployment of fibre optic connections into buildings, domestic and commercial, across most developed economies in recent years has seen fixed speeds increase to 10 gigabits per second (Gbps), fast enough for most business applications, with the option for multiple lines into a single building for more demanding users. While, no doubt, better use of the wireless spectrum for mobile and amplifiers for fixed connections will see higher speeds in the future, there is a tailing off in demand for such increases.

Connectivity is less of an issue for users, while making better use of the data that flows in and out of buildings is increasingly the focus. Webb (2024) takes up this theme with his aptly titled book, *The End of Telecoms History*, where he argues we have all the speeds we can ever need and, with the exception of some remote rural areas, there is little for infrastructure providers to do but focus on cost savings to make their operations more efficient. Beyond 50 Mbps, there is little advantage to be had for domestic users and small businesses as even streaming ultra-high-definition video requires less than 20 Mbps. There are similarities with the evolution of the internal combustion engine (ICE) motor car, which peaked a number of years ago in terms of speed, reliability, fuel economy and safety. Of course, the EV has created a new trajectory of innovation for the car, but these are already plateauing with regard to range. Like telecoms infrastructure, the focus now is on reducing costs and, as a result, prices to consumers. However, we might be a little wary of being told there is no need for any further innovation in a particular sector as it implies there is a single trajectory of development that will eventually plateau and be subject to no further innovations. This may be true to an extent, but it ignores new use cases that we cannot yet imagine and, in the case of broadband, require even higher bandwidths. Lessons from history may serve as a warning here. Henry Ford is reputed to have said that if he had asked people how he could improve their form of personal transport, they would have asked for faster horses. Similarly, it is claimed the head of the US patent office in 1899 stated 'everything that can be invented has been invented' (Crouch, 2011). Having acknowledged these lessons from the past, it is not unreasonable to agree with the sentiment of Webb's thesis. Certainly, for the foreseeable future there is little in terms of data-intensive services that may overtax our infrastructure.

This fits with Perez's influential work on innovation and technological change that builds on Schumpeter's earlier works on the relationship between transformative innovations and economic growth. Schumpeter's work in the first half of the 20th century helped economists and policy makers better understand the role that large-scale innovations such as steam power, electrical power distribution and petrochemicals played in the development and growth of economies (Schumpeter, 1994). Perez has developed Schumpeter's ideas and shown how the wave of computing-related innovations in the last 50 years has laid the foundations for a new wave of innovations that can build on the technologies and communications infrastructure we see today (Perez, 2003, 2010). She calls these 'general purpose technologies' that have been developed and deployed at considerable expense by innovating companies. From a historical perspective, these include canals, railways and the electrical generating stations and their distribution grids. Such innovations and investments have allowed companies and entrepreneurs to build new businesses that harness the capabilities of this infrastructure. While many of the companies and their investors that built these capabilities may have lost money and even gone bankrupt, the networks and technologies they left behind have powered new waves of innovation and economic growth. We can see parallels with the first dotcom bust of the early 2000s when billions of dollars were lost by companies building out the infrastructure behind the internet and the early services that sat on top of it. The rush to build national and international high-speed networks in the late 1990s by companies such as Global Crossing, WorldCom, 360networks and Level 3 saw a massive over-capacity in bandwidth being deployed with insufficient demand to light the fibre optic cables (Hogendorn, 2011). At the same time, innovations in moving data across networks by companies such as Cisco and Lucent resulted in much faster switching between and across networks. At the application level, web browsers were much improved, made more secure and offered the potential for ecommerce with Netscape leading the way. By the early 2000s, the dotcom bubble had deflated as investors realised that enthusiasm for the internet as a transformative technology had got a little ahead of itself with the Nasdaq stock exchange, the chosen place to list technology shares, falling from a high of 4798 on 17 March 2000 to a low of 1468 on 22 November 2022, a drop of 70% (Google Finance, 2024c).

From these ashes, a new wave of internet-based innovation emerged that saw a more interactive and social web develop, often referred to as Web 2.0. The technologies and infrastructure were still there for new companies to build businesses on top of. Facebook, Google, Amazon and others capitalised on this new phase that saw even greater investments and actual profits as a result. By the end of September 2024, the Nasdaq had long-since bounced back from its low of 22 years previously to reach 18082, a more than 12-fold increase (Google Finance, 2024c).

So, what might this all mean for the current data-driven AI revolution? Essentially, the necessary infrastructure is in place for this new wave of innovation. Connectivity between businesses and consumers is robust, pervasive and of sufficient speed to allow data-intensive services to flow from creators to end-users. The computing infrastructure both in businesses and within households is powerful enough to access and use the emerging AI services, most of which are run remotely in data centres and require only minimal power at the user end. However, this is changing rapidly with the next generation of smartphones from Alphabet and Apple capable of running some AI applications locally on the handset. Following Moore's Law, assuming it lasts for a few more years, computing devices will only become more capable. There is still much work to be done on developing the AI applications that businesses will adopt and demonstrating, through use cases and evidence, their value, but the underpinning technologies are in place and the investments have been made for this to happen.

Will the data run out?

If we accept the hypothesis presented in this book that data is a key driver of the current wave of AI innovation, then any claims that we may run out of data to train future generations of AI models should be considered seriously. We have seen in previous chapters where much of the data used to train existing models has come from and some of the legal issues that have arisen as a result. Chapter 2 discussed the role of synthetically generated data in training LLMs and the potential dangers of model collapse from a form of data inbreeding. The lawsuits being brought against some AI developers by content owners angry that their intellectual property has been used without their permission coupled with the dangers of an over-reliance on synthetic data is leading to claims we may be hitting a 'data frontier' that could stifle future innovations. According to the co-founder of Snorkel AI, which builds data sets for companies:

> There's no more free lunch. You can't scrape a web-scale data set any more. You have to go and purchase it or produce it. That's the frontier we're at now.
>
> (Hammond, 2024)

Data marketplaces can go some way to alleviating data shortages by opening data sets to developers that previously were inaccessible. Similarly, greater efforts by public bodies to allow reuse of their data in machine-readable formats would help, although the track record of many institutions in doing so is patchy. Budgetary constraints on public spending across many economies means investing resources in freeing up data to third parties is not a priority. Advances in synthetic data creation will be needed. AI models that make more efficient use of the data at their disposal will also help alleviate this data exhaustion issue. New approaches to creating training data such as AgentInstruct and Arena Learning are interesting developments (Labonne, 2024).

Content creators and owners can expect to see a greater value being placed on their intellectual property because of these shortages. This is already happening with the exclusive contracts they are signing with well-funded companies such as OpenAI, Anthropic and Alphabet. However, whether content creators can keep up with the almost insatiable demands of models for ingesting data remains to be seen. The quality of the data used in training is, in many ways, more important than the quantity.

The commoditisation of AI

When the first commercially viable PCs were introduced by IBM in 1981, they cost the equivalent of almost US$6,000 in 2024 money. Today, a PC that is thousands of times as powerful can be bought for one tenth of that amount. PCs, as with most digital technologies, have become commodities, with users generally choosing the cheapest model that meets their needs. Except for high-end models, smartphones have followed a similar path, with capable Android phones available for less than £100. Products that have become commoditised tend to be interchangeable with other competing products, with price often being a differentiator. This is true of many foodstuffs where the supermarkets that sell them compete fiercely on prices, particularly at the lower end of the market.

We may be at the beginning of this happening with GenAI products and services. While considerable expense and expertise has been invested in creating the frontier models from OpenAI, Anthropic, Microsoft and Alphabet, their outputs are often very similar to a non-technical audience. Models from each of these vendors have their strengths on tasks such as coding, creative writing and image creation and users may select products that suit their specific needs. However, these products are increasingly being bundled into existing applications that consumers and businesses already use, particularly the offerings from Alphabet and Microsoft. The AI element is fading into the background of Microsoft's 365 suite of applications such as Word and PowerPoint and Google's Workspace software. Just as Netscape, once the most popular web browser, rapidly lost market share once Microsoft bundled the Internet Explorer browser with Windows, so AI-focused startups like Anthropic and OpenAI may find users less willing to pay for their offerings when similar applications are already included with existing services. Having an existing customer relationship with users and providing applications they use every day is a great head start in the race to dominate AI. Google Workspace has more than 3 billion users monthly, most using Gmail, while more than 1.3 billion people regularly use Microsoft products (Google, 2022; Elad, 2023). Both these companies have the expertise, the models and the financial resources to turn AI into an embedded, background technology that we take for granted in the same way we expect our phones to take high-quality pictures and navigate us wherever we are in the world.

Another driver of AI commoditisation is the rise of open-source LLMs. Despite naming itself OpenAI, most of the company's key offerings are anything but open in the sense that third-party developers can freely access their models and adapt them for their own purposes. OpenAI offers APIs for developers to hook applications into their models, but these come at a price and the models themselves, with some exceptions for older, less powerful versions, are closed. However, there is a growing ecosystem of open-source LLMs available to developers with one of the main repositories, Hugging Face, listing almost a million models as of September 2024 (Hugging Face, 2024). Many of these are only slight variations on other models in the database, but it illustrates the vibrant community of AI developers and the resources at their disposal. Some of the most popular open models include Stable Diffusion, Meta Llama 3, Mistral 7B, Bloom and Falcon (Marr, 2024). Meta's Llama LLMs are, perhaps, the most immediate threat to the business models of OpenAI and Anthropic as they have the backing of a well-resourced company and offer performance equal to some of the commercial frontier models. By mid-2024, versions of Llama had been downloaded 350 million times by developers and it is being used to power applications designed to solve multiple business needs (Mims, 2024). There is disagreement as to how open some of these models are as the underlying data they were trained on is often hidden. Meta's Llama, for example, shows the 'weights' applied within the model during its training but not the underlying data these weights were used on. As with the requirement for scientific research to be reproduceable by others if it is to be taken seriously, so, it is argued, developers should be able to reproduce LLM models by having access to the training data, the weightings and the code (Waters, 2024). Despite these concerns about how open models are, their widespread availability and the growing community of developers adapting them to specific business and consumer needs presents a real threat to some of the startups building their futures on proprietary models. With Google reducing the price to developers of using its Gemini 1.5 Flash model by 78% and OpenAI lowering the price of GPT-4o by 71% in late 2024, perhaps the writing is on the wall for business models based around closed models (Wiggers, 2024).

AI in the real world to 2030

While the development and provision of LLMs may become commoditised with prices falling and frontier models converging on a core of features and capabilities, the applications built on top of these LLMs will be far more differentiated. Depending on its size, financial resources, location and the sector it operates in, businesses have very different needs. Some functions, such as marketing, human resources and accounting, will operate to some core principles whatever the sector but even here there will be a wide range of needs. The marketing function in a major investment bank will look very different to a food retailer's or engineering company. Similarly, the regulatory environment that governs healthcare services will place very different demands on the human resources department in a hospital to a global firm of management consultants. AI services and products designed to make workflows in these departments more efficient will need to be tailored to the specific requirements of such businesses.

A focus of innovative activity within the AI world will be applying the capabilities of LLMs and other AI and ML technologies to applications that can help businesses operate more efficiently. Recent research from Gartner on how organisations are using AI and their motivations for doing so has shown increasing operating efficiencies to be by far the most important driver. In a 2024 survey of 145 AI deployments within a wide range of businesses, the main objective for 81% of them was to increase efficiencies (Sau, 2024). At the Toyota Research Institute, for example, employees were using GenAI to produce variations of initial vehicle sketches, which reduced the time-to-design phase of vehicle development and led to more innovative vehicle designs. The Mayo Clinic used a medical chatbot to conduct dynamic interviews with patients, more efficiently gather symptom-related information and provide faster personalised care recommendations (Sau, 2024). As organisations experiment with new approaches like these and learn where AI can be deployed most efficiently, their impact will grow and, where real efficiencies impact the bottom line, encourage other companies down the same road.

We can expect to see innovative AI-based applications emerge from three main sources. Larger companies with the resources and skills to internally develop their own applications will do so and we have already seen this with a number of the larger consulting and investment banking firms such as McKinsey, BCG, JPMorgan Chase and PwC (Rinta-Kahila, 2024). However, most organisations will buy applications from software vendors, either new startups focused on a niche industry need or established providers incorporating AI functionality into existing offerings. The number of startups building AI applications has grown rapidly since 2020, with financial information provider Dealroom tracking more than 1,400 new businesses building GenAI services alone (Dealroom, 2024). Many of these will fail or be swallowed up by larger companies, but we can expect a number to succeed and it is very likely there will be a future Google or Meta among them. Perhaps the greatest initial source of AI applications to be deployed within organisations will be from established software and technology vendors who already have customer relationships and can add AI functionality into products currently being used. Sometimes, this will go unnoticed by customers as AI is employed to sit in the background of applications, making them more efficient and opening up new features. According to Evelson (2024), most business intelligence (BI) platforms now incorporate AI-based functionalities. BI systems from vendors such as SAP, Microsoft and Oracle are used by most large enterprises to gather and analyse operating data that can help managers track sales, look for market opportunities and develop corporate strategies. AI is being built into these systems to improve their predictive capabilities, make it easier for users to interrogate data via chatbots and automate alerts when specific data patterns are detected.

One of the most common instances of AI being deployed within enterprise applications is using AI assistants or copilots as they are commonly called. These help users by suggesting actions they might take, help draft documents and e-mails as well as writing software code and resolving customer issues. Their integration with widely used applications such as Microsoft Word and Google Docs is helping users become familiar with these tools across domestic and corporate use cases. The next phase of development for copilots is via AI agents, which increase the autonomous nature of such tools by acting more independently than more traditional AI assistants. Agentic AI is still at an early stage and many businesses will be reluctant to trust such systems until they have been proven reliable and safe. Removing humans from the decision-making loop may be a step too far for organisations that fear financial and reputational damage from an AI agent making bad decisions. However, we can expect to see significant improvements in their capabilities and reliability over the coming years. According to Microsoft CEO, Satya Nadella we should look on AI agents as extensions of copilots rather than a straight replacement. He claims his company's copilot and agentic offerings are evolving into an 'enterprise orchestration layer', providing a conversational interface from which employees will be able to create and use agents to carry out specific tasks (Waters and Morris, 2024).

This is a theme taken up by technology analysts, Don Scheibenreif and Mark Raskino in their thought-provoking book, *When Machines Become Customers* (Scheibenreif and Raskino, 2023). Their premise is that intelligent systems comprising connected devices, the Internet of Things (IoT), combined with AI will see new types of machine-based customers emerge. These will be able to make purchasing decisions autonomously based on pre-programmed objectives and operating parameters. At a basic level, we are already seeing this with printers that automatically order ink and coffee machines ordering new capsules when supplies run low. However, the authors argue this will extend far more deeply into homes and businesses as buildings and everyday products become embedded with sensors and communication capabilities. Like a thermostat automatically maintains the temperature in a room based on its user's settings, so the intelligent systems within businesses will be able to autonomously order new supplies and do so more efficiently than humans. Corresponding intelligent systems within suppliers will be able to tender for these contracts and purchase decisions will be made more quickly and from a wider range of offerings than a person ever could. The authors believe that by 2030, up to 20% of company revenues will be from machine customers. If sufficient use cases emerge and cost savings can be demonstrated, we should not be surprised if this figure is exceeded. We have already seen that operational efficiencies are a driving force for most AI deployments and allowing machines to act more autonomously for routine purchases seems an obvious choice for many businesses, particularly those where large numbers of goods flow through their premises, such as retailers. Agentic systems are always on and can respond to situations whatever the time. They are also able to remember and learn from their activities, which can, over time, help organisations continue to improve their business processes as AI models are adjusted to their needs. A problem for many businesses, and one that traditional knowledge management systems have never managed to resolve, is the loss of expertise and accumulated knowledge when employees leave or retire. Intelligent systems built around autonomous AI agents will be able to retain this knowledge.

The regulatory and commercial environment to 2030

We saw in the previous chapter some of the significant policy and regulatory initiatives in Europe and the US that are shaping the ways data and AI can be used across a range of commercial and public organisations. Two of the key themes of that discussion centred on protecting personal privacy through data protection regulations and attempts to curb the power of some of the largest technology companies that have emerged in the last 20 years.

In terms of the data landscape, the 2024 US judicial ruling that Google has built an illegal monopoly with its search business is likely to have the most impact. Google's dominant share of the internet search market has been achieved and maintained in part through the payments it has made to device makers, including Samsung and Apple, for its search engine to be the default choice on handsets. The trial revealed that in 2022 Google had paid Apple US$20 billion for this arrangement, which, taking into account the iPhone's 55% share of the US smartphone market, impacted many tens of millions of users (Robins-Early, 2024a). The consequences of this ruling may take several years to be fully understood and an appeal may change the outcome. However, it is relevant here because it raises several questions about the business models of software and hardware companies and their inter-relationships. Apple, for example, has probably been very happy to receive billions of dollars a year to do nothing except make Google the default search engine. The company does not have one itself and most users are generally happy to use Google so there was no opportunity cost for Apple. However, if it is no longer allowed to receive that income and new AI-powered search services such as that from Perplexity are gaining traction, perhaps there are benefits for Apple to look elsewhere for a search provider. It may even decide to build its own and reap the financial benefits that Google has had from search-related advertising. Apple's development of its own foundational AI models and integration of AI capabilities into its iPhones from late 2024 indicate its willingness to move into new areas. Whatever happens, it promises to shake up the market for information searching technologies that could deliver benefits for users. Google's dominance of this sector for two decades has given it little incentive to innovate. The combination of judicial rulings with the disruptive potential of AI may sow the seeds for a new generation of data-driven business models.

GenAI will certainly impact how consumers find the information they need. As tailor-made answers start to replace the traditional page of links (many of which are to clickbait web pages) we have become used to, there is certainly a place for new entrants. Cracks are already starting to appear in the traditional search landscape and new business models will follow for companies that are successful in providing timely and accurate answers. At the premium end, paid for services may emerge where users are happy to pay a subscription for an ad-free service that offers greater protection for personal privacy. If so, this could upend the digital advertising sector, which relies on Google and data sharing to function effectively. Many online publishers would also have to develop new revenue streams as Google may not be providing them with sufficient traffic if users are finding their information elsewhere. GenAI will be at the heart of these changes and the deals that publishers do with AI developers could determine our online searching experience as we approach 2030. On the upside, we may have to wade through less spammy sites that have gamed their way to the top of Google search results and get instant answers to our search queries. On the downside, there may be a narrower pool of information that GenAI answer engines are able to draw on in a world where content owners restrict which models are allowed to train on their data. Whether this results in a more focused and accurate set of answers or a fragmented market of answer engines that are good for certain types of questions remains to be seen. Perhaps a new breed of aggregators will emerge that pool answers from multiple services, like meta search engines from the late 1990s such as AlltheWeb, which aggregated results for users from six different search engines. Whatever happens, LLMs will disrupt the search world of 2025 and, according to industry analyst Grace Carney, 'new platforms will leverage advanced technologies to interpret richer forms of data to offer personalised and immersive search experiences' (Carney, 2024).

The impact of AI legislation is yet to be felt in that the market for AI products and services is so nascent and regulations, with the prime exception of the EU AI Act discussed in Chapter 4, are still largely in the drafting stages around the world. As was the case with the EU AI Act, there is considerable pressure on policy makers and regulators from the larger companies developing AI services to adopt a soft touch approach. This was seen in the US in late 2024 when the California governor vetoed a controversial attempt at state-level AI regulation following intensive lobbying from leading AI companies, including Meta, OpenAI and Alphabet. Had it passed, the bill would have forced developers to follow strict rules, including implementing a kill switch, to prevent catastrophic harm from AI deployments (Hammond and Criddle, 2024). The bill was vetoed by the governor on the grounds it would stifle innovation in an emerging industry.

We can expect the second half of the 2020s to witness further examples of these tensions between developers looking to make returns on their AI investments and pressure groups concerned by the threats they see emerging from AI being more widely used. As with regulatory approaches to personal data collection and use, it is likely the divergence between the US and Europe on AI policy will continue to grow wider. The main area of common ground is around controlling abuses of power through monopolistic practices, but when it comes to social concerns, the US tends to favour the interests of technology companies. Perhaps this is not surprising as most of these companies are US-based while Europe is still far behind in commercialising digital technologies.

CHAPTER 6

Pulling the Threads Together

The initial excitement as well as considerable hype from software companies, AI developers and technology commentators following the launch of ChatGPT and other GenAI products in late 2022 and into 2023 has died down to a large extent. The 'magic' of seeing text and images being created in seconds from a few simple prompts is now just another clever thing that computers can do and is becoming part of many people's daily workflows. It was the same with e-mail, the World Wide Web (WWW), mobile phones and social media when they first became available. They are all now part of the warp and weft of everyday life. In time, GenAI and the applications that incorporate it will be no different. However, 'time' is the watchword here. This will not happen overnight for all the reasons discussed in this book. Developers need to demonstrate the value AI offers to organisations through real use cases and solid evidence of a return on investment. Adopting organisations need to be confident that the benefits outweigh the risks and this requires further work from developers and vendors in removing problems such as hallucinations and privacy breaches. If agentic AI is to take hold, then trust in such systems will be key. Alongside this, regulators and public policy makers will need to adapt their approaches as the technology evolves and its opportunities and risks become clearer. Finally, education will be a vital factor in helping workers, existing and yet to enter the workforce, adapt to this transformative technology, as well as teaching all individuals what they can and cannot trust online. This last requirement is, perhaps, the most important as it touches on foundational issues such as literacy and democracy.

From an organisational adoption perspective, AI vendors and developers need to focus on the business impact of their products rather than the technical capabilities of their models. A 2023 PwC survey of over 500 executives concluded that almost 90% of respondents struggle to measure their return on investment in new technologies because they 'lose sight of the ultimate business outcome objective, and end up tempted by the latest bright, shiny objects' (A. Brown, 2024). This is where industry-focused AI vendors that are developing applications for the specific needs of a particular sector will play a key role. The frontier models from OpenAI, Meta, Alphabet and Anthropic alongside open source offerings from other developers are the foundation of the current AI revolution. However, it will be the highly focused applications that rest on these foundations that organisations will adopt and that will transform workflows and business practices. It will take five to ten years for the effects of these changes to be evident and, like the computing and internet revolutions before it, we will see some booms and busts along the way.

The opportunities that AI presents to organisations both in making efficiency gains and in leveraging their data assets are too attractive to ignore. We have seen how information is often underutilised by businesses despite ever-increasing amounts of it filling up data centres. The examples presented in previous chapters have touched on the potential of AI to better manage much of this data for both commercial and socially beneficial purposes. Following Perez's descriptions of technological revolutions and how they follow two key stages – installation and deployment – we can see we are on the cusp of the deployment phase with AI now (Perez, 2003, 2010). The installation phase is complete, with the underpinning computing and communications infrastructure in place from years of investments and innovations. Developers and software vendors, with the support of this infrastructure, are now ready to develop AI applications for organisations to deploy. As Goldman Sachs said in a 2024 note to investors:

> Historically, investors over-focus on the originators, understate the impact of competition and overstate the returns on capital invested by the early innovators. At the same time, investors tend to underestimate the growth of new entrants to the industry that can piggyback off the capex of others.
>
> (Oppenheimer et al., 2024, 8)

The ongoing digital revolution is at an inflection point triggered by the accumulation of data on an unprecedented scale alongside a new set of transformational technologies capable of adding enormous value. For anyone working with information, these are exciting, if a little uncertain, times.

References

Abernathy, W. J. (1978) *The Productivity Dilemma: Roadblock to Innovation in the Automobile Industry*, Johns Hopkins University Press.

Acar, O. A. (2023) AI Prompt Engineering isn't the Future, *Harvard Business Review*, 6 June, https://hbr.org/2023/06/ai-prompt-engineering-isnt-the-future.

Accoya (2024) Google HQ Project Update, www.accoya.com/uk/project/google-hq-project-update.

Afshar, V. (2024) Connected Cars, Powered by AI, Will Make up 95% of All Vehicles on the Road by 2030, *ZDNET*, www.zdnet.com/article/connected-cars-powered-by-ai-will-make-up-95-of-all-vehicles-on-the-road-by-2030.

Age UK (2024) Computer Training Courses – IT Training Services, www.ageuk.org.uk/services/in-your-area/it-training.

Agnew, P. (2023) Introducing AI Made for Social Media — Buffer's AI Assistant, *Buffer*, https://buffer.com/resources/introducing-ai-made-for-social-media-buffers-ai-assistant.

Allan, D. (2024) Nvidia Now Owns 88% of the GPU Market – But That Might not be a Bad Thing . . . Yet, *TechRadar*, www.techradar.com/computing/gpu/nvidia-now-owns-88-of-the-gpu-market-but-that-might-not-be-a-bad-thing-yet.

Alphabet (2024) Alphabet Annual Filings (2023), http://abc.xyz/investor/sec-filings/annual-filings/2023.

Amazon (2024) Amazon Annual Report 2023, https://ir.aboutamazon.com/annual-reports-proxies-and-shareholder-letters/default.aspx.

Ambrose, J. (2024) Ireland's Datacentres Overtake Electricity Use of all Urban Homes Combined, *The Guardian*, 23 July, www.theguardian.com/world/article/2024/jul/23/ireland-datacentres-overtake-electricity-use-of-all-homes-combined-figures-show.

Anker, D. (2017) Forecasting – Prediction is Very Difficult, Especially if it's About the Future!, *Cranfield University Blogs*, 10 July, https://blogs.cranfield.ac.uk/cbp/forecasting-prediction-is-very-difficult-especially-if-its-about-the-future.

A&O Shearman (2024) Financial Results for Legacy Allen & Overy for the Year Ended 30 April 2024, www.aoshearman.com/about-us/annual-reports/financial-results-for-legacy-allen-overy-for-the-year-ended-30-april-2024.

Apple (2024) Investor Relations – Apple, https://investor.apple.com/investor-relations/default.aspx.

Arguello, S., Crowther, P. and Vyas, N. (2024) Competition Corner, Winston & Strawn – Early Assessment of the Digital Markets Act, www.winston.com/en/blogs-and-podcasts/competition-corner/early-assessment-of-the-digital-markets-act1.

Author's Guild (2023) The Author's Guild, John Grisham, Jodi Picoult, David Baldacci, George R. R. Martin, and 13 Other Authors File Class-Action Suit Against OpenAI, 20 September, https://authorsguild.org/news/ag-and-authors-file-class-action-suit-against-openai.

AWS (2024) Structured Data vs Unstructured Data – Difference Between Collectible Data, https://aws.amazon.com/compare/the-difference-between-structured-data-and-unstructured-data.

Badke, W. (2010) Foundations of Information Literacy: Learning from Paul Zurkowski, *Online*, **34** (1), 48–50.

Badke, W. (2011) Why Information Literacy is Invisible, *Communications in Information Literacy*, **4** (2), 129–41.

Baird, G. (2024) Re-Evaluating Data Management in the Generative AI Age, *IBM Blog*, www.ibm.com/blog/re-evaluating-data-management-in-the-generative-ai-age/www.ibm.com/blog/re-evaluating-data-management-in-the-generative-ai-age.

Baker McKenzie (2019) Schrems I, www.bakermckenzie.com/en/-/media/files/insight/publications/2019/12/schrems-ibackgroundv6.pdf.

Baraniuk, C. (2024) Electricity Grids Creak as AI Demands Soar, *BBC News*, www.bbc.com/news/articles/cj5ll89dy2mo.

Barclays (2020) Digital Eagles, https://home.barclays/news/2020/04/barclays-digital-eagles- -keeping-older-people-connected-through-.

Barker, P. (2024) Platform Lets Creators Monetize Their Content for Use in LLM Training, *Computerworld*, 17 July, www.computerworld.com/article/2519026/platform-lets-creators-monetize-their-content-for-use-in-llm-training.html.

Battersby, M. (2024) Anthropic Sued by Trio of US Authors over Use of 'Pirated Books' to Train AI Chatbot Claude, *The Bookseller*, www.thebookseller.com/news/anthropic-sued-by-us-authors-over-use-of-pirated-books-to-train-ai-chatbot.

Beam (2024) Prompt Engineer, https://careers.beam.org/jobs/4640084-prompt-engineer.

Beard, T. R., Ford, G. S., Spiwak, L. J. and Stern, M. L. (2015) Eroding the Rule of Law: Regulation as Cooperative Bargaining at the FCC, *Phoenix Center Policy Paper* [Preprint], (49), https://papers.ssrn.com/sol3/papers.cfm?abstract_id=2913115.

Bell, D. (1976) *The Coming of Post-Industrial Society*, Basic Books.

Bennett Institute for Public Policy (2020) *The Value of Data: Summary Report*, Bennett Institute for Public Policy.

Berger, K. (2019) Pharmacy's Past: The Soothing Syrup Known for Causing Death in Thousands of Babies, *Pharmacy Times*, www.pharmacytimes.com/view/pharmacys-past-the-soothing-syrup-known-for-causing-death-in-thousands-of-babies-.

Berners-Lee, T. and Fischetti, M. (1999) *Weaving the Web: The Original Design and Ultimate Destiny of the World Wide Web by its Inventor*, HarperCollins.

Bhattacharyya, M., Miller, V. M., Bhattacharyya, D. and Miller, L. E. (2023) High Rates of Fabricated and Inaccurate References in ChatGPT-Generated Medical Content, *Cureus*, **15** (5), e39238, https://doi.org/10.7759/cureus.39238.

Binder, R. (2018) Disrupting the Car, *CB Insights*, 67.

Birnbaum, E. (2018) FCC Chairman Acknowledges Russia Interfered in Net Neutrality Public Comments, *The Hill*, 5 December, https://thehill.com/policy/technology/419846-fcc-chairman-acknowledges-russia-interfered-in-net-neutrality-public.

Boscovic, D., Khullar, K., Oguri, P. B., Pandey, P., Eghbali, M. and Olsen, M. (2023) Tokenization of Digital Assets for Ethical and Equitable Model Training in an AI-Based Proctoring Application. In *2023 International Conference on Computational Science and Computational Intelligence (CSCI)*, IEEE, 1691–9, https://ieeexplore.ieee.org/abstract/document/10590406.

Bousquette, I. (2023) AI Is Writing Code Now. For Companies, That Is Good and Bad, *The Wall Street Journal*, 31 May, www.wsj.com/articles/ai-is-writing-code-now-for-companies-that-is-good-and-bad-6f19ecdc.

Boyne, S. M. (2020) Data Protection in the United States: U.S. National Report. In Moura Vicente, D. and De Vasconcelos Casimiro, S. (eds), *Data Protection in the Internet*, 409–55, Springer International Publishing, https://doi.org/10.1007/978-3-030-28049-9_17.

Bradshaw, T. and Acton, M. (2024) Nvidia Shares Fall Even as Revenue More Than Doubles, *Financial Times*, 29 August, www.ft.com/content/5ea817f6-fe45-4e1d-ae30-0f4e455285cb.

Brewster, J. (2024) How I Built an AI-Powered, Self-Running Propaganda Machine for $105, *The Wall Street Journal*, 12 April, www.wsj.com/politics/how-i-built-an-ai-powered-self-running-propaganda-machine-for-105-e9888705.

Brown, A. (2024) Digital Economy Dispatch #201 – Why AI Fails, *Digital Economy Dispatches,* https://dispatches.alanbrown.net/p/digital-economy-dispatch-201-ai-fails.

Brown, S. (2024) Data Literacy for Leaders, *MIT Sloan,* https://mitsloan.mit.edu/ideas-made-to-matter/data-literacy-leaders.

Brynjolfsson, E. and McAfee, A. (2012) *Race Against the Machine: How the Digital Revolution is Accelerating Innovation, Driving Productivity, and Irreversibly Transforming Employment and the Economy,* Digital Frontier Press.

BT Group (2024) BT Group's Annual Report 2023/24, www.bt.com/bt-plc/assets/documents/investors/financial-reporting-and-news/quarterly-results/fy24/h2/h2-fy24-release.pdf.

Buller, R. (2023) 'There's Nothing More Critical': California Makes Schools Teach Kids to Spot Fake News, *The Guardian,* 5 December, www.theguardian.com/education/2023/dec/05/california-media-literacy-class-schools-misinformation.

Bureau of Labor Statistics (2024) Graphic Designers, www.bls.gov/ooh/arts-and-design/graphic-designers.htm.

Burgener, E. and Rydning, J. (2022) High Data Growth and Modern Applications Drive New Storage Requirements in Digitally Transformed Enterprises, www.delltechnologies.com/asset/en-my/products/storage/industry-market/h19267-wp-idc-storage-reqs-digital-enterprise.pdf.

Calia, D. (2022) Schrems II: The EU's Influence on US Data Protection and Privacy Laws, *Washington University Global Studies Law Review,* **21**, 247–72.

California Department of Education (2024) Fingertip Facts on Education in California – Accessing Educational Data, www.cde.ca.gov/ds/ad/ceffingertipfacts.asp.

Canalys (2024) Canalys Newsroom – Global PC Shipments up 3% in First Quarter of 2024, www.canalys.com/newsroom/global-pc-market-q1-2024.

Carney, G. (2024) The Fragmentation of Search, *Union Square Ventures,* 29 February, www.usv.com/writing/2024/02/the-fragmentation-of-search.

Carr, N. (2008) How Many Computers Does the World Need? Fewer Than You Think, *The Guardian,* 21 February, www.theguardian.com/technology/2008/feb/21/computing.supercomputers.

CBRE (2024) Global Data Center Trends 2024, www.cbre.com/insights/reports/global-data-center-trends-2024.

Cennamo, C. and Sokol, D. D. (2021) Can the EU Regulate Platforms Without Stifling Innovation?, *Harvard Business Review,* 1 March, https://hbr.org/2021/03/can-the-eu-regulate-platforms-without-stifling-innovation.

Chai, W. (2020) Who is Robert Metcalfe?, *WhatIs.com,* www.techtarget.com/whatis/definition/Robert-Metcalfe.

Chatterjee, M. and Bordelon, B. (2024) The Campaign to Take Down the Biden AI Executive Order, *POLITICO*, www.politico.com/news/2024/01/25/conservatives-prepare-attack-on-bidens-ai-order-00137935.

Chicago Housing Authority (2024) Digital Inclusion, www.thecha.org/residents/services/digital-inclusion.

Chief Digital Officer for London (2023) The London Datastore Turns 13 so Here are 13+ Data Services Important to Londoners (Plus, What's Next for 2023 . . ., *Medium*, 9 January, https://chiefdigitalofficer4london.medium.com/the-london-datastore-turns-13-so-here-are-13-data-services-important-to-londoners-plus-whats-15e833380743.

Cho, W. (2024) Artists Score Major Win in Copyright Case Against AI Art Generators, *The Hollywood Reporter*, 13 August, www.hollywoodreporter.com/business/business-news/artists-score-major-win-copyright-case-against-ai-art-generators-1235973601.

Chui, M., Hazan, E., Roberts, R. and Singla, A. (2023) Economic Potential of Generative AI, www.mckinsey.com/capabilities/mckinsey-digital/our-insights/the-economic-potential-of-generative-ai-the-next-productivity-frontier#introduction.

CIPD (2024) Preparing Your Organisation for AI Use, www.cipd.org/uk/knowledge/guides/preparing-organisation-AI-use.

Claburn, T. (2024) AI Copilots are Getting Sidelined Over Data Governance, www.theregister.com/2024/08/21/microsoft_ai_copilots.

Clarke, S. (2023) 2024 AI Outlook for Digital Agency Leaders, https://blog.duda.co/report-2024-ai-outlook-for-digital-agency-leaders.

Coase, R. H. (1937) The Nature of the Firm, *Economica*, New Series, **4** (16), 386–405.

Coatanlem, Y. (2024) Why Europe is a Laggard in Tech, *Financial Times*, 26 February, www.ft.com/content/d4fda2ec-91cd-4a13-a058-e6718ec38dd1.

Columbus, L. (2024) Deepfakes will Cost $40 billion by 2027 as Adversarial AI Gains Momentum, *VentureBeat*, 1 July, https://venturebeat.com/security/deepfakes-will-cost-40-billion-by-2027-as-adversarial-ai-gains-momentum.

Connatser, M. (2023) Intel's CEO Says Moore's Law is Slowing to a Three-Year Cadence, but it's not Dead Yet, *Tom's Hardware*, www.tomshardware.com/tech-industry/semiconductors/intels-ceo-says-moores-law-is-slowing-to-a-three-year-cadence-but-its-not-dead-yet.

Conte, N. (2024) Charted: Apple's Product Revenue (2007–2023), *Visual Capitalist*. www.visualcapitalist.com/charted-apples-product-revenue-2007-2023.

Coyer, C. (2024) The Debate on Data Scraping was Almost Over – Until Generative AI Rekindled it, *Legaltech News*, www.law.com/legaltechnews/2024/05/16/the-debate-on-data-scraping-was-almost-over-until-generative-ai-rekindled-it.

Cramarenco, R. E., Burcă-Voicu, M. I. and Dabija, D. C. (2023) The Impact of Artificial Intelligence (AI) on Employees' Skills and Well-Being in Global Labor Markets: A Systematic Review, *Oeconomia Copernicana*, **14** (3), 731–67.

Creamer, E. (2023) 'The Potential to Undermine Democracy': European Publishing Trade Bodies Call for Action on Generative AI, *The Guardian*, 19 October, www.theguardian.com/books/2023/oct/19/frankfurt-european-publishing-trade-bodies-call-for-action-on-generative-ai.

Cremer, D. D. and Koopman, J. (2024) Research: Using AI at Work Makes Us Lonelier and Less Healthy, *Harvard Business Review*, 24 June, https://hbr.org/2024/06/research-using-ai-at-work-makes-us-lonelier-and-less-healthy.

Criddle, C. and Ring, S. (2023) Allen & Overy Rolls Out AI Contract Negotiation Tool in Challenge to Legal Industry, *Financial Times*, 21 December, www.ft.com/content/f1aff4d0-b2c5-4266-aa0a-604ef14894bb.

Crouch, D. (2011) Tracing the Quote: Everything that can be Invented has been Invented, *Patently-O*, https://patentlyo.com/patent/2011/01/tracing-the-quote-everything-that-can-be-invented-has-been-invented.html.

Curry, D. (2024) Strava Revenue and Usage Statistics (2024), *Business of Apps*, www.businessofapps.com/data/strava-statistics.

Dahl, M., Magesh, V., Suzgun, M. and Ho, D. E. (2024) Large Legal Fictions: Profiling Legal Hallucinations in Large Language Models, *Journal of Legal Analysis*, **16** (1), 64–93, https://doi.org/10.1093/jla/laae003.

Data.NSW (2024) Making Data Available for Sharing, https://data.nsw.gov.au/making-data-available-sharing.

Datarade (2024) What is Synthetic Data? Discover Synthetic Datasets & Providers, https://datarade.ai/data-categories/synthetic-data.

Davenport, T. H. and Prusak, L. (1998) *Working Knowledge: How Organizations Manage What They Know*, Harvard Business Press.

Davenport, T. H. and Ronanki, R. (2018) Artificial Intelligence for the Real World, *Harvard Business Review*, **96** (1), 108–16.

Davis, J. (2019) Data Hunter: The New Sexy Technology Job, *InformationWeek*, www.informationweek.com/big-data/ai-machine-learning/data-hunter-the-new-sexy-technology-job/d/d-id/1334664.

Davis, M. (2024) *Data Discovery and Classification: Key Concepts for Data Mapping*, https://www.osano.com/articles/data-discovery-and-classification.

Daws, R. (2024) RootMetrics: Three Overtakes EE for Best UK 5G network, *Telecoms Tech News*, www.telecomstechnews.com/news/rootmetrics-three-overtakes-ee-best-uk-5g-network.

DCMS (2020) National Data Strategy, www.gov.uk/government/publications/uk-national-data-strategy/national-data-strategy.

De Saulles, M. (2024) Establishing Trust in an AI world. *11th European Conference on Social Media*, University of Brighton, 30 May, www.youtube.com/watch?v=OAq8zNlOCgM&t=1522s.

Dealroom (2024) Generative AI Startups List, https://app.dealroom.co/lists/33530.

Deloitte (2017) *Assessing the Value of TfL's Open Data and Digital Partnerships*, Deloitte.

Deloitte (2022) Skills Gaps are Slowing Down AI-Workforce Integration, https://action.deloitte.com/insight/2295/skills-gaps-are-slowing-down-ai-workforce-integration.

Department for Digital, Culture, Media and Sport (2024) Year 2 Online Media Literacy Action Plan (2022/23), www.gov.uk/government/publications/year-2-online-media-literacy-action-plan-202223/year-2-online-media-literacy-action-plan-202223.

Desjardins, J. (2017) The History of Consumer Credit in One Giant Infographic, *Visual Capitalist*, www.visualcapitalist.com/history-consumer-credit-one-infographic.

Dews, F. and Bull, E. (2014) The Decline of Newspapers, in Four Charts, *Brookings Commentary*, 23 October, www.brookings.edu/articles/the-decline-of-newspapers-in-four-charts.

Dey, V. (2023) 92% of US-based Developers Already Using AI-powered Coding Tools at Work: GitHub Report, *VentureBeat*, 19 June 19, https://venturebeat.com/ai/92-us-based-developers-already-using-ai-powered-coding-tools-at-work.

Dhuri, S. (2020) How AstraZeneca is Using Netflix Like Knowledge Graph to Discover New Drugs, *Medium*, 30 July, https://siddhuri.medium.com/how-astrazeneca-is-using-netflix-like-knowledge-graph-to-discover-new-drugs-a6cd187e5b10.

Dillender, M. and Forsythe, E. (2022) *Computerization of White Collar Jobs*, National Bureau of Economic Research, www.nber.org/papers/w29866.

Dodson, S. (2004) Trigger Unhappy, *The Guardian*, 27 May, www.theguardian.com/technology/2004/may/27/ruralaffairs.newmedia.

Donnan, C. (2011) A Brief History of Market Data. In *European Financial Information Summit*, London.

Dörner, D. (1997) *The Logic of Failure: Recognizing and Avoiding Error in Complex Situations*, revised edition, Basic Books.

Drapkin, A. (2023) Business Leaders can't Agree on Who's to Blame for AI Mistakes, *Tech.co*, 20 July, https://tech.co/news/business-leaders-blame-ai-mistakes.

Drucker, P. F. (1969) The Knowledge Society, *New Society*, **13** (343), 629–31.

Elad, B. (2023) Microsoft Statistics by Revenue, OS Popularity and Users, *Enterprise Apps Today*, 22 August, www.enterpriseappstoday.com/stats/microsoft-statistics.html.

Emsley, R. (2023) ChatGPT: These are not Hallucinations – They're Fabrications and Falsifications, *Schizophrenia*, **9** (1), 1–2.

Espinoza, J. (2023) EU Competition Chief Defends Artificial Intelligence Act after Macron's Attack, *Financial Times*, December 29, www.ft.com/content/2b18b3e7-5b92-4577-9c8e-6db2bdd016d8.

Espinoza, J. (2024) Europe's Rushed Attempt to Set the Rules for AI, *Financial Times*, 16 July, www.ft.com/content/6cc7847a-2fc5-4df0-b113-a435d6426c81.

Espinoza, J. and Acton, M. (2024) Apple Delays European Launch of AI features Because of EU Rules, *Financial Times*, 21 June, www.ft.com/content/360751cb-7a22-48e0-9b00-6a30ff41dcfe.

EU (2021) Open Data in Europe 2021, https://data.europa.eu/en/publications/open-data-maturity/2021#landscaping-map.

EUR-Lex (2020) Precautionary Principle, https://eur-lex.europa.eu/EN/legal-content/glossary/precautionary-principle.html.

European Commission (2010) EU Charter of Fundamental Rights, https://commission.europa.eu/aid-development-cooperation-fundamental-rights/your-rights-eu/eu-charter-fundamental-rights_en.

European Commission (2018) Communication From the Commission to the European Parliament, The European Council, The Council, The European Economic and Social Committee and The Committee of the Regions Artificial Intelligence for Europe, COM/2018/237 final, https://eur-lex.europa.eu/legal-content/EN/TXT/?uri=COM%3A2018%3A237%3AFIN.

European Commission (2020a) A European Strategy for Data, COM/2020/66 final, https://eur-lex.europa.eu/legal-content/EN/TXT/?qid=1593073685620&uri=CELEX%3A52020DC0066.

European Commission (2020b) *Impact Assessment of the Digital Markets Act – Shaping Europe's Digital Future*, https://digital-strategy.ec.europa.eu/en/library/impact-assessment-digital-markets-act.

European Commission (2023) About the Digital Markets Act, https://digital-markets-act.ec.europa.eu/about-dma_en.

European Commission (2024a) Apple's iPadOS Under the Digital Markets Act, https://ec.europa.eu/commission/presscorner/detail/en/ip_24_2363.

European Commission (2024b) CASE DMA.100047 – Apple – iPadOS, https://ec.europa.eu/competition/digital_markets_act/cases/202427/DMA_100047_5491.pdf.

European Parliament (2015) Regulation (EU) 2015/2120 of the European Parliament and of the Council, https://eur-lex.europa.eu/legal-content/EN/TXT/HTML/?uri=CELEX%3A32015R2120.

European Parliament (2024) Sources and Scope of European Union Law – Fact Sheets on the European Union,

www.europarl.europa.eu/factsheets/en/sheet/6/sources-and-scope-of-european-union-law.
European Union (2015) Maximillian Schrems v Data Protection Commissioner, https://eur-lex.europa.eu/legal-content/en/TXT/?uri=CELEX%3A62014CJ0362.
Europol (2024) Facing Reality? Law Enforcement and the Challenge of Deepfakes, www.europol.europa.eu/publications-events/publications/facing-reality-law-enforcement-and-challenge-of-deepfakes.
Evans, B. (2017) Asking the Wrong Questions, www.ben-evans.com/benedictevans/2017/01/11/wrongquestions.
Evans, B. (2023) Retail, Search and Amazon's $40bn 'Advertising' Business, www.ben-evans.com/benedictevans/2023/3/6/ways-to-think-about-amazon-advertising.
Evelson, B. (2024) AI is Now a Core Capability of BI Platforms, *Forrester*, 7 August, www.forrester.com/blogs/ai-is-now-a-core-capability-of-bi-platforms.
Executive Office of the President (2019) Maintaining American Leadership in Artificial Intelligence, Federal Register, www.federalregister.gov/documents/2019/02/14/2019-02544/maintaining-american-leadership-in-artificial-intelligence.
EY (2024) Data Interoperability: An Essential for the e-Mobility Ecosystem, EY and eurelectric, https://evision.eurelectric.org/report-2024.
Fediverse Observer (2024) Fediverse Observer Checks All Servers in the Fediverse and Gives You an Easy Way to Find a Home Using a Map or List, https://fediverse.observer/stats.
Ferracane, M. F., Kren, J. and Van Der Marel, E. (2020) Do Data Policy Restrictions Impact the Productivity Performance of Firms and Industries?, *Review of International Economics*, **28** (3), 676–722, https://doi.org/10.1111/roie.12467.
Fest, I., Wieringa, M. and Wagner, B. (2022) Paper vs. Practice: How Legal and Ethical Frameworks Influence Public Sector Data Professionals in the Netherlands, *Patterns*, **3** (10), 100604, https://doi.org/10.1016/j.patter.2022.100604.
Finley, K. (2017) FCC's Broken Comments System Could Help Doom Net Neutrality, *Wired*, September 2, www.wired.com/story/fccs-broken-comments-system-could-help-doom-net-neutrality.
Foucart, R. (2024) Europe's Tech Industry is Lagging Behind the US – But it Gives the Continent a Chance to Write the Rules of the Game, *The Conversation*, http://theconversation.com/europes-tech-industry-is-lagging-behind-the-us-but-it-gives-the-continent-a-chance-to-write-the-rules-of-the-game-224665.
Fox, W. (2024) Global Average Internet Speed, 1990–2050, www.futuretimeline.net/data-trends/2050-future-internet-speed-predictions.htm.
Freeguard, G. (2021) Mapping Data in the UK Government, *The ODI*, https://theodi.org/insights/reports/mapping-data-in-the-uk-government-report.

Friel, K. (2023) A Look Back on the Dartmouth Summer Research Project on Artificial Intelligence, *The Dartmouth*, 19 May, www.thedartmouth.com/article/2023/05/a-look-back-on-the-dartmouth-summer-research-project-on-artificial-intelligence.

Frey, C. B. and Osborne, M. A. (2017) The Future of Employment: How Susceptible are Jobs to Computerisation?, *Technological Forecasting and Social Change*, **114**, 254–80.

FT (2023) *Generative AI Exists Because of the Transformer*, https://ig.ft.com/generative-ai.

FTI (2024) Current Power Trends Implications Data Center Industry, www.fticonsulting.com/insights/articles/current-power-trends-implications-data-center-industry.

Gaglione, A., Capossele, A., Puschmann, D. and Gluhak, A. (2017) SynchroniCity: Delivering an IoT enabled Digital Single Market for Europe and Beyond, *European Large-Scale Pilots Programme*, https://european-iot-pilots.eu/project/synchronicity.

Gaia-X (2024) About Gaia-X, https://gaia-x.eu/about.

Gartner (2022) Is Synthetic Data the Future of AI?, www.gartner.com/en/newsroom/press-releases/2022-06-22-is-synthetic-data-the-future-of-ai.

Gartner (2024a) Data Literacy: A Guide to Building a Data-Literate Organization, www.gartner.com/en/data-analytics/topics/data-literacy.

Gartner (2024b) Gartner Survey Finds 64% of Customers Would Prefer that Companies Didn't Use AI for Customer Service, www.gartner.com/en/newsroom/press-releases/2024-07-09-gartner-survey-finds-64-percent-of-customers-would-prefer-that-companies-didnt-use-ai-for-customer -service.

Gawer, A. and Cusumano, M. A. (2002) *Platform Leadership: How Intel, Microsoft and Cisco Drive Industry Innovation*, Harvard Business School Press.

Gawer, A. and Cusumano, M. A. (2008) How Companies Become Platform Leaders, *MIT Sloan Management Review*, **49** (2), 28–35.

Gawer, A. and Cusumano, M. A. (2014) Industry Platforms and Ecosystem Innovation, *Journal of Product Innovation Management*, **31** (3), 417–33.

Gibbs, S. (2016) Mobile Web Browsing Overtakes Desktop for the First Time, *The Guardian*, 2 November, www.theguardian.com/technology/2016/nov/02/mobile-web-browsing-desktop-smartphones-tablets.

GlobalData (2024) Google's Revenue (2002–2021), www.linkedin.com/company/globaldataplc.

GM (2024) GM Releases 2023 Fourth-Quarter and Full-Year Results, and 2024 Guidance, https://investor.gm.com/news-releases/news-release-details/gm-releases-2023-fourth-quarter-and-full-year-results-and-2024

Google (2022) Year in Review: The Google Workspace Platform 2021, *Google for Developers Blog*, https://developers.googleblog.com/en/year-in-review-the-google-workspace-platform-2021.

Google Finance (2024a) Alphabet Inc Class C (GOOG) Stock Price & News, www.google.com/finance/quote/GOOG:NASDAQ.

Google Finance (2024b) Google Finance – Nvidia share price, www.google.com/finance .

Google Finance (2024c) Nasdaq Indices – 1984 to 2024, www.google.com/finance.

Grady, P. (2023) Extending AI Act's Ban on Social Scoring to the Private Sector Will Hurt Consumers, *Center for Data Innovation*, 11 January, https://datainnovation.org/2023/01/extending-ai-acts-ban-on-social-scoring-to-the-private-sector-will-hurt-consumers.

Green, R. (2023) Making Your Skills Count in a World of AI, www.cilip.org.uk/news/655238/Changing-our-perception-of-AI- - -Libraries-Rewired.htm.

Greenberg, A. (2018) The Untold Story of NotPetya, the Most Devastating Cyberattack in History, *Wired*, 22 August, www.wired.com/story/notpetya-cyberattack-ukraine-russia-code-crashed-the-world.

Gross, A. and Fisher, L. (2024) UK Data Centres to be Designated Critical Infrastructure, *Financial Times*, 11 September, www.ft.com/content/536965d5-d80f-417c-9ec6-b6dcac251a1b.

Grundy, T. (2006) Rethinking and Reinventing Michael Porter's Five Forces Model, *Strategic Change*, **15** (5), 213–29, https://doi.org/10.1002/jsc.764.

GSMA (2024) The Mobile Economy 2024, www.gsma.com/solutions-and-impact/connectivity-for-good/mobile-economy.

Guber, P. (2014) The Road Not Taken: Why Rearview Mirrors are Bad for Driving Your Career, www.peterguber.com/the-road-not-taken-why-rearview-mirrors-are-bad-for-driving-your-career.

Guelzo, A. C. (2005) *Lincoln's Emancipation Proclamation: The End of Slavery in America*, Simon and Schuster.

Gunkel, D. J. (2024) Introduction. In *Handbook on the Ethics of Artificial Intelligence*, 1–12, Edward Elgar Publishing, www.elgaronline.com/edcollbook/book/9781803926728/9781803926728.xml.

Hammond, G. (2024) AI Hit by Copyright Claims as Companies Approach 'Data Frontier', *Financial Times*, 31 August, www.ft.com/content/e6a4dcae-2bda-42de-8112-768844673cea.

Hammond, G. and Criddle, C. (2024) California Governor Vetoes Bill to Regulate Artificial Intelligence, *Financial Times*, 29 September, www.ft.com/content/b3b92693-a960-4b6c-a503-f2792c77b04d.

Harford, T. (2017) How the World's First Accountants Counted on Cuneiform, *BBC News*, 12 June, www.bbc.com/news/business-39870485.

Harford, T. (2019) How Computing's First 'Killer App' Changed Everything, *BBC News*, 21 May, www.bbc.com/news/business-47802280.

Hargadon, A. (2014) Brokerage and Innovation. In Dodgson, M., Gann, D. M. and Phillips, N. (eds) *The Oxford Handbook of Innovation Management*, 163–80, Oxford University Press.

Harkness, L. (2023) The Power of Generative AI for Marketing, *McKinsey*, www.mckinsey.com/capabilities/growth-marketing-and-sales/our-insights/how-generative-ai-can-boost-consumer-marketing.

Harrington, J. (2024) WPP Reveals £250m AI Investment, *PRWeek*, www.prweek.com/article/1859227?utm_source=website&utm_medium=social.

He, Z. (1994) Diffusion of Movable Type in China and Europe: Why were There Two Fates?, *Gazette (Leiden, Netherlands)*, **53** (3), 153–73, https://doi.org/10.1177/001654929405300301.

Herbert Smith Freehills (2024) Criminalising Deepfakes – The UK's New Offences Following the Online Safety Act, www.herbertsmithfreehills.com/notes/tmt/2024-05/criminalising-deepfakes-the-uks-new-offences-following-the-online-safety-act.

Hern, A. (2015) EU Net Neutrality Laws Fatally Undermined by Loopholes, Critics Say, *The Guardian*, 27 October, www.theguardian.com/technology/2015/oct/27/eu-net-neutrality-laws-fatally-undermined-by-loopholes-critics-say.

Hetzner, C. (2024) AI Could Gobble Up a Quarter of All Electricity in the U.S. by 2030 if it Doesn't Break its Energy Addiction, Says Arm Holdings Exec, *Fortune*, https://fortune.com/2024/04/16/ai-chatgpt-sora-large-language-models-arm-chips-semiconductors-electricity.

Hogendorn, C. (2011) Excessive (?) Entry of National Telecom Networks, 1990–2001, *Telecommunications Policy*, **35** (11), 920–32.

Holm, S. and Harris, J. (1999) Precautionary Principle Stifles Discovery, *Nature*, **400**, 398.

Houlsby, N. and Weissenborn, D. (2020) Transformers for Image Recognition at Scale, *Google Research Blog*, http://research.google/blog/transformers-for-image-recognition-at-scale.

Hugging Face (2024) Models, https://huggingface.co/models.

Hughes, A. (2023) ChatGPT: Everything You Need to Know About OpenAI's GPT-4 Tool, *BBC Science Focus*, www.sciencefocus.com/future-technology/gpt-3.

Hunter, T. (2024) 22 UK Local Newspapers Closed in the Past Two Years, *Press Gazette*, https://pressgazette.co.uk/publishers/regional-newspapers/local-newspaper-closures-uk-2022-to-2024.

IBM (2021) Structured vs. Unstructured Data: What's the Difference?, www.ibm.com/think/topics/structured-vs-unstructured-data.

IBM (2023a) What is a Knowledge Graph?, www.ibm.com/topics/knowledge-graph.

IBM (2023b) What is Prompt Engineering?, www.ibm.com/topics/prompt-engineering.

IBM (2024a) AI vs. Machine Learning vs. Deep Learning vs. Neural Networks, www.ibm.com/think/topics/ai-vs-machine-learning-vs-deep-learning-vs-neural-networks.

IBM (2024b) What is an API (Application Programming Interface)?, www.ibm.com/topics/api.

ICO (2020) The Information Commissioner's Office Response to the National Data Strategy, https://ico.org.uk/media/about-the-ico/consultation-responses/2618963/ico-response-national-data-strategy-consultation.pdf.

IDC (2021) The Data-as-a-Service Market in 2021 at a Glance, *IDC Blog*, https://blogs.idc.com/2021/04/19/the-data-as-a-service-market-in-2021-at-a-glance.

Intel (2023) *Moore's Law*, www.intel.com/content/www/us/en/newsroom/resources/moores-law.html.

International Energy Agency (2024) Electricity 2024: Analysis and Forecast to 2026, www.iea.org/reports/electricity-2024.

IPIE (2023) Platform Responses to Misinformation: A Meta-Analysis of Data, www.ipie.info/research/sr2023-2.

IPIE (2024) IPIE – International Panel on the Information Environment, www.ipie.info.

Ivanti (2024) State of Cybersecurity Trends Report 2024, www.ivanti.com/resources/research-reports/state-of-cybersecurity-report.

Jarrahi, M. H., Askay, D. Eshraghi, A. and Smith, P. (2023) Artificial Intelligence and Knowledge Management: A Partnership Between Human and AI, *Business Horizons*, **66** (1), 87–99, https://doi.org/10.1016/j.bushor.2022.03.002.

Jefferson, T. (1813) *Founders Online: Thomas Jefferson to Isaac McPherson, 13 August 1813, US National Archives*, University of Virginia Press, http://founders.archives.gov/documents/Jefferson/03-06-02-0322.

Jordon, J. , Szpruch, L., Houssiau, F., Bottarelli, M., Cherubin, G., Maple, C., Cohen, S. and Weller, A. (2022) Synthetic Data – What, Why and How?, *The Alan Turing Institute*, https://royalsociety.org/-/media/policy/projects/privacy-enhancing-technologies/Synthetic_Data_Survey-24.pdf.

Justia Law (2001) U.S. v. Microsoft Corp., 253 F.3d 34 (D.C. Cir. 2001), https://law.justia.com/cases/federal/appellate-courts/F3/253/34/576095.

Karaci Deniz, B. and Gnanasambandam, C. (2023) Unleash Developer Productivity With Generative AI, *McKinsey*, www.mckinsey.com/capabilities/mckinsey-digital/our-insights/unleashing-developer-productivity-with-generative-ai.

Kelham, C. (2014) Health Care Librarians and Information Literacy: An Investigation, *Health Information & Libraries Journal*, **31** (3), 235–8, https://doi.org/10.1111/hir.12071.

Kenny, G., Kowalkiewicz, M. and Oosthuizen, K. (2024) GenAI is Leveling the Playing Field for Smaller Businesses, *Harvard Business Review*, 6 June, https://hbr.org/2024/06/genai-is-leveling-the-playing-field-for-smaller-businesses.

Kerner, S. M. (2024) GPT-4o Explained: Everything You Need to Know, *WhatIs*, www.techtarget.com/whatis/feature/GPT-4o-explained-Everything-you-need-to-know.

Klarna (2024) Klarna AI Assistant Handles Two-Thirds of Customer Service Chats in its First Month, www.klarna.com/international/press/klarna-ai-assistant-handles-two-thirds-of-customer-service-chats-in-its-first-month.

Knight, W. (2023) OpenAI's CEO Says the Age of Giant AI Models is Already Over, *Wired*, 17 April, www.wired.com/story/openai-ceo-sam-altman-the-age-of-giant-ai-models-is-already-over.

Knudsen, J. E., Ghaffar, U., Ma, R. and Hung, A. J. (2024) Clinical Applications of Artificial Intelligence in Robotic Surgery, *Journal of Robotic Surgery*, **18** (1), 102, https://doi.org/10.1007/s11701-024-01867-0.

Kollewe, J. (2019) NHS Data is Worth Billions – But Who Should Have Access to it?, *The Guardian*, 10 June , www.theguardian.com/society/2019/jun/10/nhs-data-google-alphabet-tech-drug-firms.

Kolodny, L. (2024) Tesla Reported 485,000 Deliveries for the Fourth Quarter, Bringing 2023 Total to 1.8 Million, *CNBC*, www.cnbc.com/2024/01/02/tesla-tsla-q4-2023-vehicle-delivery-and-production-numbers.html.

Krakowski, S., Luger, J. and Raisch, S. (2023) Artificial Intelligence and the Changing Sources of Competitive Advantage, *Strategic Management Journal*, **44** (6), 1425–52, https://doi.org/10.1002/smj.3387.

Labonne, M. (2024) The Rise of Agentic Data Generation, *Hugging Face*, https://huggingface.co/blog/mlabonne/agentic-datagen.

Lalchand, S., Srinivas, V., Maggiore, B. and Henderson, J. (2024) Generative AI is Expected to Magnify the Risk of Deepfakes and Other Fraud in Banking, *Deloitte Insights*, www2.deloitte.com/us/en/insights/industry/financial-services/financial-services-industry-predictions/2024/deepfake-banking-fraud-risk-on-the-rise.html.

Lane, M., Williams, M. and Broecke, S. (2023) *The Impact of AI on the Workplace: Main Findings from the OECD AI Surveys of Employers and Workers*, OECD, https://doi.org/10.1787/ea0a0fe1-en.

Laney, D. B. (2017) *Infonomics: How to Monetize, Manage, and Measure Information as an Asset for Competitive Advantage*, Routledge.

Lange, K. (2023) IDC MarketScape: Worldwide Data Labeling Software 2023 Vendor Assessment, *IDC*, www.idc.com/getdoc.jsp?containerId=US50010523.

Laurent, L. (2024) Europe has US Tech in its Sights. It Might Miss, *Bloomberg.com*, 1 August, www.bloomberg.com/opinion/articles/2024-08-01/europe-s-new-ai-rules-have-us-tech-in-mind-they-might-miss.

Lazzaro, S. (2024) Google's Gemini Ultra AI Model May Have Cost $191 million, New Stanford AI Report Estimates, *Fortune*, https://fortune.com/2024/04/18/google-gemini-cost-191-million-to-train-stanford-university-report-estimates.

Leng, C. and Ho-him, C. (2024) Arup Lost $25mn in Hong Kong Deepfake Video Conference Scam, *Financial Times*, 16 May, www.ft.com/content/b977e8d4-664c-4ae4-8a8e-eb93bdf785ea.

Leswing, K. (2024) Nvidia Dominates the AI Chip Market, but There's More Competition than Ever, *CNBC*, www.cnbc.com/2024/06/02/nvidia-dominates-the-ai-chip-market-but-theres-rising-competition-.html.

Levy, F. and Murnane, R. J. (2004) *The New Division of Labour – How Computers are Creating the Next Job Market*, Princeton University Press.

Lewis, M. (2015) *Flash Boys*, Penguin.

Li, X., Rong, K. and Shi, X. (2023) Situating Artificial Intelligence in Organization: A Human-Machine Relationship Perspective, *Journal of Digital Economy*, **2**, 330–5.

Lime Micromobility (2024) E-scooter & E-Bike Rental in New York, www.li.me/locations/new-york.

Lingolu, N. V., Kumari, D. and Kumar, P. (2024) Evaluating the Impact of AI and ML on Modern Drug Discovery: Review Article, *Journal of Pharma Insights and Research*, **2** (4), 67–72, https://doi.org/10.69613/8tckqp18.

Lockerbie, H. and Williams, D. (2019) Seven Pillars and Five Minds: Small Business Workplace Information Literacy, *Journal of Documentation*, **75** (5), 977–94.

Luccioni, A. S., Jernite, Y. and Strubell, E. (2024) Power Hungry Processing: Watts Driving the Cost of AI Deployment?, *The 2024 ACM Conference on Fairness, Accountability, and Transparency*, 85–99, https://doi.org/10.1145/3630106.3658542.

Lyman, P. and Varian, H. (2000) How Much Information?, *University of California at Berkeley*, http://groups.ischool.berkeley.edu/archive/how-much-info.

Lyman, P. and Varian, H. (2003) How Much Information 2003?, *University of California at Berkeley*, https://groups.ischool.berkeley.edu/archive/how-much-info-2003/printable_report.pdf.

Machlup, F. (1962) *The Production and Distribution of Knowledge in the United States*, Princeton University Press.

Maddison, L. (2023) Samsung Workers Made a Major Error by Using ChatGPT, *TechRadar*, www.techradar.com/news/samsung-workers-leaked-company-secrets-by-using-chatgpt.

Malik, O. (2023) A Letter from Om, Issue #15/2023, *On my Om*, https://om.co/2023/11/18/a-letter-from-om-issue-15-2023.

Manancourt, V. (2020) Europe's Data Grab, *POLITICO*, www.politico.eu/article/europe-data-grab-protection-privacy.

Mance, H. (2024) Google's James Manyika: 'The Productivity Gains From AI are Not Guaranteed', *Financial Times*, 2 September, www.ft.com/content/2c122092-51ab-4529-b733-ac466f338cb5.

Mann, T. B. et al. (2020) Language Models are Few-Shot Learners, arXiv preprint arXiv:2005.14165, 1, https://doi.org/10.48550/arXiv.2005.14165.

Manyika, J. (2017) 10 Imperatives for Europe in the Age of AI and Automation, *McKinsey*, www.mckinsey.com/featuredinsights/europe/ten-imperatives-for-europe-in-the-age-of-ai-and-automation.

Marchant, G. E. (2003) From General Policy to Legal Rule: Aspirations and Limitations of the Precautionary Principle, *Environmental Health Perspectives*, **111** (14), 1799–803, https://doi.org/10.1289/ehp.6197.

Mardell, J. (2021) China is Securing Battery Metals on the Global Stage, https://merics.org/en/tracker/china-securing-battery-metals-global-stage.

Marr, B. (2024) 7 Essential Open-Source Generative AI Models Available Today, *Forbes*, www.forbes.com/sites/bernardmarr/2024/05/07/the-best-open-source-generative-ai-models-available-today.

Martins, D. (2023) Apple in the 1990s: Why it Nearly Went Bankrupt, *The Street*, www.thestreet.com/apple/news/apple-in-the-1990s-why-it-nearly-went-bankrupt.

Maxfield, M. (2023) Using Generative AI for Refactoring and Debugging Code Cuts Debugging Time in Half!, *EEJournal*, www.eejournal.com/article/using-generative-ai-for-refactoring-and-debugging-code-cut-debugging-time-in-half.

McCulloch, W. S. and Pitts, W. (1943) A Logical Calculus of the Ideas Immanent in Nervous Activity, *The Bulletin of Mathematical Biophysics*, **5** (4), 115–33, https://doi.org/10.1007/BF02478259.

McGee, J. S. (1958) Predatory Price Cutting: The Standard Oil (N. J.) Case, *The Journal of Law and Economics*, **1**, 137–69, https://doi.org/10.1086/466547.

McKinsey & Co. (2024) What is Prompt Engineering?, www.mckinsey.com/featured-insights/mckinsey-explainers/what-is-prompt-engineering.

Media Literacy Now (2024) *U.S. Media Literacy Policy Report 2023*, 1–32, https://medialiteracynow.org/wp-content/uploads/2024/02/MediaLiteracyNowPolicyReport2023_publishedFeb2024b.pdf.

Mehta, S. (2024) How Much Energy Do LLMs Consume? Unveiling the Power Behind AI, *Association of Data Scientists*, 3 July, https://adasci.org/how-much-energy-do-llms-consume-unveiling-the-power-behind-ai.

Meta (2024) Meta 10K Annual Filing 2023, https://d18rn0p25nwr6d.cloudfront.net/CIK-0001326801/c7318154-f6ae-4866-89fa-f0c589f2ee3d.pdf.

Miles, I. (1993) Services in the New Industrial Economy, *Futures*, **25** (6), 653–72.

Miller, H. E. and Engemann, K. J. (2019) The Precautionary Principle and Unintended Consequences, *Kybernetes*, **48** (2), 265–86, https://doi.org/10.1108/K-01-2018-0050.

Miller, R. (2024) CIOs' Concerns over Generative AI Echo Those of the Early Days of Cloud Computing, *TechCrunch*, https://techcrunch.com/2024/07/07/cios-concerns-over-generative-ai-echo-those-of-the-early-days-of-cloud-computing.

Milmo, D. (2024) Google Says UK Risks Being 'Left Behind' in AI Race Without More Data Centres, *The Guardian*, 19 September, www.theguardian.com/technology/2024/sep/19/google-says-uk-risks-being-left-behind-in-ai-race-without-more-data-centres.

Mims, C. (2024) The Threat to OpenAI is Growing, *The Wall Street Journal*, www.wsj.com/tech/ai/ai-chatgpt-nvidia-apple-facebook-383943d1.

Ministry of Justice (2024) Ministry of Justice: Better Outcomes Through Linked Data (BOLD), www.gov.uk/government/publications/ministry-of-justice-better-outcomes-through-linked-data-bold/ministry-of-justice-better-outcomes-through-linked-data-bold.

Mold, A. (2022) Food Hygiene, Public Health Education and Citizenship in Britain, 1948–1967, *Medical Humanities*, **48** (1), 114–22.

Mollick, E. (2024) *Co-Intelligence: Living and Working with AI*, W. H. Allen.

Moore, M. (2024) Google Orders Small Modular Nuclear Reactors for its Data Centres, *Financial Times*, 14 October, www.ft.com/content/29eaf03f-4970-40da-ae7c-c8b3283069da.

Morandini, S., Fraboni, F., De Angelis, M., Puzzo, G., Giusino, D. and Pietrantoni, L. (2023) The Impact of Artificial Intelligence on Workers' Skills: Upskilling and Reskilling in Organisations, *Informing Science*, **26**, 39–68.

Morley, J. (2019) Artificial Intelligence: How to Get it Right. Putting Policy into Practice for Safe Data-Driven Innovation in Health and Care, NHSX, 55, https://transform.england.nhs.uk/media/documents/NHSX_AI_report.pdf.

Moss, S. (2024) Iceland's AI Moment, *Data Center Dynamics*, www.datacenterdynamics.com/en/analysis/icelands-ai-moment.

MOSTLY AI (2024) AWS Marketplace: MOSTLY AI Synthetic Data Platform, https://aws.amazon.com/marketplace/pp/prodview-z4bb3qozmlg3c.

National Archives (2024) Open Government Licence, www.nationalarchives.gov.uk/doc/open-government-licence/version/3.

National Literacy Trust (2024) Evaluation of *Behind the Headlines* Media Literacy Ambassador Project: Executive Summary, https://theguardianfoundation.org/assets/files/behind-the-headlines-mla-evaluation-summary-2024.pdf.

Neate, R. (2019) Hubris of a High-Flyer: How Investors Brought WeWork Founder Down to Earth, *The Guardian*, 28 September, www.theguardian.com/business/2019/sep/28/hubris-of-a-high-flyer-how-investors-brought-wework-founder-down-to-earth.

New Scientist (2022) *Machines That Think: Everything You Need to Know About the Coming Age of Artificial Intelligence*, John Murray One.

NHS AI Lab (2024) The NHS AI Lab, https://transform.england.nhs.uk/ai-lab.

NHS Transformation Directorate (2024) OpenSAFELY: Secure Access to Data to Deepen Our Understanding of COVID-19, https://transform.england.nhs.uk/key-tools-and-info/data-saves-lives/improving-care-through-research-and-innovation/opensafely-secure-access-to-data-to-deepen-our-understanding-of-covid-19.

Nicol-Schwarz, K. (2024) AI Could Save Lives in the NHS – But a Lack of Adoption Pathways are Holding it Back, *Sifted*, https://sifted.eu/articles/ai-healthcare-nhs-startup.

Nilsson, J. (2024) Knowledge Graphs Improve Gen AI, *Capgemini*, 18 July, www.capgemini.com/insights/expert-perspectives/knowledge-graphs-improve-gen-ai.

Northern Light (2024) Enterprises Lag Their Employees When it Comes to Generative AI Use, https://northernlight.com/enterprises-lag-their-employees-when-it-comes-to-generative-ai-use.

Norton, R. (2018) Law of Unintended Consequences, www.econlib.org/library/Enc/UnintendedConsequences.html.

Norton Rose Fulbright (2024) AI Regulation in the UK: Will the Next Government Introduce AI Legislation?, www.nortonrosefulbright.com/en/knowledge/publications/859fb86d/ai-regulation-in-the-uk.

Nylen, L. (2024) Google's Payments to Apple Reached $20 Billion in 2022, Antitrust Court Documents Show, *Bloomberg.com*, 1 May, www.bloomberg.com/news/articles/2024-05-01/google-s-payments-to-apple-reached-20-billion-in-2022-cue-says.

OBR (2022) Cyber-Attacks During the Russian Invasion of Ukraine, https://obr.uk/box/cyber-attacks-during-the-russian-invasion-of-ukraine.

OECD (2022) *Using Private Sector Geospatial Data to Inform Policy*, OECD Regional Development Papers.

Ofcom (2023) Online Nation, www.ofcom.org.uk/media-use-and-attitudes/online-habits/online-nation.

Ofcom (2024a) A Positive Vision for Media Literacy: A Consultation on Ofcom's Three-Year Media Literacy Strategy, www.ofcom.org.uk/media-use-and-attitudes/media-literacy/bulletin.

Ofcom (2024b) Media Nations 2024, www.ofcom.org.uk/media-use-and-attitudes/media-habits-adults/media-nations-2024.

Ofcom (2024c) The Communications Market 2024, www.ofcom.org.uk/phones-and-broadband/service-quality/communications-market-2024.

Official Journal of the European Union (2024) Regulation (EU) 2024/1689 of the European Parliament and of the Council of 13 June 2024 laying down harmonised rules on artificial intelligence and amending Regulations (EC) No 300/2008, (EU) No 167/2013, (EU) No 168/2013, (EU) 2018/858, (EU) 2018/1139 and (EU) 2019/2144 and Directives 2014/90/EU, (EU) 2016/797 and (EU) 2020/1828 (Artificial Intelligence Act) (Text with EEA relevance), http://data.europa.eu/eli/reg/2024/1689/oj/eng.

OpenAI (2024a) *Delivering Contextual Job Matching for Millions with OpenAI*, https://openai.com/index/indeed.

OpenAI (2024b) Playground Prompt Length – What is Too Long?, *Prompting, OpenAI Developer Forum*, https://community.openai.com/t/playground-prompt-length-what-is-too-long/627123.

OpenSAFELY (2024) *OpenSAFELY: About OpenSAFELY*, www.opensafely.org/about.

Oppenheimer, P., Jaisson, G., Bell, S. and Peytavin, L. (2024) AI: To Buy, or Not to Buy, That is the Question, *Goldman Sachs*, 1–34, www.goldmansachs.com/pdfs/insights/goldman-sachs-research/global-strategy-paper-ai-to-buy-or-not-to-buy-that-is-the-question/GlobalStrategypaperAIredacted.pdf.

ORG (2020) Response by the ORG to the National Data Strategy Consultation, www.openrightsgroup.org/app/uploads/2020/12/Open-Rights-Group-National-Data-Strategy-consultation-response.pdf.

Orwell, G. (2021) *Nineteen Eighty-Four*, Wordsworth Editions.

Osterwalder, A. and Pigneur, Y. (2010) *Business Model Generation: A Handbook for Visionaries, Game Changers, and Challengers*, John Wiley & Sons.

Overton, M. (1996) Re-establishing the English Agricultural Revolution, *The Agricultural History Review*, **44**, 1–20.

Partridge, J. (2022) Behold London's 'Landscraper'! Google's New UK HQ – As Long as the Shard is Tall, *The Guardian*, 1 July, www.theguardian.com/business/2022/jul/01/behold-londons-landscraper-googles-new-uk-hq-as-long-as-the-shard-is-tall.

Perez, C. (2003) *Technological Revolutions and Financial Capital: The Dynamics of Bubbles and Golden Ages*, Edward Elgar.

Perez, C. (2010) Technological Revolutions and Techno-Economic Paradigms, *Cambridge Journal of Economics*, **34** (1), 185–202.

Perplexity (2024) *Perplexity Blog*, www.perplexity.ai/hub.

Peterson, M. (2006) The Precautionary Principle is Incoherent, *Risk Analysis*, **26** (3), 595–601, https://doi.org/10.1111/j.1539-6924.2006.00781.x.

Phillips, S. (2023) Focus on Creating Value: The 2023 Business Information Review Survey, *Business Information Review*, **40** (4), 158–66, https://doi.org/10.1177/02663821231214079.

Pinsent Masons (2024) International Data Transfers and Schrems II: GDPR Obligations, www.pinsentmasons.com/out-law/guides/international-transfers-schrems-ii-gdpr.

Ponsford, D. (2024) Google Takes Lion's Share of Growing UK Ad Market as Publishers Lose Out, *Press Gazette*, 25 April, https://pressgazette.co.uk/marketing/google-takes-lions-share-of-growing-uk-ad-market-as-publishers-lose-out.

Porat, M. U. (1977) The Information Economy: Definition and Measurement, Office of Telecommunications, 1–242, https://eric.ed.gov/?id=ED142205.

Porter, M. E. (1979) How Competitive Forces Shape Strategy, *Harvard Business Review*, 1 March, 137–45.

Porter, M. E. and Millar, V. E. (1985) How Information Gives You Competitive Advantage, *Harvard Business Review*, **63** (4), 149–60.

Powell, M. K. (2004) Preserving Internet Freedom: Guiding Principles for the Industry, *Journal on Telecommunications and High Technology Law*, **3**, 5–21.

Rajpurkar, P., Chen, E., Banerjee, O. and Topol, E. J. (2022) AI in Health and Medicine, *Nature Medicine*, **28** (1), 31–8, https://doi.org/10.1038/s41591-021-01614-0.

Rayward, W. B. (2014) Information Revolutions, the Information Society, and the Future of the History of Information Science, *Library Trends*, **62** (3), 681–713.

Reisinger, D. (2017) That Time Steve Ballmer Laughed at the iPhone, *Fortune*, https://fortune.com/2017/01/10/steve-ballmer-apple-iphone.

Reuters (2008) *Reuters, From Pigeons to Multimedia Merger*, www.reuters.com/article/us-reuters-thomson-chronology-idUSL1849100620080219.

Richardson Ellis, D. (2024) How and Where to Integrate ChatGPT on Your Website: A Step-by-Step Guide, https://blog.hubspot.com/website/chatgpt-integration.

Riley, J. C. (2001) *Rising Life Expectancy: A Global History*, Cambridge University Press.

Rinta-Kahila, T. (2024) Artificial Intelligence is Taking the Consulting Industry by Storm – Should we be Concerned?, *The Conversation*, http://theconversation.com/artificial-intelligence-is-taking-the-consulting-industry-by-storm-should-we-be-concerned-232149.

Roberts, H., Cowls, J., Hine, E., Mazzi, F., Tsamados, A., Taddeo, M. and Floridi, L. (2021) Achieving a 'Good AI Society': Comparing the Aims and Progress of the EU and the US, *Science and Engineering Ethics*, **27** (6), 68, https://doi.org/10.1007/s11948-021-00340-7.

Robins-Early, N. (2024a) A US Judge Ruled that Google Built an Illegal Monopoly. What Happens Next?, *The Guardian*, 6 August, www.theguardian.com/technology/article/2024/aug/06/google-antitrust-monopoly-ruling.

Robins-Early, N. (2024b) CEO of World's Biggest Ad Firm Targeted by Deepfake Scam, *The Guardian*, 10 May, www.theguardian.com/technology/article/2024/may/10/ceo-wpp-deepfake-scam.

Robinson, D. (2024) 'Hyperscale Customer' to Take Massive DC Site near London, www.theregister.com/2024/09/13/hyperscale_customer_to_take_massive.
Robinson, S. (2024) *What is Data Literacy?*, www.techtarget.com/whatis/definition/data-literacy.
Robison, K. (2024) Perplexity is Cutting Checks to Publishers Following Plagiarism Accusations, *The Verge*, www.theverge.com/2024/7/30/24208979/perplexity-publishers-program-ad-revenue-sharing-ai-time-fortune-der-spiegel.
Robles Carrillo, M. (2020) Artificial Intelligence: From Ethics to Law, *Telecommunications Policy*, **44** (6), 101937, https://doi.org/10.1016/j.telpol.2020.101937.
Rogers, R. (2024) How Google's AI Overviews Work, and How to Turn Them Off (You Can't), *Wired*, 16 May, www.wired.com/story/google-ai-overviews-how-to-use-how-to-turn-off.
Room, A. (1987) History of Branding. In Murphy, J. M. (ed.) *Branding: A Key Marketing Tool*, 13–21, Palgrave Macmillan, https://doi.org/10.1007/978-1-349-08280-3_2.
Rosenblatt, F. (1958) The Perceptron: A Probabilistic Model for Information Storage and Organization in the Brain, *Psychological Review*, **65** (6), 386–408.
Rubin, D. B. (1993) Statistical Disclosure Limitation, *Journal of Official Statistics*, **9** (2), 461–8.
Saelee, M. (2020) Research Guides: Standard Oil's Monopoly: Topics in Chronicling America: Introduction, https://guides.loc.gov/chronicling-america-standard-oil-monopoly/introduction.
Saheb, T. and Saheb, T. (2024) Mapping Ethical Artificial Intelligence Policy Landscape: A Mixed Method Analysis, *Science and Engineering Ethics*, **30** (2), 9, https://doi.org/10.1007/s11948-024-00472-6.
Sartor, G. (2020) Artificial Intelligence and Human Rights: Between Law and Ethics, *Maastricht Journal of European and Comparative Law*, **27** (6), 705–19, https://doi.org/10.1177/1023263X20981566.
Sau, M. (2024) Generative AI Use Cases Across Industries, *Gartner*, www.gartner.com/en/articles/generative-ai-use-cases.
Schatsky, D., Camhi, J. and Muraskin, C. (2019) *Data Ecosystems: How Third-Party Information Can Enhance Data Analytics*, Deloitte.
Scheibenreif, D. and Raskino, M. (2023) *When Machines Become Customers*, Gartner Inc.
Schneider, L. (2024) IDC's Worldwide Data-as-a-Service and Data Collaboration Taxonomy, 2024, www.idc.com/getdoc.jsp?containerId=US52116624.
Schumpeter, J. (1994) *Capitalism, Socialism and Democracy*, Routledge.
Science and Media Museum (2024) *A Short History of the Internet*, www.scienceandmediamuseum.org.uk/objects-and-stories/short-history-internet.

SCONUL (2024) Seven Pillars of Information Literacy, https://access.sconul.ac.uk/page/seven-pillars-of-information-literacy.

Scott, B. (2023) A Case of 'AI Hallucination' in The Air, *Leiden Law Blog*, www.leidenlawblog.nl/articles/a-case-of-ai-hallucination-in-the-air.

Select Committee on Environment, Food and Rural Affairs (2003) *House of Commons – Environment, Food and Rural Affairs – Eleventh Report*, https://publications.parliament.uk/pa/cm200203/cmselect/cmenvfru/587/58705.htm.

Shadbolt, N. (2024) Can Better Data Save the NHS?, *Financial Times*, 6 August, www.ft.com/content/b4c57347-d64d-436a-a2f1-33b7049a74b7.

Shaik, T., Tao, X., Higgins, N., Li, L., Gururajan, R., Zhou, X. and Acharya, U. R. (2023) Remote Patient Monitoring Using Artificial Intelligence: Current State, Applications, and Challenges, *WIREs Data Mining and Knowledge Discovery*, **13** (2), e1485, https://doi.org/10.1002/widm.1485.

Sherden, W. A. (1997) *The Fortune Sellers: The Big Business of Buying and Selling Predictions*, John Wiley & Sons.

Sherman, N. (2024) WeWork Set to Emerge from Bankruptcy, *BBC News*, www.bbc.com/news/articles/cljj3nxze6lo.

Shumailov, I., Shumaylov, Z., Zhao, Y., Papernot, N., Anderson, R. and Gal, Y. (2024) AI Models Collapse When Trained on Recursively Generated Data, *Nature*, **631**, 755–9, https://doi.org/10.1038/s41586-024-07566-y.

Siegel, J. (2024) The Art of the Prompt: How to Get the Best Out of Generative AI, *Source*, https://news.microsoft.com/source/features/ai/the-art-of-the-prompt-how-to-get-the-best-out-of-generative-ai.

Smyth, J. (2024) Amazon Buys Stake in Nuclear Energy Developer in Push to Power Data Centres, *Financial Times*, 16 October, www.ft.com/content/00776191-b010-4104-add4-8dc430386911.

Solomonoff, G. (2023) The Meeting of the Minds that Launched AI, *IEEE Spectrum*, https://spectrum.ieee.org/dartmouth-ai-workshop.

Solon, O. (2017) Why the Net Neutrality Protest Matters, *The Guardian*, 11 July, www.theguardian.com/technology/2017/jul/11/what-is-net-neutrality-threat-trump-administration.

SP Airbuz (2018) Boeing 787-10 Dreamliner Next-Gen Platform, www.spsairbuz.com/story/?id=784&h=Boeing-787-10-Dreamliner-Next-Gen-Platform.

Srnicek, N. (2016) *Platform Capitalism*, Polity Press.

Standage, T. (1999) *The Victorian Internet*, W&N.

Statcounter (2024a) Mobile Operating System Market Share Worldwide, https://gs.statcounter.com/os-market-share/mobile/worldwide.

Statcounter (2024b) Search Engine Market Share Worldwide, https://gs.statcounter.com/search-engine-market-share.

Stiglich, L. (2023) Understanding the Social and Economic Value of Sharing Data, *Open Data Institute*, https://theodi.org/insights/reports/understanding-the-social-and-economic-value-of-sharing-data-report.

Stonier, T. (1983) *The Wealth of Information: Profile of the Post-industrial Society*, Mandarin.

Strava (2024) About, https://press.strava.com/about.

Svyatkovskiy, A. , Zhao, Y., Fu, S. and Sundaresan, N. (2019) Pythia: AI-assisted Code Completion System. In *Proceedings of the 25th ACM SIGKDD International Conference on Knowledge Discovery & Data Mining. KDD '19: The 25th ACM SIGKDD Conference on Knowledge Discovery and Data Mining*, ACM, 2727–35, https://doi.org/10.1145/3292500.3330699.

Swapna, G. and Biradar, B. S. (2017) Information Literacy Model for Higher Education Institutions in India, *International Journal of Digital Library Services*, **7** (3), 31–50.

Tapper, J. (2024) 'Share Government Data to Boost Economy', says UK Statistics Watchdog Chief, *The Observer*, 18 August, www.theguardian.com/uk-news/article/2024/aug/18/share-government-data-to-boost-economy-says-uk-statistics-watchdog-chief.

techUK (2021) The UK National Data Strategy: How the UK Government Plans to Unlock the Value of Data Across the Economy, www.techuk.org/resource/the-national-data-strategys-policy-framework-for-mission-1-unlocking-the-value-of-data-across-the-economy.html.

Teece, D. J. (2010) Business Models, Business Strategy and Innovation, *Long Range Planning*, **43** (2–3), 172–94, https://doi.org/10.1016/j.lrp.2009.07.003.

The Economist (2017) The World's Most Valuable Resource is no Longer Oil, but Data, *The Economist*, 6 May, www.economist.com/news/leaders/21721656-data-economy-demands-new-approach-antitrust-rules-worlds-most-valuable-resource.

The Economist (2023) AI is not Killing Jobs yet, *The Economist*, 15 June, www.economist.com/finance-and-economics/2023/06/15/ai-is-not-yet-killing-jobs.

The Economist (2024) A Russia-Linked Network Uses AI to Rewrite Real News Stories, *The Economist*, 10 May, www.economist.com/science-and-technology/2024/05/10/a-russia-linked-network-uses-ai-to-rewrite-real-news-stories.

The White House (2023) Executive Order on the Safe, Secure, and Trustworthy Development and Use of Artificial Intelligence, www.whitehouse.gov/briefing-room/presidential-actions/2023/10/30/executive-order-on-the-safe-secure-and-trustworthy-development-and-use-of-artificial-intelligence.

Tobitt, C. (2024) Who's Suing AI and Who's Signing: Publisher Deals vs Lawsuits with Generative AI Companies, *Press Gazette*, 21 August, https://pressgazette.co.uk/platforms/news-publisher-ai-deals-lawsuits-openai-google.

Toffler, A. (1970) *Future Shock*, Random House.

Tong, A., Wang, E., Coulter, M., Tong, A. and Wang, E. (2024) Exclusive: Reddit in AI Content Licensing Deal with Google, *Reuters*, 22 February, www.reuters.com/technology/reddit-ai-content-licensing-deal-with-google-sources-say-2024-02-22.

Toosi, A., Bottino, A. G., Saboury, B., Siegel, E. and Rahmim, A. (2021) A Brief History of AI: How to Prevent Another Winter (A Critical Review), *PET Clinics*, **16** (4), 449–69.

Turing, A. M. (1950) Computing Machinery and Intelligence, *Mind*, **59**, 433–60.

UCL (2020) 'Deepfakes' Ranked as Most Serious AI Crime Threat, *UCL News*, www.ucl.ac.uk/news/2020/aug/deepfakes-ranked-most-serious-ai-crime-threat.

Ulnicane, I. (2022) Artificial Intelligence in the European Union: Policy, Ethics and Regulation. In Hoerber, T., Weber, G. and Cabras, I. (eds), *The Routledge Handbook of European Integrations*, Taylor & Francis, https://library.oapen.org/handle/20.500.12657/52622.

US Congress (2017) H.R.1770 – 115th Congress (2017–2018): OPEN Government Data Act, www.congress.gov/bill/115th-congress/house-bill/1770.

Uszkoreit, J. (2017) Transformer: A Novel Neural Network Architecture for Language Understanding, *Google Research Blog*, http://research.google/blog/transformer-a-novel-neural-network-architecture-for-language-understanding.

Van Der Marel, E. and Ferracane, M. F. (2021) Do Data Policy Restrictions Inhibit Trade in Services?, *Review of World Economics*, **157** (4), 727–76, https://doi.org/10.1007/s10290-021-00417-2.

WARC (2024) Instagram Forecast to Hit $71bn Revenue by 2024, www.warc.com/content/feed/instagram-forecast-to-hit-71bn-revenue-by-2024/en-GB/OGUrl.

Waters, R. (2024) We are a Long Way from Truly Open-Source AI, *Financial Times*, 22 August, www.ft.com/content/c7ab2cf3-deaf-4de4-9dc7-46eadc84e2a0.

Waters, R. and Morris, S. (2024) Move Over Copilots: Meet the Next Generation of AI-Powered Assistants, *Financial Times*, 22 September, www.ft.com/content/372536b1-08dd-4161-b6e3-4d09ba235ae8.

Waters, R. and Murgia, M. (2023) Why AI's 'Godfather' Geoffrey Hinton Quit Google to Speak out on Risks, *Financial Times*, 5 May, www.ft.com/content/c2b0c6c5-fe8a-41f2-a4df-fddba9e4cd88.

Watson Healy, L. (2017) *Information Industry Outlook 2018*, OutSell Inc.

Weatherbed, J. (2024) iPads Join iPhones in Requirement to Follow Strict EU Rules, *The Verge*, www.theverge.com/2024/4/29/24144209/ipados-ipad-eu-commission-dma-rules-compliance-regulation.

Webb, W. (2024) *The End of Telecoms History*, independently published.

Wellman, S. (2007) Google's Search Business Runs on 75% Profit Margin, *Information Week*, www.informationweek.com/it-leadership/google-s-search-business-runs-on-75-profit-margin.

Wells, S. (2023) Generative AI's Energy Problem Today is Foundational, *IEEE Spectrum*, https://spectrum.ieee.org/ai-energy-consumption.

Wertz, R. E. H., Purzer, Ş., Fosmire, M. J. and Cardella, M. E. (2013) Assessing Information Literacy Skills Demonstrated in an Engineering Design Task, *Journal of Engineering Education*, **102** (4), 577–602, https://doi.org/10.1002/jee.20024.

West, C. (2024) 10 AI Content Creation Tools that will Make your Job Easier, *Social Media Marketing & Management Dashboard*, https://blog.hootsuite.com/ai-powered-content-creation.

White and Case (2024) AI Watch: Global Regulatory Tracker – European Union, www.whitecase.com/insight-our-thinking/ai-watch-global-regulatory-tracker-european-union.

Wiggers, K. (2024) This Week in AI: AI is Rapidly Being Commoditized, *TechCrunch*, https://techcrunch.com/2024/08/28/this-week-in-ai-ai-is-rapidly-being-commoditized.

Wilson, T. D. (2002) The Nonsense of Knowledge Management, *Information Research*, **8** (1), www.informationr.net/ir/8-1/paper144.html.

Wixom, B. H. and Beath, C. M. (2023) *Data Is Everybody's Business: The Fundamentals of Data Monetization*, MIT Press.

WPP (2024) Capital Markets Day 2024, www.wpp.com/en/news/2024/01/capital-markets-day-2024.

Wu, T. (2003) Network Neutrality, Broadband Discrimination, *Journal on Telecommunications and High Technology Law*, **2**, 141–75.

Wu, T. (2016) *The Attention Merchants: The Epic Scramble to Get Inside Our Heads*, Knopf.

Xingyu Wang, T. and McLarty, M. (2021) APIs aren't just for Tech Companies, *Harvard Business Review*, 13 April, https://hbr.org/2021/04/apis-arent-just-for-tech-companies.

Yang, L. H. et al. (2021) Stigma, Structural Vulnerability, and 'What Matters Most' Among Women Living with HIV in Botswana, 2017, *American Journal of Public Health*, **111** (7), 1309–17, https://doi.org/10.2105/AJPH.2021.306274.

Yeuh, L. (2019) Don't Underestimate the Power of the Fintech Revolution, *World Economic Forum*, www.weforum.org/agenda/2019/04/dont-underestimate-fintech-it-could-be-the-next-revolutionary-technology.

Yoffie, D. B. and Cusumano, M. A. (2015) *Strategy Rules: Five Timeless Lessons from Bill Gates, Andy Grove, and Steve Jobs*, Illustrated edition, Harper Business.

Zimeta, M. (2022) *Data Literacy and the UK Government*, The ODI, https://theodi.org/insights/reports/data-literacy-and-the-uk-government-report.

Zirar, A., Ali, S. I. and Islam, N. (2023) Worker and Workplace Artificial Intelligence (AI) Coexistence: Emerging Themes and Research Agenda, *Technovation*, **124**, 102747.

Zittrain, J. (2008) *The Future of the Internet*, Penguin Books.

Zweig, J. (2014) Wall Street, 1889: The Telegraph Ramps Up Trading Speed, *The Wall Street Journal*, 7 July, www.wsj.com/articles/wall-street-1889-the-telegraph-ramps-up-trading-speed-1404765917.

Index

A&O Shearman (legal firm), AI opportunities 67
advertising
  expectations 61
  GenAI impact 133
  revenue 4–5, 7–8, 37–9, 45, 97, 103, 121, 133
  targeting 48–9, 57–8
AI and data legislation 93–106
  see also legislation
  EU AI Act 93–8
  EU Digital Markets Act (DMA) 98–101
  network neutrality 102–6
AI and data policies 80–92
  AI research and investment 83–91
  data sharing 81–3
  US data policies 91–2
AI challenges 68–72
  automation risk 68–70
  Copilot 68, 70
  dehumanising workers 74–5
  prompt engineering 72–4
  structured data 71–2
AI landscape 49–54
  context windows 52–4
  development 22–4
  effectiveness 50–1
  GenAI impact 49–50
  hallucinations 54
  large language models (LLMs) 49–54
  parameters 51–2
  training data 50–1
  variables 50–2
AI opportunities 56–69, 136
  A&O Shearman (legal firm) 67
  automation 66
  competitive advantage 65–7
  computer coding 68–9
  content creation 60–3
  customer engagement 66
  data analysis 66
  employment rates 62–3
  healthcare 63–5
  information processing 56
  knowledge graphs 71–2
  knowledge management 58–60
  legal firms 67
  marketing industry 61–2
  medical research 63–5
  prompt engineering 72–4
  retrieval-augmented generation (RAG) 58–60, 71
AI research and investment 83–7
  AI Regulation Bill 84
  AI Sector Deal 83–4
  EU AI Act 85–6
  EU AI Strategy 85
  EU policies 84–6

Executive Order: Maintaining American Leadership in Artificial Intelligence 86
US policies 86–7
Alphabet 7–9
business model 36–41
cost of AI 53–4
EU Digital Markets Act (DMA) 98, 101
platform 42–5
revenue 57, 83, 92, 95, 103
Amazon 7–9
application programming interfaces (APIs) 123
EU Digital Markets Act (DMA) 98, 101
revenue 83
answer engines v. search engines 56–8
APIs *see* application programming interfaces
Apple 7–9
business model 38–41, 132–3
EU Digital Markets Act (DMA) 98, 101
platform 42–5
revenue 83
Apple Intelligence, EU Digital Markets Act (DMA) 101
application programming interfaces (APIs) 128–9
API economy 123–4
data sharing 81
automation, AI opportunities 66
automation risk, AI challenges 68–70

Badke, W. 87
Beam (company) 73
Berman, Marc 116–17
bias, news 114–15
branches of AI research 11–12
branding 114
Brewster, Jack 112–13
Buller, R. 116–17
business impacts 135–6
Business Model Canvas 31–2
business models 30–54
Alphabet 36–41
Apple 38–41, 132–3
Business Model Canvas 31–2
business model innovation 33–4
data-driven business models 36–41
defining 30–1
Five Forces model 34–6
Gillette Company 33–4
Google 36–8
PEST (Political, Economic, Social, Technological) framework 34–5
platforms 41–9
Porter's Five Forces model 34–6
Swift Company 33
SWOT (Strengths, Weaknesses, Opportunities, Threats) framework 34–5
ByteDance, EU Digital Markets Act (DMA) 98, 101

cars, connected 25–6
challenges, AI *see* AI challenges
ChatGPT 12, 49–50, 57, 58
content creation 60–1
EU AI Act 95
fake news 113
hallucinations 54, 59–61
Claburn, T. 70
Claude 22–3, 49–50, 57, 97
EU AI Act 97
CNI (critical national infrastructure) 118
Code of Hammurabi 1–2
coding, AI opportunities 68–9
commerce 4–9
commercial environment 132–4
commoditisation of AI 128–30

competitive advantage, AI opportunities 65–7
computer coding, AI opportunities 68–9
connected cars 25–6
content creation, AI opportunities 60–3
content creation/ownership 12–13
Copilot 57
  AI challenges 68, 70
copyright issues, EU AI Act 96–8
Creamer, E. 96–7
critical national infrastructure (CNI) 118
customer engagement, AI opportunities 66
cyberattacks 117–18
cybernation 109

Dartmouth workshop, history of AI 10
data analysis, AI opportunities 66
data availability 127
data backchannel 7–9
data centres 118–21
data-driven business models 36–41
data-driven innovation 5–9
  Tesla cf. GM 6
data exchanges 47–9
data.gov.uk portal 19
data interoperability, data value chains 29–30
data literacy *see* information and data literacy
data marketplaces 121–3
data policies *see* AI and data policies
data sharing 81–3
  application programming interfaces (APIs) 81
  European strategy for data 82–3
data sources 16–24
  private sector data 16–17
  public sector data 16–20
  structured data 16–17, 71–2
  unstructured data 16–17, 23, 71
data value chains 26–30
  data interoperability 29–30
  electric vehicles (EVs) 27–30
  internal combustion engine (ICE) vehicles 26–7
Davenport, T. H. 66
Deep Blue 11
deepfakes 111–13
deep learning (DL), terminology 11–12
defining AI 10
dehumanising workers, AI challenges 74–5
digital literacy 89
disintermediation 13
DMA *see* EU Digital Markets Act
Dörner, D. 79–80
Drucker, Peter 24–5, 55

The Economist 5
education 115–17
  information and media literacy 115–17
  National Literacy Trust (NLT) 115–16
electric vehicles (EVs)
  data value chains 27–30
  Tesla 27
employment rates, AI opportunities 62–3
energy shortages 118–21
entertainment technology 4–5
ethical concerns 77–80
  legislation 77–80
  unintended consequences 79–80
EU AI Act 93–8
  AI research and investment 85–6
  ChatGPT 95
  Claude 97
  copyright issues 96–8
  impacts 95–6
  large language models (LLMs) 96–7

non-compliance penalties 94–5
objectives 93–4
Open AI 97
Perplexity 97
responses 95
EU AI Strategy, AI research and investment 85
EU Digital Markets Act (DMA) 98–101
Alphabet 98, 101
Amazon 98, 101
Apple 98, 101
Apple Intelligence 101
ByteDance 98, 101
core provisions 98–9
iPadOS 99–101
Meta 98, 101
Microsoft 98, 99–101
EU policies, AI research and investment 84–6
European strategy for data 82–3
EVs *see* electric vehicles
Executive Order: Maintaining American Leadership in Artificial Intelligence 86

fake news 112–13
ChatGPT 113
Federal Communications Commission (FCC), network neutrality 103–4
fediverse 45–7
financial markets 4
Five Forces model 34–6
Freedom of Information Act (1966) 17–18
Fulbright, Norton Rose 84

Gaia-X project 17
GenAI 12–13
advertising 133
AI landscape 49–50
impact 49–50, 133–4
terminology 12
generative AI *see* GenAI
Gillette Company 33–4
Google 7–9
business model 36–8
dominance 132–3
Knowledge Graph database 56, 57
platform 42–5
Google Workspace 128
graphics processors (GPUs), Nvidia 120
Green, Rob 73

hallucinations, ChatGPT 54, 59–61
Hammond, G. 127
Harbr, platform 49
healthcare, AI opportunities 63–5
history of AI 9–13
branches of AI research 11–12
Dartmouth workshop 10
Deep Blue 11
defining AI 10
machine learning 11–12, 16, 73
neural networks 11–12
Turing, Alan 9–10
history of the information industry 1–9
advertising 4–5
Code of Hammurabi 1–2
commerce 4–9
data backchannel 7–9
data-driven innovation 5–9
early form of transcription 1
entertainment technology 4–5
financial markets 4
mass media 4–5
printing industry 3–4
role of technology 3–5
speed of data and information 2–7
telegraph networks 4, 6, 55
telephone networks 6–7, 55, 99, 102

ICE vehicles *see* internal combustion engine vehicles

infonomics 122–3
information and data literacy 87–91
  defining data literacy 88–9
  digital literacy 89
  National Data Strategy 89–90
  Open Rights Group (ORG) 90
  Seven Pillars of Information Literacy 87–8
information and media literacy 115–17
information intensity matrix 25
information processing, AI opportunities 56
information volume 15–16
infrastructure, network 124–7
innovation
  business model innovation 33–4
  data-driven innovation 5–9
internal combustion engine (ICE) vehicles, data value chains 26–7
International Panel on the Information Environment (IPIE) 113
internet
  data backchannel 7–9
  World Wide Web (WWW) 6–7
Internet of Things (IoT) 131–2
iPadOS, EU Digital Markets Act (DMA) 99–101
IPIE (International Panel on the Information Environment) 113

Jefferson, Thomas 81–2

Klarna 60
KM (knowledge management), AI opportunities 58–60
Knowledge Graph database, Google 56, 57
knowledge graphs, AI opportunities 71–2
knowledge management, AI opportunities 58–60
knowledge management (KM) 21–2

labelling products 113–14
large language models (LLMs) 49–54
  commoditisation of AI 128–30
  context windows 52–4
  development 22–4
  effectiveness 50–1
  EU AI Act 96–7
  hallucinations 54
  parameters 51–2
  structured data 71–2
  synthetic data 22–4
  training data 50–1
  variables 50–2
LDS *see* the London Datastore
legal firms, AI opportunities 67
legislation
  see also AI and data legislation; *individual Acts*
  ethical concerns 77–80
  EU AI Act 85–6, 93–8
  EU Digital Markets Act (DMA) 98–101
  Freedom of Information Act (1966) 17–18
  impacts 134
  law of unintended consequences 79–80
  Official Secrets Act (1911) 18
  OPEN Government Data Act (2017) 18
  Schrems I and Schrems II legal cases 92
Levy, F. 109
LLMs *see* large language models
the London Datastore (LDS) 20

machine learning (ML) 11–12, 16, 73
  terminology 11–12
Malthus, Thomas 108

mapping data 18–19
marketing industry, AI opportunities 61–2
Marsman, Jennifer 73
mass media 4–5
media literacy 115–17
medical research, AI opportunities 63–5
Meta 7–9
  data marketplaces 121
  EU Digital Markets Act (DMA) 98, 101
  revenue 83, 92
Metcalfe, Robert 108
Microsoft
  antitrust case 99–101
  EU Digital Markets Act (DMA) 98, 99–101
  platform 42–5
  revenue 83
Microsoft 365 suite of applications 128
Millar, V. E. 25
Milmo, D. 120
misinformation 111–15
ML *see* machine learning
Moore, Gordon 108–9
MOSTLY AI Synthetic Data Platform 23
Murnane, R. J. 109

National Data Strategy 18, 89–90
National Literacy Trust (NLT) 115–16
network infrastructure 124–7
network neutrality 102–6
  Federal Communications Commission (FCC) 103–4
  Net Neutrality Regulation 105
  Preserving Network Freedom 103–4
  telecom providers 102–3
neural networks 11–12
news bias 114–15
  fake news 112–13
NHS AI Lab 64
NLT (National Literacy Trust) 115–16
Nvidia
  AI chips 53
  graphics processors (GPUs) 120
  revenue 83

ODI (Open Data Institute) 65
Official Secrets Act (1911) 18
Open AI, EU AI Act 97
OpenAI 12–13
Open Data Institute (ODI) 65
Open Data Maturity index 19–20
OPEN Government Data Act (2017) 18
Open Rights Group (ORG) 90
OpenSAFELY platform 63
Oppenheimer, P. 136
opportunities, AI *see* AI opportunities
ORG (Open Rights Group) 90
Orwell, George 111

Perplexity 57–8
  EU AI Act 97
PEST (Political, Economic, Social, Technological) framework 34–5
platforms 41–9
  Alphabet 42–5
  Apple 42–5
  characteristics 42
  data exchanges 47–9
  fediverse 45–7
  Google 42–5
  Harbr 49
  Microsoft 42–5
  OpenSAFELY 63
  types 41–2
Porter, M. E. 25
Porter's Five Forces model 34–6
predicting the future 108–9
  Malthus, Thomas 108
  Metcalfe, Robert 108
  Moore, Gordon 108–9

Preserving Network Freedom 103–4
printing industry 3–4
private sector data 16–17, 20–4
synthetic data 22–4
prompt engineering, AI opportunities and challenges 72–4
public sector data (PSI) 16–20
data.gov.uk portal 19
Freedom of Information Act (1966) 17–18
Gaia-X project 17
London Datastore 20
mapping data 18–19
National Data Strategy 18
Official Secrets Act (1911) 18
Open Data Maturity index 19–20
OPEN Government Data Act (2017) 18
value of PSI 18–21

RAG (retrieval-augmented generation) 58–60, 71
Ratner, Alex 97
Rayward, W. B. 3
regulatory environment 132–4
research and investment, AI *see* AI research and investment
retrieval-augmented generation (RAG) 58–60, 71
role of technology 3–5
Ronanki, R. 66

Samsung 70
Schneider, L. 122
Schrems I and Schrems II legal cases, legislation 92
search engines v. answer engines 56–8
Shadbolt, Nigel 65
Sherden, W. A. 109
Shumailov, L. et al. 23–4
Siegel, J. 73
social and economic implications 109–17
cybernation 109
education 115–17
trust 111–15
unemployment 109–11
Solar-Lezama, Armando 68–9
sources of AI-based applications 130–1
sources of data *see* data sources
speed of data and information 2–7
Stiglich, L. 81–2
structured data 16–17, 71–2
AI challenges 71–2
large language models (LLMs) 71–2
Swift Company, business model 33
SWOT (Strengths, Weaknesses, Opportunities, Threats) framework 34–5
synthetic data 22–4
aims 22–3
defects 23–4
issues to be considered 23–4
large language models (LLMs) 22–4
MOSTLY AI Synthetic Data Platform 23

telecom providers 102–3
telegraph networks 4, 6, 55
telephone networks 6–7, 55, 99, 102
terminology
AI 10, 11–12
deep learning 11–12
generative AI 12
machine learning 11–12
transformers 12
Tesla
data-driven innovation 6
electric vehicles (EVs) 27
revenue 83
Tesla cf. GM 6

transformers 12–13
  terminology 12
trust 111–15
  branding 114
  deepfakes 111–13
  fake news 112–13
  labelling products 113–14
  misinformation 111–15
  news bias 114–15
Turing, Alan 9–10

unemployment 109–11
unintended consequences
  ethical concerns 79–80
  precautionary principle 79–80
unstructured data 16–17, 23, 71
US data policies 91–2
using data 24–30
  connected cars 25–6
  data value chains 26–30
  information intensity matrix 25
US policies, AI research and investment 86–7

volume of information 15–16

WeWork 55, 56
World Wide Web (WWW) 6–7, 45
WPP Open 61–2
Wu, T. 46, 103

Zurkowski, Paul G. 87
Zweig, J. 6